THE RISE AND FALL OF PEACE ON EARTH

Also by Michael Mandelbaum

Mission Failure: America and the World in the Post-Cold War Era (2016)

The Road to Global Prosperity (2014)

That Used to Be Us: How America Fell Behind in the World It Invented and How We Can Come Back (with Thomas L. Friedman) (2011)

The Frugal Superpower: America's Global Leadership in a Cash-Strapped World (2010)

Democracy's Good Name: The Rise and Risks of the World's Most Popular Form of Government (2007)

The Case for Goliath: How America Acts as the World's Government in the Twenty-first Century (2006)

The Meaning of Sports: Why Americans Watch Baseball, Football, and Basketball and What They See When They Do (2004)

The Ideas That Conquered the World: Peace, Democracy, and Free Markets in the Twenty-First Century (2002)

The Dawn of Peace in Europe (1996)

The Global Rivals (with Seweryn Bialer) (1988)

The Fate of Nations: The Search for National Security in the Nineteenth and Twentieth Centuries (1988)

Reagan and Gorbachev (with Strobe Talbott) (1987)

The Nuclear Future (1983)

The Nuclear Revolution: International Politics Before and After Hiroshima (1981)

The Nuclear Question: The United States and Nuclear Weapons, 1946-1976 (1979)

THE RISE AND FALL OF PEACE ON EARTH

MICHAEL MANDELBAUM

OXFORD
UNIVERSITY PRESS

OXFORD
UNIVERSITY PRESS

Oxford University Press is a department of the University of Oxford. It furthers
the University's objective of excellence in research, scholarship, and education
by publishing worldwide. Oxford is a registered trade mark of Oxford University
Press in the UK and certain other countries.

Published in the United States of America by Oxford University Press
198 Madison Avenue, New York, NY 10016, United States of America.

© Oxford University Press 2019

Library of Congress Cataloging-in-Publication Data
Names: Mandelbaum, Michael, author.
Title: The rise and fall of peace on Earth / by Michael Mandelbaum.
Description: New York, NY : Oxford University Press, [2019]
Identifiers: LCCN 2018027496 | ISBN 9780190935931 (hc : alk. paper)
Subjects: LCSH: Peace—History—20th century. |
Peace—History—21st century. | World politics—20th century. |
World politics—21st century.
Classification: LCC JZ5554 .M36 2019 | DDC 303.6/6—dc23
LC record available at https://lccn.loc.gov/2018027496

1 3 5 7 9 8 6 4 2

Printed by Sheridan Books, Inc., United States of America

To Barbi and Larry Weinberg,

in appreciation for their many contributions to their community,

their country, and the world.

War appears to be as old as mankind, but peace is a modern invention.

— SIR HENRY MAINE (1822–1888)

Be it thy course to busy giddy minds
With foreign quarrels.
That action, hence borne out,
May waste the memory of the former days.

— WILLIAM SHAKESPEARE, *Henry IV, Part Two*

CONTENTS

ACKNOWLEDGMENTS

I AM GRATEFUL TO Ray Takeyh for a very useful discussion of Iran, to Thomas L. Friedman, James R. Kurth, and George Walden for stimulating conversations about the issues with which this book deals, to Charles Davidson, Adam Garfinkle, and Damir Marusic for the opportunity to explore some of the ideas that follow in *The American Interest*, to David McBride for welcoming the book to Oxford University Press, to Starr Lee for research assistance, and above all, and as always, to Anne Mandelbaum, for peerless editing, unwavering support, and endless love.

Introduction

THE QUARTER CENTURY after the Cold War, from 1989 to 2014, included some noteworthy, historically important, much discussed, and in some cases widely celebrated events and trends: the fall of the Berlin Wall and the collapse of communism in Europe; the rise of China and rapid economic growth in Asia; the worldwide spread of free markets, a process known as globalization; the surge of terrorism around the world, most spectacularly in the attacks on New York and Washington DC on September 11, 2001; the uprisings across the Middle East initially called, with what turned out to be misplaced optimism, the Arab Spring; and the burst of innovation in information technology that produced the personal computer, the Internet, and the smartphone, all of which rapidly ensconced themselves in the lives of hundreds of millions of people and changed them and their daily, even hourly, habits more profoundly, in many cases, than any of the other features of that period.

From the perspective of the twenty-second century another development, hardly noticed much less fully appreciated, will seem as consequential if not more so: the reign of peace in the world. The quarter century of the post-Cold War era qualifies as the most peaceful in history.

The Rise and Fall of Peace on Earth examines that singularly peaceful quarter century. Its initial three chapters describe how and why peace came to be established in three important parts of the world: Europe (Chapter 1), where it was most firmly embedded; East Asia (Chapter 2), which was more peaceful than at any other time in its modern history; and the Middle East (Chapter 3), the least peaceful of the three regions during those twenty-five years. These chapters also describe and explain how and why the unprecedentedly peaceful conditions in each of the three regions came to an end. The fourth and final chapter explores the prospects for the revival of peace in the future.

In what sense, the reader may well ask, can the quarter century following the fall of the Berlin Wall be regarded as uniquely peaceful? After all, inhabitants of the Balkans in southern Europe, the Congo in central Africa, and Syria in the Middle East died violently in large numbers. They died for the most part, however, because of civil war or the slaughter by governments or private militias of unprotected civilians, not as the result of the clash of the armed forces of the most powerful states, which is what makes historical periods the opposite of peaceful. Still, the great powers themselves have not, historically, fought one another unceasingly. What, therefore, distinguishes the post-Cold War era from periods when the strongest members of the international system were not engaged in open warfare?

The answer to that question may be found in perhaps the first and certainly one of the most famous descriptions of peace, from the prophet Isaiah in the Bible: "nation shall not lift up sword against nation, neither shall they learn war any more." Historical eras when swords were not actively being used—periods lacking shooting wars—are common enough; but only in the post-Cold War era did many nations cease to "learn war"—that is, to anticipate war, to prepare for war, and to gear their foreign policies to the real possibility of imminent war.

Isaiah's vision came to pass because of the presence of three features of the contemporary world that favor it: the geopolitical dominance of the United States; the growth of economic interdependence among almost all of the world's nearly 200 sovereign states; and the spread of democracy throughout much of the planet.

The book's first three chapters recount not only the establishment but also the demise of the post-Cold War peace. It came to an end in all three regions because one important country in each of them ended it through policies aimed at overturning the prevailing, peaceful, political, and military arrangements: Russia in Europe, China in East Asia, and Iran in the Middle East. They had a common motive: the need to generate domestic political support, a need that had become urgent in the face of declining prospects for a formerly reliable source of such support—economic growth—and with the most reliable twenty-first-century wellspring of domestic legitimacy, democracy, unavailable to their dictatorial governments. Aggressive nationalism destroyed the post-Cold War peace in all three regions; and in Vladimir Putin's Russia, in Xi Jinping and his Communist Party's China, and in the Shia clerics' Iran, aggressive nationalism stemmed at least in part from the domestic needs of autocratic regimes attempting to survive in a democratic age. Autocracy destroyed peace.

The book's final chapter shows that the key to a return peace on Earth lies in the advent of genuine democracy, including both popular sovereignty—free elections—and the protection of religious, economic, and political liberty in Russia, China, and Iran. Alas, democracy cannot be imposed from the outside and there is no knowing when or indeed whether it will come to any of the three, let alone to all of them. The message of *The Rise and Fall of Peace on Earth* is thus both an optimistic and pessimistic one. Happily, the world has a formula for genuine peace; unhappily, the world has no way of ensuring that all countries embrace it.

I

Europe: The Lost Peace

. . . most of the strategic white papers and plans within the [Atlantic] alliance [in the post-Cold War era] began with some version of the following sentence: "Europe is experiencing an age of prosperity unlike any in its history."

— MARTIN DEMPSEY, Chairman of
the United States Joint Chiefs of Staff[1]

Putin's support has traditionally rested on two pillars: a growing economy and Russia's international prestige, measured in terms of its confrontation with America. With incomes falling and consumption plummeting, the need to demonstrate Russia's geopolitical clout and military might was all the greater.

— ARKADY OSTROVSKY[2]

Peace

In the twenty-five years after 1989 Europe enjoyed the deepest peace in its history. In the first half of the twentieth century the bloodiest place on the planet, the site of two terrible all-encompassing wars, after the collapse of communism war became such a remote prospect there that its governments scarcely gave the prospect of fighting one any thought.

In one sense, to be sure, the post-Cold War era appears much like the Cold War before it: in neither period did Europe experience a major shooting war. During the Cold War, however, the United States and the Soviet Union did engage in virtually every other aspect of political and military rivalry: they sponsored proxy forces; they recruited or coerced third countries to assist their respective causes; they spied on each other; they raised, trained, and equipped powerful military forces; and they competed to develop ever more deadly weaponry.

During the Cold War, that is, the condition of Europe was not a shooting war but a *state* of war, in which preparations for war, the anticipation of war, and negotiations and political maneuvering with the prospect of war in the background took place constantly, even if actual war did not.[3] In the wake of the Cold War these activities, which comprise what is known as "security competition," had become dramatically less important or had disappeared entirely.

Just as in a chess match every move of every different piece stems ultimately from the twin aims of protecting the player's king and capturing the king of the opponent, so particular foreign policies almost always have their origins in the prospect of war. The state of war may therefore be compared to a chronic disease: it is ever present, and while it may not constantly disrupt normal life, on occasion it does flare into something more serious—that is, war itself. In Europe's golden quarter-century of peace the symptoms of this disease all but vanished.

How did this happy state of affairs come to pass? After all, war has been part of the human story from the beginning.[4] It has multiple, powerful, simultaneously operating causes. There are grounds for believing, in the first place, that the propensity for violence, including organized violence, is part of human nature, encoded in the genes that have survived the process of evolution that created *Homo sapiens*, along with every other living species.[5] While genes belong to individuals, it is groups that undertake serious fighting and they have always had several compelling reasons for doing so, chief among them economic gain, the defense and propagation of a particular set of ideas, both religious and secular, and the desire for honor and prestige—the familiar trio of "gold, God, and glory."

For the purposes of war the relevant group became, in the modern era, the nation, and nations have had three related incentives to fight: to gain independent statehood; to protect their state against predatory enemies, real or imagined; and to achieve what they consider their rightful borders and, more generally, their rightful place in the world. Almost every conflict of any size in the twentieth and twenty-first centuries in Europe, and elsewhere, had some connection to nationalism; and policies motivated by, or designed to exploit, nationalist sentiment brought the post-Cold War peace in Europe, and elsewhere, to an end.

Finally, war has stemmed from the pressures exerted by the wider setting in which large-scale groups have to exist. That setting is one of anarchy, meaning that no supreme authority exists to prevent one state from attacking another. Each must therefore prepare for the possibility of being attacked. That possibility, and the precautionary preparations that follow from it, create the state of war.

Peace as simply the absence of a shooting war has most often come about through the exercise of the old-fashioned virtue of prudence. Governments seldom initiate wars that they doubt they can win. When one state has sufficient strength to discourage another from attacking, it is practicing successful deterrence, as the United States and the Soviet Union did toward each other during the Cold War. In such cases, however, when a balance of power keeps the peace, security competition, far from declining in importance as occurred during the post-Cold War period in Europe, actually forms the basis for non-belligerency.

How, then, was it possible, at the end of the Cold War, for Europe to move beyond the state of war to a deeper peace, a peace less fixated than ever before the prospect of war? This happy condition came about because of three developments: the hegemony of the United States, the ongoing growth of economic interdependence, and the spread of democracy.

Historically, a single state has sometimes become powerful enough to impose order far beyond its borders. The Roman Empire brought a "Pax Romana" to the places it conquered. In the modern era the British Empire brought peace while its Royal Navy safeguarded seaborne commerce throughout much of the world. By the twenty-first century empire had fallen out of fashion. It had in fact become a major source of war: much of the conflict in that and the previous century came from national groups struggling to break free of imperial control. Still, after 1945 the United States not only used its enormous power to help keep the peace beyond its borders but also, like Great Britain before it, provided to the global economy the kind of secure military and political frameworks that every market needs.[6]

This was possible because, with rare and usually involuntary exceptions, the United States, unlike ancient Rome and modern Great

Britain, did not conquer, occupy, and/or govern other countries. It maintained overseas military bases with the consent of the countries in which the bases were located. As a consequence, the American role in Europe broke with historical precedent. Repeatedly in European history, when one power grew particularly strong on the continent others banded together to form a "counterhegemonic" coalition to oppose it. This pattern played out in response to the rise and the geopolitical ambitions of Louis XIV of France, Charles XII of Sweden, the imperial Germany of Kaiser Wilhelm II, Hitler, and the Soviet Union. The United States, however, evoked no such response.

In fact, the post-Cold War peace of Europe had its origins in the American-dominated alliance, the North Atlantic Treaty Organization (NATO), that was formed after World War II to oppose the Soviet Union and its communist satellites. That alliance had three purposes according to its first secretary-general, Hastings Ismay of Great Britain: to keep the Americans in, the Russians out, and the Germans down. NATO was thus the vehicle for assuring that the United States remained available both to deter the Soviet Union and to contain Germany, the great disturber of the European peace of the previous seventy-five years that had, as a result of the outcome of the war, become the ally of the countries with which it had recently been at war.

Over time, it became clear that the Germans had ceased to harbor any further impulses to conquer their neighbors. It became clear as well that the European members of the alliance welcomed the American role on their continent.[7] What had begun as a necessity—only America had the military force to stand up to the Soviet Union—evolved, over time, into a preference and a habit. This was hegemony not by imposition but by invitation.

Along with hegemony, post-World War II Western Europe developed another bulwark of peace: economic interdependence. Over the course of history economic considerations have usually lent themselves to war: preliterate bands of hunters, ancient states, and modern empires all used force against their neighbors to enrich themselves. The Industrial Revolution, however, created a new route to riches: the production of an unprecedented array of goods, and the cross-border trade in them, replaced the seizure of territory from others as the path to wealth.[8] Of course trade, even trade over great distances, long predated the machine age; but over great distances it involved only small, easily portable, highly valuable objects. The railroad and the steamship, both of them offspring of the Industrial Revolution, could carry far more cargo over far greater distances much more rapidly.

The expansion in commerce gave rise to the idea that because trade had become so significant economically, and because war would bring it to a halt, major trading partners not only should not but in fact would not fight one another. World War I, waged between countries with extensive economic ties with each other, demonstrated that trade cannot guarantee peace. In fact, nothing can. The events of human social and political life, including war, are determined by the interplay of many forces, which vary in strength from one era to another and from one place to another. Still, robust trade between and among countries does raise the cost of any armed conflict that puts an end to that trade. Political leaders know this, and the people who depend on and benefit from trade know it as well, which gives them a reason to oppose war.[9]

This second modern force that brought peace to Europe differs from the first one in an important way. Whereas the presence of a powerful state suppresses the *capability* of fighting, the benefits of trade suppress the *intention* to fight. Countries that trade with one another avoid war not because they fear losing but because they do not find winning an attractive prospect: they gain more economically by not fighting than by prevailing.

To be sure, while on the whole economic interdependence encourages peaceful conduct, it can sometimes be used as a weapon, an instrument of security competition. The temptation to deploy it in this way is particularly strong when the economic relationship between the wielder of the would-be economic weapon and the target is asymmetrical: when the second party has far more to lose from the interruption of commerce than the first.[10]

Economic interdependence, along with American hegemony, contributed to the European peace. At the same time that NATO was being formed, economic integration among its member countries began. The original impetus for it came in fact from the belief in the pacifying impact of international economic connections. The first step in European integration, the creation of the European Coal and Steel Community, was designed to prevent France and Germany, which had fought three wars against each other between 1870 and 1945, from engaging in a fourth. It led to the 1957 Treaty of Rome, which established the European Economic Community (EEC). By the end of the Cold War, the EEC had become the twelve-member European Union (EU), within which goods, money, and people moved freely across borders. By 2018 the EU had grown to include twenty-eight countries, nineteen of which shared a common currency. The ongoing process of economic integration coincided with, and was widely believed to have made a major contribution to, the virtual disappearance of the threat of war among them.

During this period Western Europe also became uniformly democratic, which reinforced the peace there. Democracy is the third great modern force for peace. A hybrid political system, it brings together two distinct traditions. One is popular sovereignty—rule by the people, in the modern era indirectly by electing representatives to do the governing. Popular sovereignty makes armed conflict less likely because it puts political power in the hands of those who, historically, have gained the least and suffered the most from war, namely the public as a whole.[11]

The other part of democracy, liberty, protects areas of human activity from government control and comes in three varieties: religious liberty—freedom of worship; political liberty, as encoded in the first ten amendments to the Constitution of the United States, the Bill of Rights; and economic liberty, most importantly the protection of private property. Liberty conduces to peace by fostering habits, attitudes, and values in domestic politics that, when carried over to dealings with other sovereign states, make for peaceful relations. Democratic politics involves, and therefore inculcates and reinforces, tolerance for differences, respect for the independence of others, and the practice of compromise.[12]

At its core, democracy is a mechanism for coping with political differences, which are inevitable within countries as well as among them, without resorting to violence.[13] Democracy contributes to peace in yet another way: it involves the transparent conduct of public affairs, which makes surprise attacks on other countries difficult. This, in turn, fosters in others the confidence that they do not have to fear such attacks, which diminishes their incentives to prepare for war.[14] Like economic interdependence, the presence of democracy, while it tends to make the states that practice it conduct peaceful foreign policies—especially toward other democracies—does not guarantee peace. Indeed, the presence of partial or illiberal democracy—popular sovereignty without liberty—has sometimes been associated with war.[15]

In Europe, however, where a democratic political system became a requirement for membership in the EU, democracy did reduce the incentives for armed conflict. At the end of the Cold War, because of its effects in combination with those of the American role and the economic interdependence embodied in the EU, security competition within the Atlantic alliance had not only disappeared, it had become all but unthinkable. Indeed, over four decades NATO had been transformed from a military alliance against a common adversary, a familiar feature of international politics from the time of the ancient Greeks, into something different, something more cohesive and more enduringly peaceful than an ordinary alliance. It came to be called, by scholars of international affairs, a security community.[16]

When the Cold War ended, the perpetuation of peace required extending the security community to include the countries of Central and Eastern Europe, including post-Soviet Russia. While the three forces that produced the deep peace in the West had not been present in what had been the communist world, the communist bloc, led by the Soviet Union, had concluded a series of military agreements with the Western security community that carried over into the post-Cold War era and that brought a new peace-promoting innovation to the European continent.

The agreements in question placed limits on the nuclear and non-nuclear arms that the two military coalitions could deploy. Arms control negotiations had become a regular feature of the Cold War at the outset of the 1970s. They initially yielded a number of accords of largely symbolic significance.[17] It was the existence of the agreements, not their contents, that mattered: by signing them the United States and the Soviet Union demonstrated that, despite their bitter rivalry, they could find common ground. This helped to reassure each of them, and the rest of the world, that they would keep their rivalry from triggering a nuclear war. The early accords had, however, only a minimal impact on the array of weaponry over which each side presided. By contrast, the later ones, reached at the end of the Cold War and the outset of the post-Cold War era, reduced and reshaped the two nuclear arsenals in ways that made each less threatening to the other side.[18] Specifically, the later arms control agreements embodied three principles that made Europe more peaceful.

One was unanimity. All countries on both sides agreed to the treaties' terms. They thus acknowledged that security is a common property, that the arms that one country possesses affect the security of others, and that each country, assuming it harbors no aggressive ambitions, has an interest in maximizing the security of all its neighbors.

Second, the accords provided for transparency. They gave all the signatories ways of satisfying themselves that all the others were observing the limits on nuclear and non-nuclear weapons the agreements mandated, and were not planning for, let alone about to launch, a surprise attack.[19]

Third, the terms of the accords reconfigured the military forces of both sides to make them more suitable for defending territory than for conquering it. To be sure, drawing a clear distinction between offensive and defensive weapons is not always possible: weapons of all kinds can often be used for both purposes. Still, the accords made each side less capable of attacking, which made all of them more capable of defending themselves, thus moving the military deployments of both in the direction of "defense dominance."[20] The chances that either side could launch a successful attack decreased, reducing the chances that either would launch any attack at all and so reinforcing the European peace. Because all parties to it shared in its construction and accepted its terms, what they created in Europe was a common security system.

Common security promoted peace by addressing a fundamental cause of security competition: the anarchy of the international system. Anarchy makes each state hostage to the intentions of the other, and ordinarily none of them can be sure that the others' intentions are benign. Common security addressed that problem. It provided a way for each sovereign state credibly to communicate peaceful intentions to others, thereby enhancing others' confidence that it would not attack them. Confidence-building measures are designed to convert the natural, normal, prudent suspicion with which independent political communities have always regarded one another, and that creates the state of war, into trust. That is what the three defining principles of the European common security order did.

Unanimity promoted confidence because each country knew that all the others had agreed to the measures to which it had also agreed. Transparency did so by enabling each country to see for itself that the others were doing what they had promised to do. Defense dominance provided the most convincing evidence of peaceful intent: countries voluntarily relinquished, or eschewed, the military capabilities most useful for attacking others.

At the outset of the post-Cold War period the common security system helped to compensate for the absence of the three peace-promoting features of modern life in Russia. Just as a plaster cast keeps an arm immobile while a break or a fracture heals, so the series of arms control accords that made up the common security system served to bind post-communist Russia to the European peace to gain time for economic interdependence and democracy, which had been entirely absent from the Soviet Union, to take root and begin to grow there. Their growth had the potential to make Russia, over the long term, as firmly committed to reducing security competition as its Western European neighbors already were. Unfortunately, this is not what happened. Instead, the West, led by the United States, removed the cast by violating the terms on which common security had been established, paving the way for the end of the post-Cold War peace in Europe.

The Blunder

Having prevailed in the Cold War, having created a zone of deep peace among themselves, and having extended part of the scaffolding of peace eastward by means of the late-Cold War arms control agreements, the Western coalition faced the task of sustaining, strengthening, and spreading the conditions that suppressed security competition across the continent. The phrase commonly used to describe the Western aspiration—"a Europe whole and free"—implied a third adjective: peaceful.

The countries of Central Europe that the Soviet Union had occupied in the course of World War II, on which it had imposed communist rule, and that had been compelled to join the military coalition that it dominated, the Warsaw Treaty Organization, quickly became part of the zone of peace. By opting for membership in the EU these countries committed themselves to two of the pillars of peace: economic interdependence and democracy.[21] Russia followed a different course. Ultimately, it put an end to the peace of Europe. It did so principally because of the kind of government it had come to have, but also because of what the United States and its allies foolishly did in the early years of the post-Cold War era.

While the government in Moscow had played a key role in negotiating the components of the common security order, post-Soviet Russia lacked each of the three modern sources of peaceful conduct. It did not fully share the Western (and Central and Eastern) European view of the United States as a benign hegemon. During the Cold War, Russia's predecessor, the Soviet Union, had regarded America as anything but benign; and while anti-American sentiment diminished sharply as the military and ideological conflict between the two nuclear-armed titans ended, the Russian political elite did not adopt the Europeans' deference to the United States in matters of security. America had not, after all, defeated their country militarily. Russia still had the largest territory of any sovereign state on the planet; it had inherited its Soviet predecessor's considerable stockpile of nuclear weapons; and, although far weaker than the United States, in size and strength it towered over its neighbors.[22]

Nor could post-communist Russia immediately integrate itself into the global economic order. To do so it had to rid itself of the centrally planned economic system of the communist era, which did not mesh with the free-market economies of the West, and then build a market economy of its own. The first was a painful and disruptive process, the second a protracted and difficult one. Economic interdependence, of the kind that bound together the countries of Western Europe and thereby promoted peace among them, would at best take time to achieve.

As for democracy, Russia had had virtually no experience with either popular sovereignty or the protection of economic, religious, and political liberty. Democratic government requires a particular set of values, habits, and institutions. At the end of the Cold War Russia had none of them. It had to start from scratch.

At the dawn of the post-Cold War era Russia found itself, in relation to the rest of Europe, in the position it had occupied for most of the previous four centuries: at the lower end of what the historian Martin Malia described as a downward-sloping west-to-east "cultural gradient."[23] Historically, Russia lagged behind the countries to its west in the development of political and economic practices and institutions, but generally, and with exceptions, followed—at a distance—the Western path.

Modern developments made peace in Europe possible but Russia was, at the end of the Cold War, as Russia had always been, less modern than the countries to its west. That made it all the more important to reinforce the common security order that it had joined—indeed had helped to construct. The West, led by the United States, instead pursued the opposite policy.

The administration of Bill Clinton, the first post-Cold War American president, took the initial, fateful step in this policy by expanding NATO eastward to include formerly communist countries and former parts of the Soviet Union while making it clear that the single country whose membership would have made the greatest difference in the decades to come—Russia—would not be invited.[24] Expansion came as an unpleasant surprise to the Russians, to whom Western officials had given assurances, more than once, that no such thing would occur.[25]

The Clinton administration portrayed NATO expansion as a measure that would consolidate democracy in the newly admitted countries.[26] The claim was absurd. The new members were firmly committed to democracy for their own reasons; and if they had not been, membership in a military organization would not have catalyzed such a commitment.[27] Moreover, if belonging to NATO did in fact promote democracy, the country that should have been offered membership, the one in which the prospects for democracy were shakiest and the direction of whose domestic politics would have the widest impact, was precisely the country that was being kept out: Russia. What tipped Bill Clinton in favor of NATO expansion was his calculation that it would work to his short-term political advantage, winning him the votes of

Americans with family backgrounds in the new member countries in his 1996 campaign for reelection.[28]

Russians came to believe that the United States had adopted a policy of deliberate hostility to their country and was seeking to weaken and humiliate it. In fact, the Clinton administration did not, for the most part, harbor hostile intentions toward Russia. Rather, the Americans felt free to ignore Russian protests because, as they saw it, Russia had become too weak to make trouble in Europe. The Russian government could complain about NATO expansion, the Clinton administration believed, but could not stop it. This proved correct—up to a point.[29] Russian complaints had little effect, as well, because with the end of the Cold War, the Americans also assumed, Russia would reconcile itself to what the United States proposed to do.[30] This assumption proved to be entirely mistaken.

NATO expansion eroded the European peace in several ways. It weakened the forces of democracy in Russia by discrediting the country's democrats, who were identified with the United States.[31] It undercut the common security order by violating one of that order's three defining principles, unanimity. The United States and its allies altered the basic security arrangements on the continent without the consent—indeed, over the explicit objections—of the largest European country.

NATO expansion also disregarded history, ignoring what had happened after the other great conflicts of the modern period. Of these the Cold War was the fourth, after the Napoleonic Wars of the late eighteenth and early nineteenth centuries and the two world wars of the first half of the twentieth. In all four, one of the two opposing sides decisively prevailed over the other: after each, the losing party relinquished territory and moved to adopt the domestic political system of the winners. The winners, for their part, were eager to prevent another such conflict.

Their success in preventing one turned out to depend heavily on how they treated their defeated opponents. In the wake of the Napoleonic Wars, and again following World War II, the winners managed to integrate the loser—France after Napoleon in the first case, Germany after Hitler in the second—into the postwar order in a way that was acceptable to all parties.[32] The victors, that is, made a conciliatory peace.

After World War I, by contrast, the victorious allies imposed what the defeated Germans regarded as a harsh peace. This created German resentment, which helped Hitler come to power. That in turn led to the outbreak of another, even bloodier and more destructive conflict.

The lesson that emerges from the four cases is that generous conditions for the vanquished party are more likely than harsh treatment to preserve a postwar peace. With NATO expansion the United States flouted that lesson, treating Russia more like post-World War I Germany than Germany after World War II—or so the Russian political establishment and the Russian public came to feel.[33] In the end, rather than uniting Europe, the proclaimed goal of the United States and its allies, NATO expansion redivided the continent, with Russia, like the Soviet Union before it, separated from and ultimately in active opposition to the West.

In alienating Russia from the post-Cold War settlement, expansion combined with other Western policies to which the Russians took exception. In the second half of the 1990s, NATO went to war in Bosnia and Kosovo against the Serbs, a people with whom many Russians felt a cultural and historical affinity, without consulting Russia[34] and without the authorization of the United Nations Security Council (where Russia retained a veto). In Kosovo, the West supported the secessionist aspirations of the Muslim Kosovars, again over Russian objections and in contravention of the international norm against unilateral secession.[35]

The administration of George W. Bush withdrew from the three-decades-old ABM Treaty, which had survived the end of the Cold War and that the Russians regarded as a guarantee of their continuing and highly valued post-Soviet status as a great nuclear power. The Russian president was among the first world leaders to offer support to the American government after the attacks on New York and Washington D.C. of September 11, 2001, but the Russians came to believe that the United States had failed to reciprocate appropriately for that support.[36] Instead, it launched, again without the sanction of the UN, an attack on Iraq, a one-time Soviet client,[37] and eight years later went beyond a UN mandate authorizing the protection of endangered civilians in Libya to bring down the government of that country, which then became a haven for terrorists. In Russian eyes (and not theirs alone) the

American government had decided that it could depose any government it did not like whenever it chose.

NATO expansion, combined with these subsequent American and Western policies, had the unintended effect of persuading the Russian political class, and much of the Russian public, that they could not trust the United States and that America in fact wished to do them harm.[38] As a consequence, opposition to American initiatives became the default response of Russian foreign policy and resistance to the United States its major goal. Both weakened the peace in Europe.

The United States and its allies could have adapted the arrangements for European security to the new realities of the post-Cold War era in ways other than expanding NATO eastward. Alternatives were possible that could have gained the approval of Russia and been consistent with the principles of common security while keeping the United States actively engaged in Europe so as to furnish reassurance to the Europeans. First Soviet and later Russian leaders had already agreed to a continuing American presence on the continent, perhaps in part because they valued the reassurance this would give them that a newly united Germany would not become a threat.

The victorious side in the Cold War could have retained, and built upon, its initial institutional response to the end of that conflict, a loose association that involved all the countries of Europe, including Russia, called the Partnership for Peace. NATO's members could also have invited Russia to join the Western alliance. Russian membership would certainly have transformed NATO; but since the basic circumstance in which it had been established and had operated for four decades had disappeared, transformation of some kind was in order if the alliance was to survive. Indeed, NATO did add a new feature—military missions beyond Europe—in an effort to retain its relevance.[39] Including Russia would have given the alliance a border with China, which would have complicated relations between America and Europe on the one hand and the world's most populous country on the other; but those relations became complicated anyway.[40] The countries of North America and Europe might, as yet another option, have come together to redesign the security architecture of the continent. The Russian government suggested doing precisely this in the second decade of the post-Cold War era, when, however, the evolution of Russia's domestic politics and foreign policy made it too late to act on the suggestion.

At the end of the Cold War, therefore, which, like the aftermaths of other great wars, was a moment when the range of possible futures was unusually broad, a number of roads to security lay open to the United States and its allies that they did not take. The road they did take led to the end of the European peace because it intersected with the drift of Russian domestic politics. The Russian animus and resentment toward the United States and the West, which had its roots in NATO expansion, then combined with the political needs and the geopolitical inclinations of the Russian leadership in the second decade of the twenty-first century to overthrow the peace that was the Cold War's outstanding legacy.

From Yeltsin to Putin

Russia was both fortunate and unfortunate in having Boris Yeltsin as its first post-Soviet leader. It was fortunate because Yeltsin proved successful at dismantling the communist system that Lenin and Stalin had set in place and that had endured for three-quarters of a century. He did more than anyone else to put an end to the political supremacy of the Communist Party of the Soviet Union, the centrally-planned Soviet economic system, the Soviet-era military-industrial complex, and the Soviet Union itself.

On the other hand, Yeltsin proved far less adept at the more difficult project of constructing the institutions of democratic politics and free-market economics. He was committed to that project and made a start on it. His successor lacked that commitment and, far from reinforcing and expanding what Yeltsin had built, he sought, with considerable success, to tear it down.

Yeltsin accomplished less than he might have during his nine years as the president of Russia, in part because he became unpopular with the Russian public. This weakened him politically and discredited his agenda for making Russia a more Western country. His unpopularity stemmed from his erratic, alcohol-fueled personal behavior[41] but also from the fact that he presided over a period of economic distress. This was all but unavoidable. The transition from a centrally-planned to a free-market economy was bound to be rocky, and Russia suffered as well from high inflation, the result of a money-printing spree during the final months of the Soviet Union.[42] The Yeltsin administration also pursued an imprudent fiscal policy, borrowing recklessly, which produced a fiscal crash—the government defaulted on some of its obligations and sharply devalued the ruble—in August, 1998. This too made Western institutions and practices seem unattractive to the people of Russia.[43]

Perhaps the most politically damaging feature of the Yeltsin era was its massive corruption, which the president tolerated and from which he and his family were widely believed to have benefitted. Without a tradition of either transparency or honesty in the conduct of public business, without the well-established rule of law, and with one of the world's largest endowments of immensely valuable natural resources the disposition of which rested ultimately with the government, Russia was vulnerable to the abuse of public office for private gain; and such abuse took place on an enormous scale. Corruption became, in fact, the fundamental underlying principle of, and the main driving force behind, Russian politics.[44]

Along with corruption, and indeed as a direct consequence of it, the Yeltsin years saw the development of a sharply unequal distribution of the wealth that became available with the end of a communist economic system that had prohibited private property. A handful of particularly favored individuals amassed vast fortunes by gaining control, with the connivance of the Russian government, of much of the country's resources. By one twenty-first-century estimate, 110 individuals controlled 35 percent of the nation's total wealth.[45] They used their wealth to exercise political influence, on some notable occasions for the benefit of Boris Yeltsin. These individuals became known as "oligarchs."[46] Their rise, which Yeltsin tolerated and in some ways made possible, further undercut his standing with the Russian people.

Yeltsin's most important legacy turned out to be his hand-picked successor. Vladimir Putin had made his early career in the KGB. The Soviet espionage and secret police organization sent him to East Germany, where he attained the far-from-lofty rank of lieutenant colonel. When the East German communist government fell, he returned to his home town, whose name reverted from Leningrad to the pre-Soviet St. Petersburg, and found work with its mayor. The contacts he made in that position helped him get to Moscow. There he rose, through a series of appointments (including as the head of the KGB's successor, the FSB) to become prime minister and Yeltsin's designated political heir. At the end of 1999 Yeltsin resigned and Putin became acting president, winning election to the office in May, 2000. In a decade and a half in charge of the Russian government—the first eight as president, then four as a prime minister more powerful than Dimitri Medvedev, the subordinate he had tapped to fill the presidency for a term, and then again as president—Putin did more to shape his country's politics, economics, and foreign policy than any single individual since Josef Stalin.[47] The changes he made led, ultimately, to the collapse of the peace of Europe.

Almost from the start he took steps to make the Russian political system less free. By 2014, according to Freedom House, an organization that tracks and assesses the status of political liberty in the world, Russia was comparable, for the freedom its citizens enjoyed, to Afghanistan, Burma, the Democratic Republic of Congo, and Iran, none of them a bastion of democracy.[48] Where his predecessor had delegated considerable power to regional governments, Putin took it back. He asserted control, directly or indirectly, over the country's major media outlets, notably its television stations, from which most Russians got their news. He permitted no effective political challenges to his policies or his rule. Organized political opposition, a growing part of Russian politics in the Yeltsin years, vanished under Putin. Potentially formidable opponents suffered harassment, imprisonment, and in some cases assassination.

Putin exercised supreme authority,[49] becoming what Yeltsin had not been and had not, by all appearances, aspired to be: a dictator. The country continued to stage elections, but these were neither free nor fair.

At the outset of his tenure Putin did preside over economic reforms designed to enhance the efficiency of the newly established free market.[50] Soon enough, however, he reversed Yeltsin's practice of putting economic assets in private hands, returning more and more of them to the control of the state.[51] In particular, he made sure that the government—meaning he himself and his associates—controlled the country's reserves of oil and natural gas. A turning point came in 2003 and 2004 when the regime imprisoned Mikhail Khodorkovsky, the owner of the largest privately-held Russian oil company, Yukos, and seized its assets. The Yukos affair demonstrated not only Putin's determination to control Russia's energy riches himself but also his intolerance of any independent center of wealth and potential political power and his disdain for the institution of private property, on which a free-market economy rests.[52]

Putin moved to dispossess some of the oligarchs who had flourished under Yeltsin, driving several into exile. He created oligarchs of his own, however, a number of whom he had known in St. Petersburg and many of whom came from the security services.[53] They became known as the *silovikii*—from the Russian word *sil* for strength—and formed the core of his regime. For them, and for Putin himself, the highest priority was the preservation of the political arrangements from which they derived such immense personal economic benefits. The goal of regime protection suffused everything Putin did, including the foreign policies he carried out.

The regime he built called itself a "sovereign democracy," meaning that Russia counted as one of the few countries that could act independently—unlike the Europeans, who, in this view, were subservient to the United States.[54] Putin's Russia did have elections and a parliament and unlike the Soviet communist regime the president and his colleagues did not aspire to control every aspect of social and economic life. The country was not, however, a democracy.[55] The people did not choose the government: the government chose itself. Post-Cold War Russia became a dictatorship, with supreme power vested in one person, Vladimir Putin.

The purpose of his regime, insofar as it had one beyond holding and exercising power for its own sake, was to enrich the small clique of favored people designated by the president.[56] Their wealth came not from providing goods or services that consumers wanted but from using the power of the government that they controlled to divert resources to themselves. Membership in this privileged group amounted to a license to steal;[57] and its members stole on a very large scale. The political party created to support Putin, officially named "United Russia," was given, by one of the regime's vocal critics, the title "the party of crooks and thieves," which became a rallying cry for its opponents.[58] Corruption became the core principle of the Russian political system. As a result, Vladimir Putin's Russia had one of the most unequal distributions of wealth in the world.[59] The most accurate term for the political system over which he presided, therefore, was "kleptocracy."[60]

Responsibility for the sharp deviation from Boris Yeltsin's preferred path for Russia does not fall entirely on the will and the whim of one person, important though these were in the case of Vladimir Putin. It would have been difficult in the best of circumstances to endow Russia with Western political and economic institutions, practices, and values during the Yeltsin era. These do not spring up overnight: in the West they are the work of generations. Because post-communist Russia had no experience at all with democracy[61] and none in the previous seventy-five years with free markets, creating them would have taken considerable time even under optimal conditions. The Russia over which Putin came to preside, and that he did so much to shape, represented a reversion to the country's historical norm.[62] Power had always been concentrated in a few hands. The public had never chosen the government or enjoyed political rights.

Compounding the difficulty for Russia of moving up the centuries-old cultural gradient that separated it from the countries to its west[63] were its energy resources. They made it possible for the government to earn income from abroad without creating a well-functioning free-market economy. They also provided the country's rulers with both the incentive to remain in power indefinitely, in order to divert to themselves the riches from the sale of oil and gas—Putin himself was estimated in 2007 to have a net worth of $40 billion[64]—and the means to do so, by bribing the public at large with welfare benefits and repressing any opposition with a well-funded security apparatus. For this reason energy-rich countries—"petrostates," a designation for which Russia qualified—tend not to be democracies; and the roots of their authoritarian politics lie in geology rather than history.

Finally, the experience of the average Russian in the 1990s, which included the instability of the Yeltsin presidency and the erratic conduct of the president himself as well as the sharp decline in individual economic fortunes, gave democracy and free markets, which Russians were told were being established in their country, a poor reputation. These

Western institutions did not seem to Russians, as they most certainly did to most Central and Eastern Europeans, to be worth promoting and defending.

While Russia was not swiftly going to become an orderly, prosperous facsimile of a Scandinavian country under any post-Soviet conditions, neither did its politics and economics have to develop as they did. Some moments in a country's history offer a wider range of possible futures than others, and the end of the Soviet Union and the emergence of a non-imperial, non-communist Russia presented an unusually broad spectrum of possibilities. These included the best opportunity in Russian history if not to discard entirely then at least to lighten the burden of the country's autocratic political tradition.

At such moments the personal predilections of leaders can make a large difference in the trajectory of the political communities they lead, for worse as well as for better. Twentieth-century Germany, Russia, and China would have perpetrated and suffered far less bloodshed if Hitler, Stalin, and Mao had never come to power. On the other hand, the United States, Turkey, India, and South Africa would have had less freedom, and been less united and probably less peaceful, without George Washington, Mustafa Kemal, Jawaharlal Nehru, and Nelson Mandela.

Vladimir Putin's accession to supreme power, moreover, was not inevitable. Six prime ministers held office before Putin during the Yeltsin presidency, each of whom would have become president had Yeltsin resigned or died in office. Not all of his predecessors shared what turned out to be Putin's dictatorial and kleptocratic preferences. At one point Yeltsin considered designating as his successor Boris Nemtsov, a genuine liberal from the Volga River city of Nizhny Novgorod who became threatening enough to the Putin regime to be assassinated in the shadow of the Kremlin in February 2015.[65]

All apart from the identity of Yeltsin's successor as president, events outside the country's borders had an impact on its political direction. The Asian financial crisis of 1998 spread to Russia and helped precipitate the August, 1998 financial meltdown, which destroyed the remaining political support for both economic reform and the reformers responsible for it. Had Asians managed their finances better, Russians might have been spared their own economic crisis, and public attitudes toward Western-style politics and economics and the leader who embraced them might have been more favorable.[66]

In the end, however, the deep currents of Russian history and the contingent developments of the 1990s combined to give Russia a vicious, kleptocratic government. That government's overriding aim was to perpetuate itself, which meant that it required a strategy for creating and sustaining the support, or at least the tolerance, of the Russian people.

Putin's tsarist predecessors had held power on the basis of a long, religion-based tradition, the Russian version of the pre-modern European principle of the divine right of kings. The communists claimed the right to rule by virtue of their mastery of the "scientific" ideology of Marxism-Leninism. In case anyone doubted its truth or their prerogatives, they also carried out mass terror, whose intimidating effects persisted for decades. The leaders of the Western democracies, of course, derive their political legitimacy from the democratic process by which they are chosen.

None of these was available to Vladimir Putin; but he did rely heavily on the approval of the Russian people. He and his political circle came to be obsessed with polls tracking his popularity with the public.[67] They saturated the airwaves, which they controlled, with pro-Putin propaganda. During his first stint as president he registered consistently high ratings, not so much because of the artistry of the propaganda but because he received credit for delivering something of surpassing importance to the average Russian: prosperity.

Russia's gross domestic product (GDP) grew by 7 percent a year between 2000 and 2008, almost doubling in that period. Between 2004 and 2008 wages increased by 400 percent.[68] Repairing a shortcoming of the Yeltsin years, the regime paid, indeed increased, pensions. It expanded government employment. Economic activity in the major cities picked up, creating a middle class of consumers.[69] The government channeled revenues to the cities and towns, many located far from Moscow and St. Petersburg, in which large, obsolete industrial enterprises provided most of the employment. The goods that these places produced had no buyers, and without the subsidies they received from Moscow they would have suffered even greater economic hardship than they actually experienced. In these places Putin maintained particularly high levels of support.[70]

In the Soviet era, the saying went, Russians had a kind of social contract with the communist authorities: "We pretend to work and they pretend to pay us." In the first decade of the twenty-first century Vladimir Putin struck a different bargain with the Russian people. He stayed out of their private lives and gave them a rising standard of living and they accepted his and his cronies' monopoly of power and large-scale thievery.[71]

Russian prosperity depended on the price of oil.[72] Like the man who happened to be playing the bass tuba on the day it rained silver dollars, Putin had the personal good fortune to hold power when the price of hydrocarbon-based energy skyrocketed. In 1998 oil sold for $12.76 a barrel. By 2008 its price had risen to $132. The sale of energy produced two-thirds of Russia's export earnings and funded half its budget.[73] The rise in price generated a massive increase in the revenue that flowed to the Russian government. Its president rode the wave of oil money, which he himself had done nothing to create, to heights of popularity that Boris Yeltsin, especially in his second term, had never approached.

If oil revenue and the uses to which he put it accounted for Vladimir Putin's popularity during the initial period of his presidency, from 2000 to 2008, another basis for public approval grew substantially in importance when he returned to that office in 2012. This second source of legitimacy was the Russian version of the most powerful political sentiment of the modern era: nationalism.

Nationalism can take at least three forms: the demand that a national group have its own sovereign state, which began with the Germans and the Poles in nineteenth-century Europe and, at the end of the twentieth, helped to undo the Soviet Union; the claim that the nation is in danger and must be defended against its enemies, a rallying cry during the first great outburst of nationalism, the French Revolution; and the assertion that the nation deserves more power and prestige than it has, that it is being denied its rightful place in the world, which Germans believed during both World Wars.

Nationalist sentiment was not particularly strong in Russia when the Soviet Union ended. Russians had always lived in a multinational state—first the tsarist empire and then the Soviet Union[74]—which they themselves dominated. The disintegration of the Soviet Union made 25 million ethnic Russians, who had been part of the ruling majority in the communist multinational state, suddenly minorities in newly-independent countries where other nationalities predominated. Similar circumstances had given rise to irredentist claims and ultimately to war for the purpose of reincorporating their fellow nationals into the mother country, on the part of the Germans and Hungarians after World War I and the Serbs after the collapse of Yugoslavia.[75] During the Yeltsin years, by contrast, Russia showed no sign of wishing to annex ethnic Russian populations in newly independent Ukraine, Belarus, or Kazakhstan.

In part because the collapse of communism left an ideological vacuum, however, an aggressive, resentful variety of nationalism germinated in post-Soviet Russia, and in the second decade of the new century that nationalism became an increasingly important source of popularity for Vladimir Putin. It served, in fact, as the pretext for the policies he undertook that ended the post-Cold War European peace. The decisive initiative was Russia's 2014 invasion and occupation of neighboring Ukraine.

The End of Peace

Of all the fourteen non-Russian republics of the Soviet Union that became independent after 1991, Ukraine was the most important to Russia. It had the largest population and contributed the most to the Soviet economy. Russians felt more attached to, indeed possessive of, Ukraine than any of the others. They traced the origins of the Russian state to Ukraine's capital, Kiev, in the ninth century. Most of what emerged as independent Ukraine had been part of a larger Russian-dominated state, first the tsarist empire and then the Soviet Union, since the seventeenth century. That long history, combined with extensive intermarriage between Ukrainians and Russians, the marked similarities between their two languages, and the large number of ethnic Russians living in Ukraine—especially its eastern part, in the basin of the Don River known as the Donbass—made it difficult for Russians, apparently including Putin, to regard Ukraine as a separate country.[76]

The government of independent Ukraine turned out to be corrupt and ineffective, and in 2004 large-scale peaceful demonstrations protesting a rigged presidential election succeeded in forcing a freer vote. In that second election the candidate illegitimately chosen the first time, Viktor Yanukovich, was defeated by a would-be reformer, Viktor Yushchenko. Yushchenko failed to improve the country's governance, however, and in 2010 Yanukovich won what was regarded as a genuinely free contest. He then proceeded, however, to govern in a corrupt and autocratic fashion.

Putin had actively supported Yanukovich's candidacy in both 2004 and 2010. He urged (and reportedly bribed) the Ukrainian leader to join a Russian-sponsored economic grouping, the Eurasian Union. At the same time, Yanukovich was negotiating an Association Agreement with the European Union, something that other countries had used as a way station on the path to full membership in the EU.

In this bidding contest Yanukovich at first seemed prepared to tie Ukraine to the EU. On November 21, 2013, however, he abruptly announced the end of negotiations with the Europeans and the resumption of talks with Russia for Ukraine to join Putin's Eurasian Union. Demonstrations even larger than those in 2003 erupted in Kiev and other major Ukrainian cities and continued into the first two months of 2014. To those who took to the streets, an association with the West offered the hope of prosperity and Western-style democratic politics in Ukraine. Opting to link the country's economic future with Putin's Russia, as Yanukovich seemed poised to do, portended, by contrast, economic stagnation and political domination by the country's large and increasingly undemocratic eastern neighbor.

The biggest rallies, involving as many as 800,000 people, took place in and around the Maidan Square in Kiev. Violence broke out there in February and at least eighty-eight people died, in all likelihood killed by snipers working for the Yanukovich government. Negotiations between the regime and the demonstrators produced a political compromise on February 21 but the following day Yanukovich fled the country. In May a new, pro-Western Ukrainian president, Petro Poroshenko, was elected.

The triumph of the Maidan Revolution administered a major political setback to Vladimir Putin. The Russian president responded with war. He launched two military operations against Ukraine. The first had as its target the Crimean peninsula, which the Soviet leader

Nikita Khrushchev had put under Ukrainian jurisdiction in 1954, a time when the transfer of authority within the centralized, totalitarian Soviet state had purely symbolic significance.[77] After 1991, Crimea became part of the newly-independent Ukraine, to which, unlike Russia, it is geographically contiguous. A plurality of the Crimean population, however, consisted of ethnic Russians and Russia retained a large naval base there.

Soldiers wearing Russian combat fatigues but no insignia (they became known as "little green men")[78] infiltrated Crimea at the end of February and, with the cooperation of locally-recruited personnel, ousted Ukrainian officials there and took control. A plebiscite of dubious propriety, held on March 16, 2014, produced what was reported as a large majority in favor of making Crimea part of Russia.[79]

In April, Russian-sponsored forces in the Donbass seized control of government buildings, attacked local authorities, and declared the territory no longer part of the Ukrainian state. This time the Ukrainian army fought back and between May and July gained the upper hand over the rebels. Russia resupplied the insurgents and in August sent in regular forces of its own, turning the tide of battle against the Ukrainians. More than 9,000 people died in the fighting.[80] Two rounds of negotiations to try to settle the conflict followed in the city of Minsk, the capital of Belarus—the first in September, 2014, the second, after fighting had resumed, in February, 2015. The Minsk Agreements called for the end of hostilities, the withdrawal of armed forces from the disputed areas, and changes in the Ukrainian constitution to give the Donbass an unspecified form of political autonomy.

The assault on Ukraine marked the end of an historical era. By invading, occupying, and annexing part of another sovereign state Russia engaged in a classic case of aggression, the first time such a thing had happened in Europe since World War II. As a result, the European continent became what it had been before the collapse of communism: a place where armed conflict was always a possibility and occasionally a fact, and where governments' foreign policies therefore had, in a variety of ways, to take the possibility of such conflict into account. Europe had returned, that is, to the state of war.

The blow that destroyed the post-Cold War European peace did not come out of the blue. Russian unhappiness with, sliding into outright opposition to, the security arrangements in place after the Cold War had become apparent well before February, 2014. In 2007 Putin told a security conference in Munich that included American officials: "Today we are witnessing an almost uncontained hyper use of force—military force—in international relations, force that is plunging the world into an abyss of permanent conflicts . . . One state and, of course, first and foremost the United States, has overstepped its national borders in every way."[81]

In August of 2008 Russian armed forces conducted a kind of dress rehearsal for the assault against Ukraine. In that month Russia waged a brief war against the neighboring country of Georgia, in the Caucasus, which, until the end of 1991, had been a Soviet republic. The borders of independent Georgia, which Soviet officials had originally drawn in the 1920s, encompassed two ethnic minorities, the Abkhaz and the Ossetians. The two groups did not wish to be part of the new Georgian state. Both managed to achieve de facto independence and looked to Russia as their protector. In 2004 Mikheil Saakashvili assumed the Georgian presidency with an agenda that included bringing Abkhazia and South Ossetia (North Ossetia was located in Russia) under the control of the central Georgian government and moving his country as close as possible to the West, including through membership in NATO. Both positions put him sharply at odds with Putin.[82]

On the night of August 7-8, 2008, fighting erupted between the Georgian armed forces and the far more powerful Russian military. It is not clear which side fired first: each accused the other of doing so and an EU study reached an inconclusive verdict on the question. (Even if the Russians did not initiate hostilities, they may have goaded Georgia into launching the initial attack.[83]) Whatever its origins, the war ended in a swift and decisive victory for Russia. Russian troops occupied part of Georgia, coming within 40 miles of the capital, Tbilisi, which Russia's air force bombed. The Russian government withdrew its troops but recognized Abkhazia and South Ossetia as independent from Georgia.

The West responded in restrained fashion. Georgia had no strategic or economic importance and belonged neither to NATO nor to the EU. Nor was it clear that the Russian claim to have acted in self-defense rather than to have committed an unprovoked act of aggression was entirely false.

In the wake of the Georgia war Russia undertook an expansion of its military forces, reversing the pattern of the Yeltsin years.[84] It also violated the terms of two of the arms control accords—the agreement on Intermediate Nuclear Forces (INF) and the Treaty on Conventional Forces in Europe (CFE)—that were part of the European common security order. The attacks on Ukraine, therefore, were in keeping with, rather than a break from, the general approach to Russia's neighbors and to the West that Putin had adopted.

The end of the post-Cold War peace was important for Europe and the world, of course, but the timing of the events that ended it and the underlying condition that predisposed the Russian government to attack and occupy its neighbor have a particular significance. They bear on the staying power of peace in the contemporary world and on the prospects for reviving it in Europe and elsewhere. Putin's war against Ukraine caused the end of peace: in order to begin to appreciate the twenty-first-century challenge to the kind of deep peace that the modern era has made possible, it is necessary to understand what caused that war.

Like all wars, indeed like all major political events, the Russian conflict with Ukraine had more than one cause. It represented a reversion to an historical norm. Just as the Putin autocracy resembled the country's previous systems of governance, so, too, the assault on Ukraine followed a familiar pattern. Historically, Russia had conducted itself as an empire, expanding in all directions to subjugate other peoples, including the Ukrainians. Even before 2014 Dimitri Medvedev, Putin's one-term successor (and then predecessor) as Russia's president, had declared the territory of the former Soviet Union, which included fourteen independent countries, to be a "zone of privileged interest" for Russia.[85]

The war had another basis in Russia's history. In its tsarist and communist incarnations the country had enjoyed a lofty international status, first as one of Europe's several great powers and then as one of the world's two nuclear superpowers. The Russian elite in particular resented the loss of this status, which the end of the Soviet Union had imposed. The war against Ukraine entailed, among other things, an effort to restore it, or to pretend that post-Soviet Russia still had it.

Vladimir Putin himself, and his government, explained the assault differently. Russia was responding, they claimed, to an insidious, illegal coup against the Ukrainian government plotted and carried out by "fascist" elements in Ukraine in cooperation with Western governments, especially the government of the United States. The malign forces that ousted Viktor Yanukovich, according to this account, sought to weaken and threaten Russia and they intended to make Ukraine a NATO outpost for this purpose. Russia's military operations, it followed, qualified as justified, indeed necessary, acts of self-defense.[86]

The Putin version of events was almost entirely untrue. The United States and other Western governments had welcomed the downfall of a corrupt, illiberal leader in Kiev but had done nothing to bring it about. The Ukrainian people were wholly responsible for the movement that overthrew him. That movement did include some politically dubious elements, and the Ukrainian parliament did annul a law that designated Russian as one of the country's two official languages,[87] but these were of minor significance. The principal goals of the Maidan Revolution were national independence and democracy.

Did Vladimir Putin himself believe what he and his government said about the events in Ukraine and Russia's response to them? Someone whose formative experience is service in the KGB is surely capable of deep cynicism, and Putin certainly knew many of the specific allegations he and his colleagues made were false. On the other hand, he may well have subscribed to the broader narrative of a rapacious West out to enfeeble and even destroy Russia. Such a view of the world, and of the West, would come easily to a veteran of the KGB.[88]

Whether the Russian government believed its own explanation for its attack on Ukraine was true, that explanation proved to be very useful for the people who propounded it. This was so because, whatever Putin's private attitude, the Russian people believed it. The Putin regime unleashed a barrage of propaganda, through television and other media, asserting, reiterating, and purporting to document its own partisan account of what was happening in Ukraine.[89]

This account gained wide credibility among Russians, and not only because the government saturated the airwaves with it: they were already disposed to believe it. The series of Western and particularly American affronts to Russia, crucially beginning with NATO expansion, had created a widely held perception in the country that a deep anti-Russian animus motivated the policies of the United States and the countries of Western Europe. The Putin version of events, willfully inaccurate though much of it undoubtedly was, conformed to that general perception. Putin and his associates' allegations that America and its allies had engaged in devious manipulations in Ukraine seemed plausible to Russians, given what had happened before, as only the latest in a series of measures intended to isolate and diminish their country.[90]

In this way NATO expansion contributed, disastrously, to the end of the European peace. Without it Putin's aggression would not have earned him the wave of approval and support among Russians that it did. He could not have portrayed it as successfully as he did as an act of self-defense to the audience that mattered most to him: the Russian public. Whether, without expansion, Russia would not have adopted the aggressive foreign policy that culminated in the invasion and occupation of Ukraine cannot, of course, be known. Counterfactual historical scenarios do not admit of proof—or disproof. What is clear is that the impact of NATO expansion on Russian opinion gave Vladimir Putin an incentive to invade Ukraine—to bolster his own popularity by exploiting anti-Western sentiment—that he would not otherwise have had. What can also be said is that including Russia in the organization at the heart of the post-Cold War security order, which the Clinton administration rejected, would have created a disincentive— perhaps a powerful one—to aggression that was conspicuously missing in 2014.

Because of NATO expansion and subsequent American initiatives, the account he propounded made Putin himself the heroic defender of Russia and its interests. That is indeed how the Russian public came to see him. His popularity soared;[91] and from Putin's perspective the sharp upturn in the public approval of him was perhaps the most important consequence of the assault on Ukraine and indeed an important reason for it.

The public perception that he was battling, with skill and determination, a major threat from the West was more than useful for Vladimir

Putin: it was politically necessary. The kleptocracy over which he presided rested on his personal popularity. His popularity had, in turn, rested, during the first decade of the twenty-first century, on Russians' rising standard of living, for which their president received considerable if largely undeserved credit. Then their well-being stopped rising and started falling.

The reversal began with the American-centered financial crisis of 2008. The fallout from that crisis adversely affected most of the world but Russia suffered greater economic damage than any other major country.[92] As Russians were struggling to recover from the crisis-inflicted economic downturn, the price of oil, the source of the economic bounty that Putin had ridden to strong public approval,[93] began to drop. From a high of $145 per barrel it moved unevenly but ultimately sharply downward, touching $30 in 2014.[94] Like the rise in its price during Vladimir Putin's first stint as president, its decline stemmed from developments far beyond his control. Global supply and demand determined how much Russia earned from its oil. With the worldwide recession following the crisis of 2008, which the ongoing crisis of Europe's common currency, the euro, aggravated beginning two years later, demand dropped. More or less simultaneously the global supply of energy increased, largely through the expansion of production in the United States as the result of the availability of new techniques of exploration and recovery.

The Russian government's revenues followed the price of oil downward. This gave Putin fewer resources with which to buy popularity and, accordingly, he became less popular. Polls showed public approval of him declining.[95] Even more worrying for the regime, public protests took place, sparked by a 2011 election for the Russian parliament—the Duma—marked by obvious signs of fraud, and then by the announcement that Putin would run for the presidency again the following year. More than 50,000 people rallied in Moscow against the regime on December 10, 2014, and nearly double that number assembled two weeks later,[96] with many chanting the slogan "Russia without Putin." Notwithstanding the protests, Putin was duly elected to a third presidential term in 2012 and then, after an increasingly repressive term in office, to a fourth in 2018, with neither election a model of democratic propriety.

It was surely not difficult for Putin and his colleagues, in 2011 and thereafter, to imagine themselves being swept away by popular protests, as had happened twice to Viktor Yanukovich in Ukraine,[97] to unpopular leaders in Georgia and Kyrgyzstan, both former Soviet republics, in the first decade of the twenty-first century, and to the communist governments of Central and Eastern Europe in the fateful year 1989. For the sake of its survival, the Putin regime needed to distract the Russian public from its economic difficulties and rebuild public support for its leader. Attacking Ukraine, annexing Crimea, and occupying the Donbass offered a way to do both.

In this the regime succeeded: Putin's popularity rose sharply. The actions of individuals and governments typically have multiple motives that are not easy to disentangle or to compare in strength, but bolstering the regime's domestic standing certainly counts as an important— perhaps the most important—motive in this case—as Russians and other observers noted at the time and afterward.[98]

The Ukrainian operations enhanced Putin's popularity because, portrayed as they were as defensive responses to Western aggression, they mobilized the other major source of support for the regime besides prosperity—nationalism. The war against Ukraine was therefore, among other things, a way of compensating for the damage to the regime's reputation that its poor economic performance had inflicted. Unable to deliver bread to the Russian people, Putin doubled down on circuses.

The wars gave Putin the opportunity to capitalize on both the defensive and the aggressive versions of nationalism. The regime's depiction of his role cast him as both protecting the Russian nation against the rapacious West and reasserting Russia's familiar status as a major presence in international affairs.

The American president John F. Kennedy once observed of the public support that dispatching American troops to trouble spots abroad normally produces that "It's like taking a drink. It wears off and then you have to have another."[99] In that spirit, the year after the invasion of Ukraine Putin launched another military operation that cost Russia little, that he could claim defended vital Russian interests, and that he could depict as a success. Syrian dictator Bashar Assad had come under assault from a large, heterogeneous resistance movement that prominently included Islamic fundamentalists. Putin ordered the Russian air force into action in support of Assad, announcing that in doing so he was fighting terrorism and defending the principle of national sovereignty. Russian bombing did not in fact aim mainly at the Islamic fundamentalists, but it did strengthen Assad's position; and the Syrian intervention reinforced the elevated standing with the Russian public that the attack on Ukraine had earned for the Russian president.

The tactic of using force outside the country's borders to strengthen an unpopular regime at home did not originate with Vladimir Putin. It has recurred in Russian history,[100] not least because of the cultural gradient with the European countries to its west.[101] Authoritarian Russian governments have feared the contagion of political ideas and practices from the west that could subvert their rule and have acted to snuff them out. In 1793 Polish constitutional reform provided an alternative model of governance to Catherine the Great's absolute monarchy in Russia, and she took part in the partition that ended Polish independence.[102] In the nineteenth century Poland became a gateway to Russia for political ideas and practices that threatened tsars,[103] and in 1830 the Russian government put down an insurrection there and abolished the autonomy the Poles had retained after the partition.[104] In 1863 the tsar repressed another Polish uprising, which had the professed aim not only of restoring independence but also of establishing democracy.[105] In the twentieth century the unyielding Russian policies in the Balkans that contributed to the outbreak of World War I stemmed in part from the fear that a more conciliatory approach would encourage resistance to the regime in Russia itself.[106] In 1968 Soviet troops put an end to a movement to make Czechoslovakia freer, initiated by the Czech communist leader Alexander Dubcek, which was known as the "Prague Spring," and for the same reason.[107]

Like these historical precedents, the Maidan Revolution did present a genuine threat—of a particular kind. The events in Kiev did not threaten Russia's territorial integrity or economic well-being: Ukraine was not about to join NATO and, even if it had, NATO was not going to attack Russia; and its invasion of Ukraine made Russia worse off economically because of the economic sanctions that the Western countries imposed in response. Rather, the Ukrainian upheaval threatened the Russian regime of the moment: it threatened Putin.

The association with the EU, Viktor Yanukovich's discontinuation of negotiations for which touched off the demonstrations in Kiev (and that his elected successor subsequently embraced), was designed to import Western political and economic standards to Ukraine, to make its government more transparent and less corrupt. Those favoring the association assumed, plausibly, that improved national economic performance would follow such changes. Where Putin-style governance had brought economic decline to Ukraine, which lacked Russia's energy resources to compensate for mismanagement and theft, Western practices promised to trigger economic growth. Precisely because of the long ties and marked similarities between Ukraine and Russia (which the Russian political elite believed gave them a kind of *droit de seigneur* over their neighbor), the Russian people were bound to take notice of developments next door. Over the long term the most powerful force in human social life, including international affairs, is the power of example. From the beginning of human civilization individuals and collectives have copied what they have observed and admired. There was every reason to believe that Russians would admire and seek to emulate the economic and political institutions and practices of a democratic, prosperous Ukraine.

Putin could not afford that. The goal of the assaults he launched, it became clear over time, was not to incorporate any part of Ukraine beyond the special case of Crimea. Instead, it was to create problems in the Donbass that would preoccupy the government in Kiev, divide the people of Ukraine, and generally obstruct the development of what the Association agreement with the EU was intended to foster. Here he had some success: he managed to create a regional version of a failed state in eastern Ukraine, with its status contested,[108] its economy in ruins, and many of its people living elsewhere as refugees.

At the same time, Putin used the atmosphere of crisis that he had artificially created in Russia to protect his regime in another way. He cracked down on demonstrations[109] and on the Russians who took part in them, and moved to restrict even further the scope for independent civic and political activity.[110] He created a National Guard of 400,000 troops, to be subordinate, and presumably personally loyal, to him.[111] He and his associates alternately insinuated and declared outright that anyone who opposed him was a traitor.[112]

All this meant that among the causes of the Russian foreign policies that put an end to the post-Cold War peace in Europe was democracy— both its absence in Russia and its looming presence almost everywhere else. The twenty-first-century Russian political system lacked the war-resisting features that democracy brings with it: transparency, trust-worthiness, and a disposition to friendly, peaceful relations with others. It lacked them because Putin had deliberately constructed a political system without them, the better to monopolize power and use it to en-rich himself and his friends.

Of the other two bulwarks of the deep European peace, Russia did not welcome the hegemony of the United States and Russian economic engagement beyond its borders, dominated by the sale of energy, did not match the degree of interdependence that bound the countries of Western Europe and North America to one another. A democratic political system might have reduced the resentment at NATO expan-sion and the other measures to which Russians took exception, but for reasons of history as well as the deliberate policies of the person who came to power from the beginning of the new century, Russia did not have one.

The Putin regime feared democracy, especially the prospect of a stable democratic government in a neighboring country that had the poten-tial to create a powerful demand for a similar government in Russia. This would have posed a threat to the kleptocracy from which its senior officials benefitted so handsomely. Democracy—or rather the lack of it—contributed to the end of the European peace in yet another way. Democracy is a source of legitimacy. Without it, Putin had to rely for his hold on power first on economic success, over which he exercised no control, and then on assertive nationalism, which produced the in-vasion of Ukraine. A democratic government would not have had to go searching for legitimacy in what turned out to be, from the standpoint of peace, all the wrong places. That search ended by bringing back to Europe something at once unwelcome to the governments of every country there except Russia and unhappily familiar to them all: secu-rity competition.

The New/Old Europe

European security in the wake of the Russian occupation of Ukraine had a doubly familiar appearance. It was generally familiar because the sovereign states of the continent had lived in a "state of war"— that is, with the constant possibility of armed conflict—for most of recorded history. It was specifically familiar because the version of security competition that emerged from the post-Cold War peace resembled, in important ways, Europe's most recent experience of it, the Cold War itself.

As in the Cold War, the United States opposed Russia. As in the Cold War, the United States had a coalition of like-minded allies: indeed, the post-Cold War American alliance, NATO, had come into being in the late 1940s to wage the Cold War.

The competition between the United States and Russia had an economic as well as a military dimension. At the beginning of the Cold War, in fact, before it became a military conflict, the United States had provided economic assistance to the war-damaged economies of Western Europe in the form of the European Recovery Program, popularly known as the Marshall Plan after the Secretary of State, George C. Marshall, who announced it. Its goal was to catalyze economic growth and thus to prevent distressed economic conditions in which local, Moscow-affiliated communists could thrive politically. Similarly, thwarting Putin's aims in Ukraine required that Ukraine become more stable politically, less corrupt, and more prosperous economically than it was during the first quarter century of its post-Soviet independence. Western economic assistance would not, by itself, reverse Ukraine's political and economic trajectory, but it would be an indispensable part of any formula for such a reversal.

European security after the Russian assault on Ukraine bore a military resemblance to its Cold-War predecessor as well. On both occasions the Russians sought to overturn the status quo, and the United States to preserve it. That made the Western military mission in post-Cold War Europe the same one that it had undertaken during the Cold War: deterrence. In both periods a secure and peaceful Europe required that Western armed forces, in concert with Western diplomacy and Western economic weight, dissuade Russia from doing to other countries what it did in 2014 to Ukraine.[113] As from the late 1940s to the early 1990s, the policy of deterrence had to be carried out under the shadow of American and Russian nuclear weapons.

Nuclear weapons contributed to a particular twenty-first-century strategic problem for the United States and NATO that echoed one of the major Cold War challenges with which they had had to cope. In the earlier period, the NATO allies were committed to defending West Berlin, a Western island with free elections and economic, religious, and political liberty located 80 miles inside communist East Germany, which enjoyed none of these freedoms.[114]

Surrounded as it was by communist-controlled territory, West Berlin could not be defended successfully against a determined attack by troops and tanks. Only a token Western force was stationed there, and if a war broke out adequate reinforcements would not be able to reach the western part of the city to keep it from being overrun and conquered. The security of West Berlin therefore rested on deterrence based on the Western threat, usually an implicit one, to resort to the use of nuclear weapons in response to a concerted attack. Once begun, there was no telling how a nuclear war would end.[115]

Similarly, post-Cold War NATO came to include Estonia, Latvia, and Lithuania, three tiny countries that had once been part of the Soviet Union. All three had borders both on the Baltic Sea and with Russia, as well as minority populations of ethnic Russians.[116] Russia conducted campaigns of harassment against the three countries,[117] and Putin was quoted as saying that "If I wanted, Russian troops could not only be in Kiev in two days, but in Riga, Vilnius, Tallinn [the capitals of Latvia, Lithuania, and Estonia respectively], Warsaw or Bucharest too."[118] Defending them against a determined Russian attack would encounter some of the same logistical difficulties that the defense of West Berlin had presented, including, in the worst case, a perilous choice between accepting a military defeat and bringing nuclear weapons into play.[119]

Another issue, economic in nature but with political considerations and a staple of intra-alliance politics in the West during the Cold War, resurfaced with the return of security competition in Europe. Known as burden-sharing, it concerned the contribution each NATO member made to the common task of deterring Russia. As during the Cold War, the Europeans, although more directly threatened by reason of geography, spent a smaller proportion of their national outputs on defense than did the United States.[120] The recurrent Cold-War-era effort by successive American administrations to coax, cajole, bully, and shame them into spending more emerged from its post-Cold War hibernation.

While the new security competition in some ways resembled the Cold War, it did not fully duplicate the twentieth-century rivalry. The later conflict differed from the earlier one in important ways. Not the least important was the fact that post-Soviet Russia was smaller and less powerful than its Soviet predecessor. It had lost one-quarter of the territory of the Soviet Union and one-half of its population—most of it non-Russian. Despite its energy resources, it had an economy of only modest size.[121] The formidable Soviet military-industrial complex had fallen into disrepair, and Putin's infusion of money failed to restore it to its Soviet dimensions. The Soviet Union had sustained a rivalry with the West of global scope. Post-Soviet Russia lacked the capacity to do this.

The line of division between the two opposing camps, which in the Cold War had run through Germany, had moved eastward, to Russia's disadvantage, all the way to its western border. In fact, Russia did not really have a camp—that is, a coalition of supporters. The non-Soviet members of its Cold War alliance, the Warsaw Treaty Organization, had all joined NATO.

Nor did sharply conflicting ideologies with universal claims divide the two sides, as they had during the Cold War. Post-communist Russia had no equivalent of the Soviet Union's Marxism-Leninism. Putin and his coterie did try to portray their rivalry with the West as, among other things, a conflict of ideas. He cast himself as the defender not only of Russia's territory and its international status but of traditional, socially conservative Russian values as well. He claimed that these were under assault from the militantly godless, libertine countries of Europe and North America. The regime placed particular emphasis on the alleged threat to Russia from homosexual conduct.[122] On the basis of the supposed chasm between Western values and Russia's it asserted that Russia was a unique "civilization," separate and distinct from the West, and that Western political institutions and practices, which the United

States and its allies were perpetually attempting to spread around the world, were entirely inappropriate for Russia.[123]

All this fell far short of communism's elaborate doctrine and extensive, well-organized network of cadres, not to mention the intense dedication Marxism-Leninism inspired in the first half of the twentieth century.[124] Putin occasionally cited a few Russian writers of the past as the sources of his view of the country and its place in the world, but his regime never seriously tried to elevate them to the near-sacred status that the theories of Marx, Engels, Lenin and (for a time) Stalin had enjoyed. Vladimir Putin's new doctrine for Russia, such as it was, seemed to be, in the main, just another device for warding off the specter of democracy that haunted, and threatened, his kleptocracy.[125]

Post-Soviet Russia's principal military challenge to the West also differed from the threat that the Soviet Union had posed. During the Cold War, Western military planners had worried about, and prepared for, a massive Soviet-led attack originating in the middle of Europe that would sweep aside the opposing Western forces and push all the way to the English Channel and the Atlantic Ocean. Their nightmare scenario, that is, reprised Germany's successful blitzkrieg attack on France in the spring of 1940. Not only would a comparable twenty-first-century Russian campaign have to begin almost 800 miles farther east, but post-communist Russia was far too weak to have even a hope of success in such an attack.[126]

Instead, Russia adopted a strategy of "probing"[127]—taking hostile steps and making threats that, while unwelcome, were not serious enough to elicit a forceful response from the West. Such measures included provocative military maneuvers, flights of Russian warplanes near or over the territory of other countries and Russian warships sailing near these countries,[128] and bellicose rhetoric. Like the tactics Germany employed in Europe in the 1930s,[129] these measures carried with them the potential to shift the balance of military and political advantage in favor of Putin's Russia at the expense of its neighbors.

Prominent among the anti-Western stratagems that Russia adopted as part of its attack on the European status quo was one that had been unavailable to its Soviet predecessor because the necessary technology did not yet exist. Cyberwarfare involves the use of twenty-first-century information technologies and the information they carry to deceive, confuse, disrupt, and even physically damage an adversary.[130] Far weaker than the West on almost all other dimensions of power, here Russia could compete on something close to equal terms and could harm other countries without either firing a shot or sending a single Russian soldier across a sovereign border.

In 2007, apparently in retaliation for the removal of a statue of a Soviet soldier in downtown Tallin, Russian hackers shut down websites in Estonia.[131] During the assaults on Georgia and Ukraine, Russia broadcast wave after wave of propaganda on the Internet and social media as well as on television, much of it untrue, in order to generate support for Putin's policies among Russians and sow confusion and doubt elsewhere.[132] Russians engaged as well in "trolling," posting inflammatory and often false information on the Internet to cause distress to people disfavored by the Kremlin.[133]

Most notoriously, Russian hackers were reported to have stolen information from the computers of the Democratic Party in the United States and released it in the final days of the 2016 presidential election. Some of it embarrassed the Democratic candidate, former Secretary of State Hillary Clinton. The impact of the purloined information, if any, was more or less impossible to trace and measure, but it certainly did not help Mrs. Clinton, who lost the election to the Republican businessman Donald Trump.

Russia's exercises in cyberwarfare did not have, or at least did not achieve, the goal of inflicting physical damage, as would a cyberattack on an electrical grid, for example, and as did the American-Israeli insertion of the "Stuxnet" virus into the ongoing Iranian nuclear weapons program, which was identified in 2010. They were designed, rather, to confuse, mislead, and disrupt other countries and their citizens; and in this they enjoyed some success.

Because Russia was weaker than the Soviet Union and posed no comparable challenge to the way Western countries organized their own politics and economics, the members of NATO almost all regarded the new security competition as less urgent and less dangerous than its Cold War predecessor. It occupied a less important place in their foreign policies: many of them regarded Islamic fundamentalist terror as a greater problem. Most of the European members of the Atlantic alliance had long since ceased to spend significantly on defense; almost none possessed formidable military forces. Even in the wake of the Russian attack on Ukraine and the end of the post-Cold War peace, the governments of these countries did not bestir themselves to achieve greater military readiness.[134]

Nor did Europe have a uniform view of the new Russian threat.[135] The countries closest geographically to Russia were more alarmed about the end of peace and more strongly in favor of enhancing the Western military presence on Russia's borders than were those situated farther away.[136] The invasion of Ukraine understandably concerned Estonia more than it did Italy.

The two most important members of the Western coalition, Germany and the United States, approached the new Russian threat with less determination than they had brought to the contest with the Soviet Union and international communism. The German attitude had several sources: gratitude to Russia for permitting the unification of the eastern and western parts of their country; lingering guilt over the brutal Nazi assault on Russia during World War II; reliance on natural gas from Siberia for some of Germany's energy requirements; and the lucrative commerce with Russia that some German firms conducted. These combined to create a constituency within Germany in favor not of endorsing the Russian presence in Ukraine but rather of ignoring it. According to one poll, moreover, a substantial majority of Germans believed their country should not come to the aid of a fellow NATO member under attack, as the NATO treaty their government had signed obligated it to do.[137]

The American public, for its part, displayed a certain weariness with international engagement, the result of disappointing twenty-first-century experiences in Afghanistan and Iraq. Donald Trump, the man American voters elevated to the presidency in 2016, made a point during his campaign of criticizing the nation's allies for making insufficient contributions to the cost of the common defense, a sentiment that, polls showed, a significant proportion of his fellow Americans shared.[138]

In its intensity, in the level of political, economic, and military mobilization it elicited, and in the degree of solidarity it produced in the Western coalition, therefore, the security competition into which Russia's attack on Ukraine ushered Europe did not match the Cold

War. That fact, the one-sidedness of the rivalry, and the absence of an ideological dimension to it did not necessarily mean, however, that the new conflict between the West and post-Soviet Russia would be free of direct military clashes between the opposing parties.

Precisely because the rivalry was less intense, one or both parties might become complacent, or careless, or overly optimistic about the chances of avoiding war, and so stumble into one.[139] Because the rivalry was lopsided, in a crisis the weaker party, Russia, might feel pressure to resort to the use of force lest it be defeated or humiliated, or both.[140] Because Vladimir Putin had come to depend on conflict with the West to sustain the popularity with the Russian public on which he relied to remain in power, a decline in his approval ratings might push him to ever more aggressive and reckless international initiatives.

On the other hand, one significant difference between the Cold War and the twenty-first-century security competition in Europe did weigh, on the whole, on the side of peace: economic interdependence. The Soviet Union had practiced economic autarky. Its centrally planned economy, without free markets or prices set by supply and demand, made normal economic interaction with the non-communist world all but impossible. Post-Soviet Russia abandoned central planning for a system of economic organization that, although riddled with corruption and subject to extensive government control, did in fact operate according to a distorted version of the basic principles of the economies of the West.

Russia could and did, therefore, establish economic connections with the NATO countries. In breadth and depth they did not match those between and among those countries themselves, but they were far more extensive than they had been during the Cold War. Russia did have ostensibly private banks that, although often of dubious reliability and subject to government pressure, did interact with their Western counterparts, thus becoming part of the global financial system. Large Russian enterprises, usually controlled by people with Putin's stamp of approval, took out loans from commercial banks in the West. Wealthy Russians, their wealth generally obtained by corruption and access to political power, bought property in Europe and North America, especially in Great Britain and the United States, and sent their children to expensive schools and universities there, as insurance against the day when they might fall from favor in Moscow and have to flee their homeland.[141] The country's plutocrats also stored money in relatively opaque Western financial jurisdictions such as Switzerland and Cyprus. The most important economic connection of all, of course, involved energy, with Russia as the seller and Europe as the buyer.

In short, one of the three modern forces for peace, economic interdependence, although present in a relatively weak form, did affect Russia's relations with the rest of the world. Conflict with other countries did place economic gains at risk for both sides. Because Russia's international economic ties were unusually asymmetrical, however, they cut both ways: they served both as an incentive for peace and as an instrument of conflict.[142] The Putin regime calculated that it could use the asymmetries that worked in its favor to its own political advantage. Thus, in 2006 it sought to punish the former Soviet republics Georgia and Moldova for their pro-Western inclinations by banning their imports to Russia.[143]

Even in the Yeltsin era Russia styled itself an "energy superpower." On several occasions it cut off energy supplies to Ukraine for the purpose of exerting pressure on the government in Kiev, reckoning that this would move the Ukrainians in Russia's direction because while the Ukrainians needed what Russia had, Ukraine exported nothing important to Russia and so had no countervailing leverage.[144] Because Europe imported natural gas from Russia in considerable volume, Putin seemed to have expected that his assault on Ukraine would not evoke serious economic punishment from the West.[145]

His expectation proved incorrect. A number of NATO countries expressed their reluctance to do so but in the end, on the heels of the invasion, all of them imposed sanctions on both individuals and particular economic sectors in Russia.[146] They stiffened these sanctions in response to the shooting down of a Malaysian Airlines passenger airliner on July 17, 2014, which killed all 298 people aboard including 193 from the Netherlands. The plane was hit by a Russian-supplied missile fired by Russian-supported insurgents in eastern Ukraine apparently under the mistaken impression that they were aiming at a Ukrainian government aircraft. The sanctions had an impact: the value of the ruble against the dollar fell by 40 percent.[147] The Europeans did not, however, deny the Putin regime hard currency by refusing to purchase Russian energy. In this way, at least, interdependence put limits on the Western conflict with Russia.[148]

Western sanctions did inflict economic harm on Russia—in 2015 its economy declined by between five and six percent[149]—although its post-2014 economic travails had more to do with the decline in the global price of oil[150] and with Putin's economic mismanagement than with the Western economic penalties. This meant that the conflict-resisting effects of commerce might have a delayed reaction: over the long term, the economic losses Russia suffered as a result of the war it started might make its leaders more cautious about launching acts of international aggression. Indeed, the sanctions may in fact have indirectly done so, by discouraging the Putin regime from widening its war in Ukraine.[151] Still, the mere fact of a measure of economic interdependence, in the absence of the third modern peace-promoting force, political democracy, did not suffice to make Russia a peaceful citizen of Europe.

In one respect the security competition of the twenty-first century both reproduced and differed from the Cold War. As during the first half of the twentieth-century conflict, Russia was aligned with China. Although not united, as in the earlier period, by a common allegiance to Marxism-Leninism (in the Chinese case Marxism-Leninism-Maoism), they both belonged to the Shanghai Cooperation Organization, a loose assemblage of countries the Chinese founded in 2001.[152] Moscow sold arms and energy to China and the two conducted joint military exercises. Since the Cold War, however, the geopolitical status of the two countries had reversed: China was now rising and much stronger, while Russia was declining and far weaker. For all the bonhomie the two powers professed, they retained long-harbored suspicions of each other and competed for influence in the Central Asian countries that had once belonged to the Soviet Union and that Russia regarded as properly within its sphere of influence. In this competition China's economic prowess gave it an advantage.[153]

What brought Russia and China together was not a common ideology but a parallel interest. Central Asia aside, neither played a significant role in the other's home region: Russia was a minor presence in Asia; China was economically but not strategically significant in Europe. In Asia, however, China, like Russia in Europe, was mounting a challenge to the political and military arrangements in place at the end of the Cold War. As with Russia, the Chinese challenge stemmed in no small part from the assertive nationalism that its undemocratic regime adopted to bolster its standing with the people it governed. As Russia had done in Europe, China put an end to the post-Cold War peace in Asia.

2

East Asia: The Commercial Peace

[The day will come when China will] take back from foreigners everything foreigners have taken from China, will pay off old grudges with interest, and will carry the Chinese flag and Chinese arms to many places . . . thus preparing for the future disasters and upheavals never dreamt of.

— SIR ROBERT HART, Inspector General,
Imperial Chinese Customs Service, 1863–1911[1]

China is clearly militarizing. You would have to believe in a flat earth to think otherwise. I believe China seeks hegemony in east Asia.

— ADMIRAL HARRY HARRIS, Commander-in-Chief,
United States Pacific Fleet, 2016[2]

Peace

As in Europe, peace reigned in East Asia during the post-Cold War era. The two regions both enjoyed a golden age of international harmony—a suspension, if not the final disappearance, of security competition.[3] The peace of Asia had the same origins as the peace of Europe, and suffered the same fate: as in Europe, by the middle of the second decade of the twenty-first century the Asian peace had ended, and for much the same reason. As in Europe, moreover, Asia's post-Cold War peace had its roots in the region's post-World War II geopolitical pattern, with a non-communist coalition opposing a communist bloc. As in Europe, where the United States and West Germany became allies, in East Asia an alliance between the United States and the country it had defeated in World War II, in the Asian case Japan, formed the spine of the anti-communist coalition. As in Germany, the United

45

States stationed military forces in Japan, and with them came the protection of the American nuclear arsenal. As with Germany in Europe, the American alliance with Japan served not only to deter a communist attack but also to reassure Japan's Asian neighbors, which only a few years previously it had brutally occupied, that they did not have to fear a revival of Japanese aggression.

Unlike in Europe, however, the American commitment to Japan was not part of a broader, multilateral, regional alliance. East Asia lacked the equivalent of NATO. Instead, the United States established bilateral security ties with individual East Asian countries: in addition to Japan with South Korea, Taiwan, and a number of the countries of Southeast Asia that did not, however, have comparable commitments to one another, as NATO's members did. The Asian arrangements came to be known as a "hub-and-spokes" pattern.

Like hegemonic powers throughout history, the American military presence in East Asia suppressed security competition among the non-communist countries. The United States did not, however, attract the animus that imperial powers aroused in the twentieth century because it functioned, in Asia as in Europe, not as an oppressive overlord but as a generous protector. The East Asian countries' connections to America were voluntary. They wanted the United States in their region because it had the military might, including nuclear weapons, to offset the Soviet Union and communist-ruled China. Like the Western Europeans, the Asians could count on America to safeguard rather than dominate them. The Asians' confidence stemmed in part from distance: the world's largest ocean separated them from United States. Of course, the European powers that had conquered and governed Asian societies in the nineteenth and twentieth centuries were geographically remote as well; but as a full-fledged democracy in the post-imperial era, the United States was disposed to respect the independence of other countries, as the imperial powers of the past and the communist giants of the twentieth century were not.

As did its European counterpart, the American-centered East Asian anti-communist security order turned, over the first quarter century of the Cold War, into a security community, with security competition among its members not only in abeyance but increasingly unthinkable.[4] Then, in the early 1970s, that community expanded. The United

States and the People's Republic of China, which had fought each other directly in Korea two decades earlier and had remained estranged since, effected a dramatic rapprochement. Common opposition to China's onetime ally, the Soviet Union, brought them together when the post-1949 Sino-Soviet partnership turned to hostility,[5] hostility that reached its peak with several military skirmishes between the armies of the two countries along their common border in 1969.

The Sino-American relationship never became a formal alliance, but after their rapprochement in 1972 the two countries brought their foreign policies in Asia into alignment and launched programs of intelligence-sharing and military cooperation. The collapse of the Soviet Union left the American hub with its Asian spokes, including China, as the sole surviving security arrangement in East Asia. In the wake of the Cold War, its allies continued to value the role of the United States as the region's hegemon.[6] The communist government in Beijing tolerated it.[7] In the wake of the Cold War, the first pillar of peace—benign hegemony—was firmly in place in Asia, as it was in Europe.

Also as in Europe, in post-Cold War East Asia the second pillar—economic interdependence—reinforced the deep peace. American naval and air forces, in addition to providing a protective shield against aggression for Japan, South Korea, Taiwan, the countries of Southeast Asia, and ultimately China, guaranteed the free passage of shipping over what became, in the decades after World War II, the world's most important maritime trade route.[8] American military power made Asia safe for cross-border commerce. The strategy of economic development that the East Asians adopted emphasized trade, at first mainly with the United States but then among themselves as well. American military hegemony sheltered the development of economic interdependence and that interdependence had major economic consequences.

Before World War II most of the countries of Europe had been, by global standards, rich. Afterwards they set out to restore the prosperity the war had destroyed and their strategy for restoration included ever-increasing cross-border trade and investment. Both expanded steadily over the four and one half decades of the Cold War and contributed to the post-Cold War peace on the continent. By contrast, before the second world war Asian countries, with the sole exception of Japan, were poor. In the wake of that war they set out to become wealthy, and their strategies for doing so brought them, by a somewhat different path than the one the Europeans adopted, to steady and substantial increases in trade, measured both by volume and value, as well as increases in cross-border investment. In East Asia, as in Europe, economic interdependence bolstered and deepened peace.

In economic matters the other countries of East Asia followed the Japanese example. Japan recovered from the devastation of war after 1945 and went on to create the second largest economy in the world by emphasizing exports. While poor countries outside the region often adopted what became known as the "import-substitution" strategy for economic growth, building up local industries and protecting them from foreign competition with tariffs and other measures, South Korea, Taiwan, many Southeast Asian countries and ultimately China, following the Japanese example, entered global markets and prospered. They took advantage of their relatively low labor costs to manufacture textiles, automobiles, and electronic equipment that they sold to consumers beyond their borders. This strategy paid off: the East Asians grew faster, and so became richer, than did the practitioners of import-substitution.[9] For two centuries the gap in wealth between East Asia and the countries of Western Europe and North America had expanded. Now it began to narrow.

In the East Asians' successful economic strategy the United States played an indispensable role, not only as protector of their trade but also as the principal consumer of their exports. America offered the dual advantages, for this purpose, of a population with the inclination and the resources to buy consumer products and fewer barriers to imports than virtually any other country. For much of the Cold War, the pattern of Asian trade resembled the hub-and-spokes configuration of the region's security arrangements, with the Asian countries having closer economic ties with the United States than with one another. Over time, however, intra-regional trade in Asia grew, especially with China. When the Cold War ended, the economic conditions that can act as an antidote to hostility, security competition, and war between and among sovereign states were firmly in place in East Asia.

The peace-promoting power of trade reached into the domestic politics of the countries of the region. Each of the East Asian governments based its claim to govern in no small part on the delivery of prosperity to the people over whom it presided. Prosperity in turn, depended heavily on exports—that is, on trade. Anything that interrupted trade, as war inevitably does, would risk costing these governments what was most important to them: their own incumbency.

In Europe, in addition to benign American hegemony and substantial and growing economic interdependence, the post-Cold War peace had the modern era's third peace-promoting mechanism. At the outset of the period every significant country there had, or aspired to have, a democratic political system. In East Asia as well, democracy contributed to the unprecedentedly peaceful character of post-Cold War international relations—but only up to a point.

Before 1945 East Asia had no democracies. Democratic governance originated in the West, and while the West brought many things to Asia, before 1945 economic, religious, and political liberty and popular sovereignty were not among them. To the contrary, the Portuguese, the Dutch, the British, the French, the Spanish, and the Americans imposed imperial rule on much of the region. After 1945, however, and with the end of the era of Western imperial dominance around the world, democracy began to take root in the Asia-Pacific region. It appeared first in Japan, then spread to South Korea, Thailand, Taiwan, the Philippines, and Indonesia. Continuing Western, especially American, cultural influence and military protection encouraged the adoption of democratic institutions and practice. So, too, did the free-market economic systems through which the Asians carried out the strategy of export-promotion: to function effectively, free markets require economic liberty, one of democracy's defining features.[10]

With democracy as well as economic interdependence more recently established among them and thus more fragile than in Europe, without Europe's common experiences and common institutions, and without, in particular, the treaties and rules that together constituted Europe's common security order, peace was not as firmly grounded or widely accepted in the Asia-Pacific region as it was in Europe. Still, East Asia did enjoy a deeper, wider peace—it was further from war and had less intense security competition—than ever before in its modern history. The peace of Asia shared one more feature with the peace of Europe. It did not last.

In Europe, the country that ultimately destroyed the post-Cold War peace, Russia, was never as fully reconciled to American hegemony, or as fully integrated into cross-border trade and investment, and was never as committed to democracy, as the other countries of the continent. Russia began the post-Cold War era as a new and tentative member of the European security order, drifted into the status of outlier, and then emerged as full-fledged opponent of the status quo. The country analogous to Russia in Asia, China, participated much more extensively in the region's economic life, becoming, in fact, something close to its hub. The second modern peace-promoting condition, economic interdependence, had greater force in Asia than in Europe. The third such condition, democracy, however, was weaker. Far from embracing democracy, as Russia's first post-communist leader Boris Yeltsin tried to do, the ruling Chinese Communist Party kept a tight grip on power and adamantly resisted yielding power to a government freely elected and committed to respecting and protecting liberty. In the end, despite the first difference and because of the second, in the security affairs of East Asia China took a path similar to Russia's in Europe. This happened for one of the same principal reasons—the domestic needs of the regime—and with the same result: the end of the post-Cold War peace.

China's Singularity

The world's oldest continuous political community, China has three and one-half millennia of history, but in no period in its long and eventful past, which includes numerous wars and dynastic upheavals, did it experience as much change as in the three decades after 1979. That year saw the beginning of free-market reforms of the centrally-planned economic system imposed after 1949 by Mao Zedong and his communist regime. The reforms touched off an extraordinary era of economic growth. The statistics are impressive, indeed startling. The country's economy expanded by at least 10 percent in every year of the next thirty, and continued at lower but still robust rates thereafter. China's gross domestic product (GDP) doubled every seven years, growing from $70 billion in 1980 to $9 trillion in 2014.[11] Per capita annual income increased from $210 in 1978[12] to $4940 in 2011 and to $6900 in 2016. By the estimate of the World Bank five hundred million Chinese—roughly the equivalent of the entire population of the European Union—rose out of poverty. When the reforms began, China had a negligible presence in the global economy. By 2016 it was producing 16.4 percent of global GDP and 20 percent of global manufacturing, contributing 35 percent of global growth, and engaging in 11 percent of global trade.[13] Even allowing for inaccuracy and exaggeration in official Chinese statistics, these figures have the power to astonish.

China produced this economic surge by using exports as the engine of growth, as had Japan and other East Asian countries before it. In addition, the Chinese government invested heavily in infrastructure, especially roads and ports. In contravention of communist principles, it created special economic zones that welcomed foreign investment. Despite the fundamental Marxist-Leninist-Maoist opposition to individual ownership, the regime created the functional equivalent of private property. All of these measures made indispensable contributions to the country's economic surge.

This most miraculous episode of the larger, post-1945 East Asian economic miracle had sweeping consequences for Chinese society, which acquired the main features of modern life—urbanization, a middle class, and mass consumption—in a single generation. As the most populous country not only in Asia but in the world, China's explosive growth was also bound to have an impact beyond its borders. By the end of the post-Cold War era it had made the People's Republic the leading trading partner of the other countries of the region. It also supplied China with the foundation of greater military power than any of its neighbors possessed, and ultimately for sufficient military power to challenge the United States for primacy in the Asia-Pacific region.

Chinese economic growth therefore opened the way to a kind of geopolitical competition with troubling historical antecedents. More than once the political ambitions of a rising power have brought it into direct conflict with others. The pattern is historically familiar enough to have earned a distinctive title—the "Thucydides Trap"[14]—after the diagnosis of the ancient Greek historian Thucydides of the reason for the great war between Athens and Sparta in fifth-century-B.C. Greece: "What made war inevitable was the growth of Athenian power and the fears that this caused in Sparta." More recently, Germany's aspirations for greater global power and influence, fueled by rapid economic growth in the last three decades of the nineteenth century, led to a collision with Britain, France, and Russia that became the first world war. The conviction, or fear, that the Chinese communists would follow, in the twenty-first century, the path of the German emperor in the nineteenth gave rise to the term "Wilhelmine China."[15]

Because wealth forms the basis for political and military power, and because powerful countries often develop ambitions to remake their regions in accordance with their own preferences,[16] it was hardly unrealistic to anticipate that China's extraordinary growth would come to threaten other countries. Under these circumstances it would have been logical for the others to do whatever they could to arrest that growth, or at least to take steps to counterbalance it. For most of the post-Cold War period, however, the United States and its East Asian friends, clients, and allies did neither. To the contrary, those who had the most to lose from it politically abetted, and even celebrated, China's economic rise.

Democracies such as the United States and its post-Cold War East Asian allies have on occasion tried to inhibit the economic performance of other countries, usually through the imposition of economic sanctions, but they have invariably done so only in response to actual misdeeds. In the late 1930s and early 1940s, for example, the United States placed a series of trade restrictions on Japan as punishment for the Japanese invasion and occupation of north China. The sanctions culminated in an embargo on the sale of oil in July 1941, which helped to trigger the Japanese attack on Pearl Harbor, Hawaii, on December 7 of that year. To inflict economic—or political, or military—punishment on an individual or a group in anticipation of acts it might commit at some time in the future, however, violates the democratic commitment to fairness and due process. That is what the East Asians and the Americans would have been doing had they acted to curb China's economic progress.

Moreover, that progress brought economic benefits to the others: investment in and trade with China raised the incomes of business owners and the standards of living of consumers in East Asia and the United States, which made reducing these cross-border economic flows

politically difficult. Upon assuming office in 1993, the Clinton administration proposed to deny China access to the American market[17]
unless the communist regime began to respect the human rights of
the people it governed. Not only did the regime flatly reject this demand, American businesses, fearful of retaliation from Beijing that
would deny them access to the Chinese market, opposed it. Clinton
dropped it.

The United States, especially, refrained from attempting to restrict
China's economic growth for yet a third reason. Conditioned by their
own deepest political beliefs and their interpretation of the course of
recent history, the Americans were convinced that the continuation of
China's economic ascent would remove the danger of the Thucydides
trap. Economic growth, according to this "liberal theory of history"[18]—
not a formal doctrine but a widely shared set of beliefs—would foster
democracy. Because democracies conduct peaceful foreign policies,
China would not seek to assert itself beyond its borders at the expense
of its neighbors. It would, rather, become part of the rules-based economic and security orders in East Asia and the wider world that the
United States had done so much to create and support.

Optimistic though this point of view undoubtedly is, and naive
as it may appear in retrospect (at least as applied to China), it had a
solid basis in twentieth-century history. In the last three decades of
that century a "democratic wave"[19] had swept across the world, with
dozens of countries in Europe, Asia, Latin America, and Africa (the
Arab Middle East was the exception) acquiring, or seeking to acquire,
systems of governance featuring popularly elected governments committed to respecting and protecting economic, religious, and political liberty. Almost all of these countries had, like China, previously
adopted free-market economic systems and had thereby substantially
increased their rates of economic growth. The success of free markets
in comparison with rival forms of economic organization made the
Western set of economic practices and institutions almost universally popular: only a tiny number of sovereign states spurned them.[20]
Logic and experience, moreover, suggested that economic growth and
the market practices that produce it will foster democratic politics, a
point that found its way into the public rhetoric of American political
leaders.[21]

Contemporary history furnished compelling evidence that democracy, in turn, made for peace. The Western European democracies created, over the course of the Cold War, a security community free not only of war but also of war's underlying catalyst, security competition, in no small part *because* they practiced democratic politics and governance.[22] In addition, studies showed a consistent pattern of peaceful conduct toward one another by democracies.[23] So a democratic China, which the working of its reformed economy could, history showed, be expected ultimately to deliver, would carry out a foreign policy more like Germany's after World War II than before World War I. Thus the liberal theory of history: free markets beget democratic government, and democracies conduct peaceful foreign policies.

Not only the general worldwide experience of the twentieth century, moreover, but also the evolution of Chinese politics and foreign policy during the country's economic ascent supplied supporting evidence for this theory. As the country's GDP rose, its people became freer. Religious observance expanded, for Christians at least, and irregular harassment of believers replaced the systematic persecution of the Maoist era.[24] In increasing numbers, Chinese owned their own homes, bought stocks, and started businesses. They could travel and study abroad, activities that Mao had forbidden. China did not become a democracy: the Communist Party continued to hold a monopoly of political power and to repress any individual or group that challenged it; but it was not fanciful to regard the country as heading in a democratic direction even as daily life for the average Chinese became far less oppressive and considerably more prosperous.

As for foreign policy, here China, even without democratic politics and governance, showed signs of becoming what its neighbors hoped it would be: a good citizen of the existing international order. The Maoist commitment to fomenting revolution across Asia and in other poor countries disappeared. The Chinese government joined most international organizations for which it was eligible. Deng Xiaoping, the communist leader who followed Mao and who authorized and defended the country's economic reforms, decreed that even as it grew richer and politically more influential China should "hide the brightness"[25]—that is, practice modesty in its relations with other countries. As its expanding economy became the central feature of Asian affairs, the Chinese government proclaimed itself dedicated to a "peaceful rise."

Americans especially had entertained the hope of transforming China to make it richer and freer ever since missionaries and traders from the United States had made their ways there in the nineteenth century.[26] The liberal theory of history expressed that hope in contemporary terms. It had a particular appeal in the West because, by its logic, China and other countries would make themselves over in the Western image without the West, and the democracies of East Asia, having to make any sacrifices or indeed exert themselves in any way. All they had to do, according to this theory, was to take advantage of the economic opportunities that China offered.

This happy perspective had the additional virtue of being true— or at least being valid for many countries. It was neither delusional nor purely wishful thinking to believe that China's extraordinary economic growth generated social and political forces that were propelling the country toward a peaceful foreign policy. To the extent that this was accurate it made any effort to impede that growth not only morally dubious, politically difficult, and economically costly, but also, from the standpoint of its neighbors' hopes for China's geopolitical direction, counterproductive. While faith in the liberal theory of history was not entirely misplaced, however, twenty-five years after the Cold War ended it had not produced the kind of China the other East Asians and the Americans had hoped would evolve.[27] Even as these benign, peace-promoting forces were at work, a powerful feature of Chinese history and Chinese political culture, nationalism, was pushing the country in a direction that its neighbors and the United States not only did not favor but that in fact threatened them.

China's version of nationalism stemmed from its singular history. During much of it, China had been geographically the largest, politically the most powerful, economically the richest, culturally the most influential, and militarily the strongest political community on the planet. It considered itself to be located, politically and culturally as well as geographically, at the center of the world: hence China's term for itself—the Middle Kingdom.

For much of recorded history China dominated East Asia. Its neighbors acknowledged its primacy by adopting aspects of Chinese culture, and through various rituals and payments, an arrangement known as the tribute system. The Chinese regarded their hegemony in the region, both at the time and in retrospect, as natural, normal, proper, and benign. Those peoples unfortunate enough to live at great distances from the Chinese capital were deemed to be barbarians— inferior in every way to the world's leading civilization.[28]

This longstanding Chinese view of the world envisioned a hierarchy of political communities with China at the top. To put it differently, China, like Russia, dwelled at one end of a cultural gradient, but in the Chinese case, unlike that of the Russians, at the apex. While the Russians lagged behind the European countries to their West, in Chinese eyes (and for much of history in the eyes of other Asians as well) China led the world.[29]

Then, beginning in the nineteenth century, things changed. For China, the world turned upside down: the Middle Kingdom experienced a great fall. The European powers, which Chinese officials had regarded as inconsequential insofar as they had noticed them at all, became, through the mastery of the Industrial Revolution, far more powerful than China. The Europeans sent troops and gunboats to East Asia, encroached on Chinese territory, carved out privileged zones along its coast known as treaty ports, and even, in 1860, laid waste to the imperial residence and complex of elaborate gardens and buildings outside the center of Beijing known as the Summer Palace.

From the middle of the nineteenth century to the middle of the twentieth China suffered one defeat after another. At the beginning of what the Chinese came to call their "century of humiliation,"[30] Great Britain defeated China in the two Opium Wars—conflicts over trade and sovereignty—in 1842 and 1860. The settlement of the first ceded Hong Kong and five treaty ports to the British; the end of the second led to the establishment of even more Western enclaves. The Taiping Rebellion, from 1850 to 1864, whose leader drew mystical inspiration from the West and sought, unsuccessfully, Western assistance against the emperor, devastated much of the central and southern parts of the country, further weakening the imperial government in Beijing.[31] The Japanese victory in the Sino-Japanese War in 1895 ended the long

Chinese reign as the leading power in East Asia and gave Japan both possession of the island of Taiwan and a privileged position on the Korean peninsula. In 1900 Chinese mounted an anti-Western, anti-Christian uprising known as the Boxer Rebellion, which Western troops firmly suppressed. At the Paris Peace Conference of 1919, which followed World War I, the victorious powers gave the German territories on the Chinese coast to Japan rather than restoring them to China, sparking protest demonstrations by students that became known as the May 4 Movement.[32] Finally, in 1937 Japan invaded China and imposed a murderous occupation on much of the country that lasted until the end of World War II.

In the face of this series of crushing defeats, humiliating concessions, and widespread human suffering, the goal of every Chinese leader, whether imperial or—after the end of the monarchy in 1911—republican, became the reversal of the erosion of Chinese sovereignty, of the decline of Chinese power, and of the loss of China's global status. Chiang Kai-shek, the principal Chinese leader from 1928 to 1945, inscribed a daily reminder in his diary beginning in 1928 with the character *Xuechi*, meaning "to avenge humiliation."[33]

It became a communist goal as well. Mao Zedong's communists defeated Chiang's forces in the civil war that followed World War II. Like their fellow communists who had taken control of the Russian empire three decades earlier. Mao and his henchmen were committed to the radical reshaping of Chinese society in accordance with the Maoist version of Marxism-Leninism. They persecuted people they deemed their class enemies, brought industry and agriculture under the control of the state, and concentrated all power in the hands of the Communist Party. They rejected all of the political ideas their predecessors had embraced over a century and a half, with a single exception: the imperial and republican idea of China's proper place in the world.

Orthodox Marxism considered nationalism at best a distraction from the historically-prescribed task of world revolution, at worst an obstacle to achieving that goal because it divided workers in different countries from one another, blinding them to their common interests. The Russian Bolsheviks believed this, but unlike them, the Chinese communists appealed from the outset to nationalist sentiment.[34] A declaration attributed to Mao at the dawn of the communist era, which achieved wide currency in the country, made the point: "China has stood up."[35] The Chinese took it to mean that their country had at last confronted the foreign powers that had preyed on it for a century but that henceforth would not be permitted to do so.

Even as they went about dismantling all political and economic structures inherited from the past and replacing them with new and what they believed to be superior communist ones, the Maoist regime sought to demonstrate its fitness to rule China by associating itself with nationalism. Of nationalism's three aims, the Chinese had enjoyed the first—their own sovereign state—almost uninterruptedly for 2,000 years. The second, possession of all the territory that properly belonged to the nation, had been lost in the century of humiliation and the communists depicted themselves as having consistently dedicated themselves to achieving it.[36] In particular, they insisted that they had put up stiffer and braver resistance to the occupying Japanese than had their civil war adversaries, the Kuomintang, a claim that historians have not found credible.[37]

Once in power they evidently saw advantages in perpetuating popular hostility to the Japanese, even when, as a result of its economic reforms, China began to trade with, and accept investment from, Japan—to the economic benefit of both countries. Even then, the Chinese communists presented themselves as vigilant against the continuing Japanese efforts, or at least aspiration, to subjugate China again. The demonization of impeccably peaceful postwar Japan became a staple of official Chinese propaganda.[38] The occasional visit of a Japanese leader to a shrine to his countrymen killed in World War II, where several former officials considered war criminals lay buried, became occasions for public reminders from Beijing of Japanese aggression in the 1930s and 1940s, warnings about the dangers of a recurrence, and assertions that the Chinese Communist Party stood ready to oppose it.[39] China's territorial disputes with Japan in the western Pacific touched off anti-Japanese demonstrations, often encouraged by the authorities once they began but apparently spontaneous in origin, which testified to the depth and durability of anti-Japanese feeling.

The communist regime made the United States an object of its nationalist propaganda as well.[40] America presented an obvious target as the leading military and economic power in East Asia, a position that the Chinese believed rightfully belonged to them. The Chinese aspiration to restore their primacy constituted, along with the determination to evict foreigners from Chinese territory, one of the two main themes of Chinese nationalism.[41]

Still, both the regime and the Chinese public had mixed feelings about the United States, which had, after all, supported China in its mid-twentieth-century struggle with Japan and then against the Soviet Union in the second half of the Cold War. American military predominance in the Asia-Pacific region, moreover, in combination with the openness of the American market, the world's largest, to exports from other countries, notably including China, had made possible the country's three decades of hyper-rapid economic growth, something many Chinese recognized.[42] In addition, hundreds of thousands of young Chinese studied in the United States, with many of the communist leaders sending their own children to America for this purpose. Still, the regime periodically accused the United States of trying to contain and isolate China. The accusation played on nationalist feelings through the implication that the Americans were seeking to prevent China's return to its rightful position of primacy in the region and the world. The broadly held and emotionally resonant Chinese desire to restore their country's previous status went hand in hand with another aspect of Chinese nationalism that worked against the peace-promoting forces of the post-Cold War era: irredentism.

In its long history China's borders have changed many times. When the communists came to power in 1949 they asserted their sovereignty over territory as expansive as any previous government had ever controlled. Their definition of China included lands to the west— Tibet and Xinjiang—where relatively few Han Chinese lived in 1949 but that were the homelands of non-Han Buddhists and Muslims. Ninety percent of the population of the People's Republic of China was and is ethnically Han Chinese, but because the Tibetan Buddhists and Uighur Muslims of Xinjiang did not wish to be part of a Chinese-dominated state, and periodically mounted small-scale (and invariably unsuccessful) rebellions against it, communist China became, despite its fierce anti-imperial rhetoric, a multinational empire, just at the time when the Europeans were relinquishing the empires they had assembled in the eighteenth and nineteenth centuries.

The new regime claimed as a province an island that it did not control and that had not been governed from the Chinese capital for most of the country's history and not at any time since 1895. The communist claim on Taiwan became a source of political friction and occasionally even low-level military conflict with other countries, especially the United States. Situated about 100 miles off the southeast coast of the mainland, Taiwan became a major issue in Chinese foreign policy, and in the international relations of East Asia.

This occurred, in the first place, because of an historically unusual feature of China's civil war and communist revolution. Whereas the losing side in other such conflicts had fractured, with its adherents fleeing abroad—French nobles took shelter in the surviving European monarchies after 1789, the Russian upper classes decamped to Berlin and Paris after 1917, and much of the Iranian middle class relocated to Los Angeles and other Western cities after 1979—following its defeat in 1949, Chiang Kai-shek's Kuomintang (KMT) moved its cadre of officials and much of its army to Taiwan and established a government there. It proclaimed itself the legitimate government of all of China. In the eyes of the Maoist regime this made it an ongoing threat to communist rule on the mainland, and the communists declared their intention to conquer Taiwan.

Its distance from the mainland made the island a plausible target for invasion but not an easy one. It was close enough for the communist government to make capturing it militarily a plausible goal, but far enough away to make achieving that goal formidably difficult. Then, the outbreak of the Korean War on June 25, 1950, froze Taiwan's status in place: self-governing but not formally independent. In response to the attack by communist North Korea on the non-communist South, the American president, Harry S Truman, ordered the American Seventh Fleet to the Taiwan Strait that separates the island from the mainland. Chinese entry into the war against the United States and South Korea in November of that year set the seal on a bitter estrangement between the United States and the communist regime in Beijing that lasted for two decades. Washington recognized Chiang's island regime as the legitimate government of all of China and signed a defense treaty with it, thus eliminating any chance that the communist Chinese could seize it without engaging in war with the far more powerful United States.

Despite the American guarantee, Mao made the determination to gain control of Taiwan a conspicuous part of his foreign policy. In the 1950s he launched limited military operations against it, shelling some tiny islands in the Taiwan Strait that both the communists and KMT claimed. In response, the American administration of President Dwight D. Eisenhower made veiled threats of nuclear retaliation.[43]

As part of their rapprochement in 1972, the Chinese and American governments issued a joint statement putting to one side the Taiwan question. What became known as the Shanghai Communique noted that Chinese on both sides of the Taiwan Strait asserted that there was but one China—that is, that both the communists and the KMT agreed that a single government should control both the mainland and the island while disagreeing on which of them should be that government—and that the United States did not dispute this. In December, 1978, the Carter administration announced that it would accord full diplomatic recognition to Beijing, and broke formal ties with Taiwan. The American Congress, however, passed the Taiwan Relations Act, mandating a continuing connection with the island, including arms sales, although without a full defense treaty.

Despite de-recognition by the United States, and by other countries seeking to cultivate good relations with Beijing, Taiwan thrived economically,[44] building the eighteenth largest economy in the world. Along with its export-led growth, and no doubt partly because of it, the island joined the late-twentieth-century democratic wave. Democracy in Taiwan threatened the communists on the Chinese mainland because it led the island's newly democratic government to give up its claim to power on the mainland. The next logical step was to declare Taiwan a separate, independent country. Such a declaration would clash with and, if successfully carried out, undermine the communist claim to sovereignty there. The communist authorities in Beijing asserted that a Taiwanese declaration of independence would provoke a military response from them. Democracy on Taiwan was additionally threatening because it might prove contagious, and threaten what the communists valued most: their own monopoly of power.

As Taiwan held its first free and fair election for president in 1996, Beijing expressed its displeasure by conducting military exercises near the island, firing artillery shells into the surrounding waters. In response, the American government dispatched two aircraft carriers along with other ships to the region.[45]

While it did not trigger a shooting war in East Asia during either the Cold War or the post-Cold War period, the Taiwan issue did create the threat of war, a threat that Beijing assiduously kept alive. This meant that the kind of common security arrangements that Europe enjoyed at the end of the Cold War were not possible in East Asia. Common security is based on the premise that no country is prepared to change the status quo by force: to the contrary, over the status of Taiwan, the communist regime repeatedly advertised its willingness to do precisely just that. The dispute over Taiwan also prevented the peace of Asia from becoming as solid and deep as it became in Europe. It gave rise to security competition, including one of its most familiar manifestations: an ongoing arms race between the mainland and the island. Beijing amassed a fleet of 1200 ballistic missiles on the coast opposite Taiwan[46] that was ready to be launched in retaliation for a declaration of independence. The Taiwanese tried to counterbalance China's growing military prowess by procuring armaments, particularly high-performance aircraft, from the United States, as provided for in the Taiwan Relations Act. While more peaceful than at any other time in the modern era, therefore, the Taiwan issue prevented the relations among the sovereign states of East Asia from achieving the depth of peace on the European continent.

Although the communist authorities were willing to defer their goal of governing Taiwan, it was politically unthinkable for them to do what deep peace would have required: namely, to renounce it. The claim to rule the island stood at the heart of the Chinese Communist Party's assertion of its entitlement to govern the country. The Party based this claim, after all, on its frequently reiterated commitment to the restoration not only of China's lost greatness but also, and more concretely, of territory stolen by foreigners during the century of humiliation. Of this historical wrong, which the Communist Party had undertaken to right, Taiwan became the outstanding example. Its Taiwan policy demonstrated the regime's reliance for legitimacy, support, the good opinion of the Chinese public, and its hold on power on Chinese nationalism.[47]

During the post-Cold War period the Chinese government was therefore subject to pressure, from the nationalist sentiment that the regime itself encouraged, to change the existing economic and political arrangements in East Asia. It was pledged to take control of Taiwan, which, given the Taiwanese refusal to be controlled from Beijing, could only be accomplished by force. More broadly, the regime had inherited, and had embraced, the conviction that Chinese primacy in the region was the natural order of things and that it was China's mission to resume its rightful place atop the hierarchy of Asian countries. The other countries of the region did not subscribe to the doctrine of Chinese superiority, which would therefore, as in the case of mainland control of Taiwan, have to be forcibly imposed on them.

The other East Asians preferred the existing institutions, procedures, and distribution of power in their region. The communist regime in Beijing itself had good reasons to go along with them. American hegemony, however inconsistent with the Chinese view of their place in Asia, underpinned the peaceful conditions in which trade and investment crucial for Chinese prosperity flourished. Moreover, the United States, with its long head start in building a modern military and its mastery of advanced technology, had a large advantage over mainland China's ground, naval, and air forces.

Pressures pushing China in opposite directions therefore weighed on the country's foreign policy and for most of the quarter century after the Cold War ended, the balance between them favored prudence, patience, and acceptance of the economic benefits of the status quo over the deeply rooted impulse to reshape the region according to Chinese lights. By the middle of the second decade of the twenty-first century, however, the balance had shifted. China was working to overturn the status quo. Like Russia in Europe, the People's Republic was carrying out policies and pursuing goals that other countries opposed, and was relying heavily on military force to do so.

Chinese Revisionism

Maoist China saw itself as a revolutionary force, bent on both upending the international order and establishing communist political and economic systems in other countries. Deng Xiaoping's China abandoned

Mao's aspirations for global revolution in favor of membership in the world's principal international organizations and active participation in the Western-dominated global economy. It functioned as an international "free rider," taking advantage of the benefits that the existing international order offered, especially the trading system and the American-supplied military guarantee of it, while contributing nothing to its upkeep. Western officials expressed the hope that the Chinese government would recognize the value of the institutions and practices of which it had made such good use and, by becoming a "responsible stakeholder," begin to help sustain them.[48]

Instead, the communist regime in Beijing launched efforts that aimed not to eradicate every trace of the existing political and economic arrangements, as Mao had proclaimed his intention to do, but to change them in ways that would give China greater power. The People's Republic became an actively revisionist country, and that put an end to the post-Cold War peace of East Asia.

In economic affairs the Chinese sought to establish new institutions, with the ultimate aim of displacing those put in place by the West. In response to the financial crisis of 2008, which lax American financial practices had triggered, the Chinese government, among others, expressed doubt that the United States should continue to play as large a role in the world's monetary affairs as it had since World War II. The Chinese made it clear that they wanted their own currency, the renminbi (rmb), to be used more widely and that they aspired for it one day to rival in international status, or even to supplant, the American dollar.

In matters of investment and trade the Chinese took concrete steps to enhance their regional and global importance. They launched the Asian Infrastructure Investment Bank (AIIB), with its headquarters in Beijing and with China as the largest contributor to its stock of capital, for the purpose of making the kinds of loans in which the Washington-based World Bank specialized. The United States declined to join and urged its allies to steer clear of the AIIB as well, but a number of them did become founding members. At the same time, China announced ambitious plans to expand trade. Its "New Silk Road Initiative" was designed to upgrade, or build from scratch, transportation links from China through Central Asia to Europe. It envisioned construction on a large scale of roads, railways, ports, and other forms of infrastructure. The project was to follow, roughly, the route over which silk and other commodities traveled west from China beginning two millennia ago. Beijing also announced a plan for a maritime version of the Silk Road, to connect China to Southeast Asia, the Middle East, and Africa, putting the overland and transoceanic projects together under the heading "One Belt, One Road (OBOR)."[49]

These initiatives[50] grew logically out of China's rising economic strength. They arose as well out of the failure of other countries to offer China a role in international economic institutions commensurate with its rising importance: the United States Congress blocked an increase in Chinese voting power in the International Monetary Fund and the Trans-Pacific Partnership, an American-sponsored trade agreement that included most of the major countries in Asia, excluded China.[51] They also bespoke China's ambition to assume a dominant role in Asian economic affairs, in keeping with the country's self-image as the region's natural leader.[52]

The success of these initiatives, which was far from assured,[53] would enhance Chinese power and influence in East Asia and beyond.[54] Yet they did not, in and of themselves, qualify as acts of aggression or even threats to China's neighbors. Economics is, after all, an activity that social scientists call a "positive-sum game": a gain for one country need not mean a loss for others. To the contrary, when one of them grows economically others typically do as well: that was certainly the East Asian experience in the post-Cold War era, and especially the impact on its neighbors of China's meteoric economic rise. Beijing's China-centered international economic initiatives had the potential to bring economic benefits to other countries as well. The AIIB promised to increase the capital available for growth-supporting projects in Asia, while the New Silk Road sought to expand trade: both would, if they functioned properly, make the region, and thus the world as a whole, richer.

Moreover, China's international economic program fostered competition with the existing, Western-sponsored institutions and practices; and in free-market economies competition is desirable: it drives the engine of progress. Security competition, however, does not have comparably benign effects; and by seeking to revise the existing political rules and distribution of power, China reintroduced security competition to East Asia.

Unlike its economic initiatives, China's challenge to the political status quo took a military form, and the form it took broke with Chinese precedent: the communist regime contested the region's political rules and norms, and its distribution of power, at sea rather than on land. For the first time in more than 500 years,[55] China built a formidable navy. While it has 14,000 miles of land borders, with four-teen adjacent countries,[56] it was not disputes about them that broke the post-Cold War peace. In fact, China settled some of those disputes. Instead, the Chinese initiated security competition with its neighbors through maritime measures of several kinds.

It made, or revived, sweeping and provocative territorial claims, which conflicted both with established international norms and with the claims of other East Asian countries. China began actively to assert its long-standing but previously dormant claim to small, uninhabited islands located northeast of Taiwan and controlled by Japan, which the Japanese called the Senkakus and the Chinese the Diaoyu. In 2010 a Chinese fishing trawler deliberately rammed two Japanese Coast Guard vessels near the islands. The Japanese took the trawler's captain into custody, touching off a diplomatic dispute between the two countries and anti-Japanese demonstrations in five Chinese cities. In 2012 tensions over the islands spiked again, with military maneuvers and heated diplomatic exchanges.[57]

To the south, Beijing asserted that almost all of the strategically and economically important South China Sea[58] belonged to China. In 2009 it began to place public emphasis on a map charting that assertion, which the Kuomintang had initially put forward in the 1940s. The cartographic depiction of China's claim came to be known as the nine-dashed line, or "cow's tongue," because of its elongated U-shape. The extraordinarily expansive definition of its sovereign waters brought China into conflict with Vietnam, the Philippines, Indonesia, and Malaysia because it encroached on their own claims of maritime sovereignty.[59]

In 2013 the Philippines filed a case with the World Court in The Hague disputing the legal validity of the nine-dashed line. On July 12, 2016, the Court issued its verdict in the Philippines' favor. The Chinese government immediately announced that it would not accept or abide by the Court's judgement.[60]

In addition, China began using dredging equipment to build artificial islands in the South China Sea, declared them to be Chinese territory, and started to build military facilities on them.[61] Beijing asserted that the seas surrounding what they had built counted as Chinese territorial waters, with the privileges that come with that designation accruing to China.[62] Other countries rejected this assertion on the grounds that, according to international law, such privileges go with natural but not manmade islands. The net effect of all this was to create at sea the kind of issue over which wars are traditionally fought: territorial disputes.

In another departure from widely accepted international law, in 2013 Beijing proclaimed the existence of a Chinese Air Defense Identification Zone, through which aircraft from other countries needed Chinese permission to pass, that extended across the East China Sea to encompass the Senkakus and included what Japan had long claimed as its own air space. By the terms China announced, American aircraft, upon which Japan depended for its defense, could only operate there with China's assent, a condition hardly acceptable to either the Japanese or the American government.[63]

A substantial expansion of Chinese naval and air forces made these aggressive policies possible. For much of its history the People's Republic had had armed forces of modest capacity at best. Mao Zedong presided over a very poor country and professed his faith in the ability of the revolutionary fervor and willpower of the Chinese masses to overcome the technology of Western armed forces.[64] When Deng Xiaoping assumed power after Mao's death, he made national defense a low priority. It became the fourth of the "four modernizations" that he announced the country would pursue, after agriculture, industry, and science and technology.[65]

Military spending constituted only a small fraction of the overall national budget during the first decade and a half of the period of economic reform; but defense expenditures rose during that time because they made up a fraction of a rapidly growing national economy. Beginning in the latter part of the 1990s, moreover, the Chinese government increased the proportion of its budget devoted to the armed forces, with defense spending increasing, by one estimate, by 16 percent per year.[66]

To be sure, the Chinese had legitimate uses for a navy. Their economy relied on unfettered maritime access to the rest of the world: it depended heavily on transoceanic trade and on the 65 percent of its total oil consumption that came from beyond its borders, much of it shipped from the Persian Gulf. While the United States had, since the end of World War II, guaranteed the sea routes to and from East Asia, no country, especially no large country such as China, is likely to feel entirely comfortable relying on others for transactions vital to well-being. To the extent that its government distrusted the Americans, China had an incentive to provide for the security of its own maritime commerce. China's decision to equip itself with the means to protect its own exports and imports was therefore at least understandable and did not, in and of itself, qualify as inherently aggressive.

What did make Chinese policy aggressive in the eyes of other East Asian countries and the United States was its claim to maritime territory that, by custom, tradition, and international law, belonged to others. The specific features of China's military buildup reinforced others' image of the People's Republic as a revisionist power whose ambitions threatened its neighbors. The weapons China acquired and the naval strategy it was apparently pursuing seemed to have as their principal goal negating America's naval advantage in the East and South China Seas, in the Yellow Sea between the Chinese mainland and the Korean peninsula, and in the Taiwan Strait.

To this end China invested in submarines to combat the American surface fleet and in missiles, both based on land and carried by aircraft, capable of crippling America's aircraft carriers and striking American military bases in the region. China also began to acquire aircraft carriers of its own.[67] The American military referred to the Chinese strategy that these weapons served by the acronym A2/AD, which stood for anti-access area denial. Its purpose, in the American view, was to prevent the American navy from operating in waters east of the China coast, where, as it happened, a number of America's allies were located. China was seeking to exclude American naval forces from within the "first island chain," a perimeter stretching from Japan in the north through Taiwan and the Philippines to the Indonesian island of

Borneo in the south. The aim was to make these waters a kind of maritime "no-go" zone for the United States Navy, tilting the balance of power there in China's favor. China referred to the program to contest the superior American military forces in the western Pacific by a term borrowed from its long military history and associated with thwarting a stronger power: "the assassin's mace."[68]

China sought, in short, to make itself the master of the seas over an area reaching as far into the Pacific as possible.[69] Such a state of affairs would go a long way to fulfilling the deeply and widely held nationalist ambition to resume the regional prominence it regarded as rightfully belonging to China, which the century of humiliation had stripped away. Taiwan's capacity to retain its independence would be severely weakened. China would dominate East Asia and other countries would acknowledge and adjust to Chinese hegemony just as they had for much of the previous two millennia. The United States would no longer have significant influence in the region, an outcome anticipated by Xi Jinping, the most powerful Chinese leader, in May, 2014, when he said that it was time "for the people of Asia to run the affairs of Asia, solve the problems of Asia, and uphold the security of Asia."[70] The communist regime's territorial claims and military buildup, that is, were in keeping with, indeed in a sense followed logically from, the version of nationalism embedded in Chinese political culture.[71]

Its usefulness in realizing an enduring Chinese political aspiration partly explains why China's peaceful rise turned, suddenly, into a forceful one. Three decades of rapid economic growth, underwriting first steady and then rapid expansion in its armed forces, gave China the military basis for moving to fulfill its long-held ambition of resuming its place at the top of the hierarchy of East Asian countries.[72] In this sense China acted—and some Chinese no doubt saw their country as acting—like the small child who is bullied by other, older ones and who, upon growing up to be bigger and stronger than they, turns on them to repay their insults.

On this account it was only a matter of time before China's approach to its neighbors turned assertive and aggressive; but that account is not the whole story. China's twenty-first-century revisionism had other causes as well. Events provided an opportunity for a larger Chinese regional and global role. In the first decade of the new century the United States, the principal obstacle to Chinese supremacy in East Asia and beyond, found itself preoccupied with and bogged down in Iraq, far from East Asia. Then, in 2008, an American housing bubble burst, a large investment bank, Lehman Brothers, failed, and the country's financial system teetered on the brink of a catastrophic melt-down. Emergency measures by the American Federal Reserve and the national government prevented a complete collapse, but the financial crisis triggered a deep recession that spread around the world, and two years later, the common currency of the European Union, the euro, entered a protracted, indeed seemingly open-ended, crisis.

All the advanced industrial economies of the West sputtered, undercutting the status of the Western economic and political models as the ideals that other countries aspired to emulate. The United States, already burdened with costly, frustrating military interventions in Afghanistan and Iraq, appeared in Chinese eyes (and not theirs alone) to be less a wise, decisive, and successful leader of the global economy and the international political system than a flawed, accident-prone country in economic and political decline. American political and mil-itary hegemony, an important part of the foundation of the post-Cold War peace in Europe and East Asia, suddenly looked shaky.

While tolerating, and drawing benefit from, the hegemonic role of the United States, China had never fully accepted it; but American dominance had seemed to the Chinese, since the Western triumph over the Soviet Union, to be impervious to effective challenge. After the financial debacle of 2008 the world looked different; the American co-lossus appeared vulnerable.

China, by contrast, looked—and its leaders felt—stronger. It escaped the serious economic damage that every other major country suffered. The communist government provided a huge stimulus to the Chinese economy, much of it in the form of large loans from government-controlled banks to state-owned enterprises[73] and for the construction of housing. In the short term, the medicine worked. Economic growth, which came to a halt everywhere else, continued in China.

The events of 2008 and thereafter gave the Chinese government, and the Chinese people, reason to believe that the tectonic plates of interna-tional power were shifting, altering the regional and perhaps the global hierarchy in China's favor. The crisis of 2008 marked a turning point, if not in world history then at least in the Chinese perception of the direction in which history was moving.[74]

Another event contributed to the switch in China's international personality from passive free rider to active revisionist: a change of leadership in Beijing. In any political system a new leader can and often does initiate new policies. It is one of the strengths of democracy that the regular opportunity to change the personnel steering the government brings with it the opportunity to change the government's course. The People's Republic of China did not have a democratic political system but the installation of Xi Jinping as the head of the ruling Communist Party, and therefore of China itself, in 2012 did have an impact on Chinese foreign policy. Xi showed himself, upon assuming power, to be more forceful and more determined to expand both his own authority at home and his country's influence abroad than his predecessor, Hu Jintao. He identified himself more closely with the military and with nationalist themes.[75] He concentrated power in his own hands and restricted individual initiative and dissent.[76] The Communist Party Congress in 2017 elevated Xi to a status higher than that of his immediate predecessors and comparable, in the history of the Party, only to that of Mao Zedong himself. The next year the Party's Central Committee voted to abolish the term limits for leaders that Deng Xiaoping had established, paving the way for Xi to hold power indefinitely.

Following the Chinese communist tradition of coining epigrammatic slogans signaling the regime's goals, he announced a new one: "the Chinese Dream." It presumably referred, obliquely, to a common expression of China's chief rival, the United States. Whereas the phrase "the American Dream" has to do with individual aspirations for upward mobility and prosperity, however, Xi meant his slogan to denote the national goal of recovering China's lost—or, in the Chinese view, stolen—greatness; and because of the way that China defined greatness, this would have to come at the expense of other countries.[77]

While short-term trends—China's surging growth and the missteps of the United States—favored the achievement of the Chinese Dream, Xi and his colleagues were certainly aware that troubles lurked on the horizon. Economic growth, while still robust when he took office, was beginning to fall below the double-digit annual levels the country had achieved for three decades. In addition, the ban on more than one child per couple that Mao had imposed and his successors had continued was on the verge of having a powerful demographic and therefore social and economic impact. In a few years the population would cease to grow[78] and the ratio of retired Chinese to the working population that had to support them would rise. This would further slow the rate of economic growth and create the need to devote more money to those not in the labor force, leaving less for expanding Chinese power and influence beyond its borders. Fewer males of military age would be available to fill the ranks of China's army, navy, and air force, the regime's principal instrument for enhancing its regional power.[79]

Thus, while Xi inherited conditions ripe for the realization of Chinese ambitions, he could not ignore the fact that future circumstances would be unfavorable for this purpose. The deliberations of China's communist leaders are shrouded in secrecy, so it is not possible to document how heavily the prospect of future weakness influenced Chinese foreign policy; but the increased regional assertiveness over which Xi presided was consistent with, and may well have been motivated by, a calculation that China confronted a window of opportunity for reestablishing what it considered its rightful international standing, a window that would begin to close in a decade or even less.[80]

The communist regime faced, moreover, a more immediate challenge, and China's aggressive international conduct seemed plainly to be part of the Party's response to it. Here Xi Jinping had something important in common with Russia's Vladimir Putin. Both their governments confronted the prospect of eroding popular support and therefore a looming crisis of legitimacy. Indeed, Xi's major initiatives suggested that he believed that such a crisis had already arrived.[81] For both Russian and Chinese authoritarian rulers, aggressive nationalism was attractive as a way of bolstering their public support, one that had become all the more important because other sources of that support were becoming steadily more fragile.

Xi and the rest of the communist leadership did not have to search far to find signs of disaffection with their rule. The number of public protests by workers and villagers in China reached a reported 180,000 in 2012.[82] The country's middle class, which economic growth had created, did not join them in large numbers, nor did the widespread student-led demonstrations of 1989 recur, but neither group could be counted as enthusiastic supporters of the regime. As for the wealthiest Chinese, many of them voted against the regime with their money, sending a great deal of it abroad.[83] Many of them also sent their children abroad, for the purpose of receiving Western educations but also to establish residence in Western countries to which their parents, who often bought property there, could relocate.[84]

The most visible indicators of the existence of serious political disaffection in China were the steps the Party took to thwart expressions of it. In extending the limits on public discussion of politically sensitive topics, jailing activists and their lawyers, and even kidnapping dissidents living outside the mainland, Xi presided over the most repressive version of communist rule in China since the (far worse) days of Mao.[85] For all the resources the government devoted enhancing China's military, it spent even more on internal security.[86] Xi's government ordered the intensification of "patriotic education"—that is, the glorification of the Communist Party—in China's schools that the regime had mandated since the nationwide demonstrations of 1989.[87] It attempted, with considerable success, to restrict access to Internet sites it considered subversive through an elaborate system of monitoring and filtering known as the "Great Firewall."

Most prominently, Xi launched a major campaign against perhaps the most unpopular feature of communist rule in China: massive corruption. Undertaken to demonstrate to the Chinese people that Xi's government was acting decisively against a widely noted and widely disliked practice, the anti-corruption campaign ousted, and in many cases incarcerated, hundreds of thousands of people, many of them Communist Party officials.[88] Just what impact this campaign had on the ongoing corruption of those who retained their positions, prominently including Xi's own political allies, was not clear; but because it targeted his political rivals and their followers the campaign did enhance Xi's own personal political power.

The sources of discontent with the Party predated Xi's arrival at the summit of the Chinese political system. For almost all of the preceding three decades, however, the Party had had a powerful antidote to it: the surging economic growth over which it presided.[89] During that period most Chinese, indeed most Party officials, ceased to believe in the precepts of Marxism-Leninism-Maoism, on the basis of which the communists had claimed the right to govern China. As the wellspring of their political support, prosperity replaced ideology.[90] In the era of double-digit annual growth, no matter how arbitrary and irrational the Chinese people found the Party's monopoly of power to be, and no matter how much environmental pollution and financial corruption the communists' policies brought with them, most Chinese benefitted from, and so appreciated, the rapid ongoing economic improvement over which the Party presided. For this the Party received credit. Lacking the political legitimacy that the emperors had wielded by virtue of tradition, that Mao had claimed on the basis of his ideology, and that democratic leaders enjoy because the people they govern have freely given them power, China's post-Mao rulers counted on "performance legitimacy," earned by their economic record.

When Xi assumed supreme power in 2012, however, those earnings were falling and were seemingly destined, as he and his colleagues well knew, to fall further. China's extraordinary economic surge had come about as the result of conditions that were, in the second decade of the twenty-first century, becoming weaker.[91] China had taken advantage, as had other countries before it, of the movement of workers from the countryside to the city, and from farms to factories where they could work more productively and where their relatively low wages made the products of Chinese manufacture or assembly competitive on world markets. The country's supply of rural labor was by no means exhausted but was not as plentiful as it had been three decades earlier. Labor costs had begun to rise, driving some production to lower-cost countries such as Bangladesh and Vietnam.

The Party's substantial investment in education, producing widespread literacy, and its spending on infrastructure, especially roads and ports, had also yielded economic dividends; but the volume of investment, including in housing, had reached, and exceeded, the point of diminishing returns. The growth through exports on which post-Mao China had relied requires foreign markets; but the capacity, and political willingness, of other countries, notably the United States, to absorb Chinese products had their limits. To sustain its economic advance, China would have to rely less on exports and on the building of infrastructure and more on consumer purchases by the Chinese people themselves, which accounted for a far lower proportion of total economic activity than in rich countries.[92]

To compound the difficulties that Xi and his colleagues confronted, in order to avoid the negative consequences of the post-2008 global recession, the government had increased its already considerable investments in infrastructure, which it financed by massive borrowing. This had created a large and dangerous volume of debt hanging over the economy.[93]

Finally, Xi's China faced a challenge that comes with economic success. This is known as the "middle income trap," in which a country's products become, with rising labor costs, uncompetitive with those of low-wage producers but also, because they are of insufficiently high quality, uncompetitive with the products of rich countries.[94] China had to move from "extensive" economic growth based on adding inputs, mainly labor, to "intensive" growth, which comes from making better use of the inputs that are available. That meant shifting to the production of higher-value products and entering the more valuable parts of the production process, such as design and marketing.

The Chinese government was well aware of these challenges. It announced its intention to meet them and unveiled plans for doing so. The changes required to sustain the economic growth on which the regime had been able to count for three decades proved, however, easier to describe than to achieve.[95] Political obstacles stood in the way. Sustaining growth required, for example, continuing the policy of closing large, inefficient state-owned enterprises, which had the political strength to resist being liquidated. The necessary kinds of economic activity involved individual creativity and initiative, which in turn required freedom from government control; but government control was precisely what the Communist Party was determined to maintain in China.

In short, Xi Jinping faced what he regarded as a perilous moment for communist rule. What had become, over three decades, the foundation of that rule, economic growth, was slowing, with the prospects for accelerating it uncertain at best. Xi thus found himself in a position similar to that of the Russian leader Vladimir Putin upon his return to that country's presidency in 2012:[96] with the familiar economic sources of public support for their undemocratic regimes increasingly unreliable—in Russia because of a lower international price for oil—the principal alternative source, aggressive nationalism, became increasingly appealing.

Each autocrat had reason to expect that nationalist success beyond his country's borders, at the expense of neighboring countries, would compensate for the damage to his political standing that reduced economic growth was bound to inflict. As in Russia, in Xi's China nationalist themes assumed increasing prominence in official discourse.[97] The perceived need to bolster the Communist Party's popularity at home was not the only reason for the transformation of China's international conduct from free riding to active revisionism, but it was surely an important one.[98]

While that transformation ended the post-Cold War peace in East Asia by reviving security competition, and thus posed the ultimate threat of a major, destructive war in the region, an even more immediate threat came from another quarter, a threat for which China bore partial responsibility not because of what it was doing but because of what it refused to do. Communist North Korea, a bizarre and ugly combination of an old-fashioned despotism and a modern Stalinist political system, embarked on a program to develop nuclear weapons. By the end of the post-Cold War era the success of that program had become a source of danger in East Asia. The North Korean regime had one supporter, albeit an ambivalent one: China. The regime's nuclear weapons program had the potential to trigger a war that no country including China wanted, but that China was unwilling to take the necessary steps to prevent.

The Korean Conundrum

United from the fourteenth century onward, for most of that time a nominal tributary of China that was largely cut off from the rest of the world and thus known as "the hermit kingdom," Korea came under Japanese domination after Japan's victories over China in 1895 and Russia in 1905. With Japan's defeat in World War II, the United Nations developed a plan for a trusteeship on the peninsula, with the Soviet Union administering the part of it north of the 38th parallel and the United States assuming responsibility for the south. This led to the establishment of two separate governments, and on June 25, 1950, one of them, the northern, communist regime, attacked the other, in the south, with the aim of seizing control of all of Korea. The Northern forces made initial gains, but the United States intervened on the side of the South and rolled back the communist army, advancing all the way to Korea's border with China. At that point Mao sent 250,000 Chinese "volunteers" to assist North Korea. (Overall, an estimated 3 million Chinese fought there.) The war became a bloody stalemate, with an armistice in 1953 leaving the line of division between the two Koreas more or less where it had been before the North Korean attack.

Thereafter the two countries followed radically different paths. The North became a kind of impoverished penal colony, with strict controls on all information and all activities. The communists' centralized system of economic management produced dismal results. The regime isolated the society it ruled from the rest of the world and fostered a Stalinesque cult of personality around the state's founding leader, Kim Il-sung.

In stark contrast, South Korea adopted a free-market economic system and the same strategy of export-led growth that worked so well for other East Asian countries, including China. The Republic of Korea (ROK) became an economic powerhouse, fully integrated into the global economic order with a prosperous consumer society and the eleventh largest economy in the world. In the late 1980s, following four decades of autocratic rule during which the military had dominated the political system, South Korea joined the ranks of the world's democracies.

While largely isolated, during the Cold War North Korea did receive military, political, and economic support from both the Soviet Union and the People's Republic of China. With the end of that global conflict the Democratic People's Republic of Korea (DPRK), as it called itself, became a kind of orphan: both post-Soviet Russia and economically reformed China established diplomatic relations and economic ties with South Korea. In the 1990s, moreover, the creaky, constricted North Korean economic system failed even to provide enough food for the people of the country. While reliable statistics are not available, during the famine of that decade between 600,000 and 2.5 million North Koreans are estimated to have starved to death.

In the post-Cold War era, for all its travails, the North Korean regime in Pyongyang did record two successes. It managed to perpetuate
its ruling dynasty. Kim Il-sung died in 1994 and his son, Kim Jong-il,
replaced him. While the second Kim had spent two decades preparing
to led the country, the son whom he designated as his political heir,
Kim Jong-un, and who succeeded him upon his death in 2011, had
had very little relevant experience. Moreover, at thirty-two, the third
Kim was twenty years younger at that time than his father had been
when he, the second Kim, had assumed supreme power in Pyongyang.
Nonetheless, Kim Jong-un consolidated power following Kim Jong-il's
death, in part by ordering the executions of senior officials and close
family members.

Post-Cold War North Korea enjoyed yet another success. It acquired
nuclear weapons. It had received a nuclear reactor from the Soviet
Union in 1965 and had signed the Nonproliferation Treaty (NPT) as
a non-nuclear-weapon state in 1985. It built a reactor on its own the
next year, however, and provoked a crisis with the United States in
1993 and 1994 by announcing its intention to withdraw from the NPT,
shut down the reactor, and remove its fuel rods, which contained the
fissionable material from which nuclear explosives are made. With
the prospect of an American strike against the North Korea looming,
the United States negotiated an "Agreed Framework" with Pyongyang
by the terms of which the North Koreans agreed to forsake their quest
for nuclear weapons in return for economic benefits. In 2002, however,
a secret North Korean facility for enriching uranium, in violation of
the 1994 agreement, came to light. The next year the DPRK did shut
down the reactor and remove its fuel rods. This time the diplomatic response came in the form of Six Party talks, involving the United States,
North Korea, South Korea, China, Japan, and Russia. These, too,
failed to halt Pyongyang's nuclear weapons program,[99] which yielded
tests of nuclear explosives in 2006, 2009, 2013, and twice in 2016. In
June 2018 the American president Donald Trump and the North Korea
leader Kim Jong-un held a well-publicized meeting in Singapore that
produced, however, only very modest near-term changes in the North
Korean nuclear program.

Its dogged and ultimately successful pursuit of the bomb was expensive for a very poor country, and all the more so because it brought

economic sanctions that compounded its poverty. While the North Korean leadership did not disclose its motives, it seems fair to infer from its actions that nothing had a higher priority for it—certainly not the well-being of the people it governed—than becoming, with the United States and China, the third country in East Asia to possess these weapons of mass destruction. This had such cosmic importance for the ruling Kims, it is reasonable to speculate, because they regarded nuclear weapons as the most reliable guarantors of what was most valuable to them: the continuation of their regime, with themselves in control of it.[100]

Beginning with its intervention in the Korean War, the communist government in Beijing had an historically close relationship with its communist counterpart in Pyongyang—as close, as Mao Zedong put it, "as lips and teeth." The post-Maoist Chinese government, to all appearances, lacked any sympathy for North Korea's refusal to undertake Chinese-style economic reforms and had little enthusiasm for the Kim dynasty's efforts to join the nuclear club.[101] China's disappointment in and disapproval of North Korea's economic and military policies did not, however, produce any serious Chinese efforts to change them.

This was significant for the security of East Asia because China was far better positioned than any other country to stop Pyongyang's nuclear program without attacking it directly.[102] With the world imposing stringent economic sanctions, and with its meager endowment of natural resources and the shortcomings of its economy, North Korea depended on cross-border shipments of food and fuel from its giant neighbor. Without them the North Korean economy, such as it was, would grind to a halt, the North Korean people would go hungry, and the North Korean regime might well collapse.[103]

Having continually refused to join the sanctions regime, in 2017 the Chinese government changed its policy and put pressure on North Korea by substantially reducing the flow of oil and coal crossing the border between the two countries.[104] This change may have been aimed at compelling North Korea to fall in line with Chinese policy preferences rather than at forcing the Pyongyang regime to give up its entire nuclear weapons program, a step that would require, for the purpose of verification, the most intrusive international inspections ever undertaken anywhere in the world's most tightly closed country.

China retained, moreover, an important incentive for keeping the North Korean government a going concern, which it shared with South Korea: neither country wanted North Korea to collapse, because each would have to pay some of the costs of that collapse. Refugees would flood into both countries. The South Koreans would have to pay a higher financial and social price because the responsibility for 25 million destitute, backward North Koreans would fall on them. For China, more of the potential costs were geopolitical: the end of the Pyongyang regime would likely lead to a reunited Korea on its doorstep, armed with nuclear weapons and allied with the United States.[105]

Moreover, while they regarded North Korea's drive for nuclear weapons without enthusiasm, China's leaders could not help but appreciate the difficulties it posed for the power that posed the chief obstacle to their own aspirations in East Asia. The North Korean nuclear weapons program annoyed and distracted the United States, which served what the Chinese communists considered to be their own country's interests. In addition, and not least important in Beijing's calculations, a tougher Chinese policy toward North Korea would run afoul of the very nationalism on which the regime increasingly relied for support from the Chinese public. During the Korean War and thereafter, the regime had portrayed China's role in Korea as a selfless exercise in patriotic sacrifice, and tens of thousands of Chinese soldiers had died there.[106] To turn its back on the fruit of their sacrifice—an independent, communist North Korea—would undercut the way that the Chinese government sought to present itself to the people it governed, and, as the communist leaders increasingly believed, that it had to present itself in order to continue to govern.[107]

As the North Koreans violated agreements they had signed and proceeded along the path to nuclear weapons, the other countries of East Asia became increasingly concerned. They escalated their public rhetoric of disapproval and their private pleas to China to put pressure on Pyongyang. They tightened the sanctions they imposed on North Korea. This did not stop the Kim regime from producing more fissionable material and testing missiles of increasing range. The more fissionable material North Korea accumulated, moreover, and the more bombs it fabricated, the more likely it was to sell either or both to another country, or even to a terrorist group.[108]

Still, the initial North Korean nuclear explosions did not mark a turning point for the international relations of East Asia. American nuclear weapons, after all, were available to deter those of the DPRK. A moment of transformation loomed, however, and would arrive when the North Koreans demonstrated the ability both to fabricate a nuclear explosive compact enough to fit on the tip of a ballistic missile and to build and launch a missile capable of reaching North America. Such a combination had the potential to alter the strategic calculations, and the military policies, of the countries of East Asia.

A North Korean capacity to deliver a nuclear strike on the United States would reproduce, in East Asia, the circumstance that provoked the most serious crisis of American military strategy in Europe during the Cold War. At the outset of that conflict both the United States and the Soviet Union had a way of preventing the other from launching an attack. The Soviet Union had—or was widely believed to have—a large advantage in non-nuclear forces, which the Kremlin could have used to conquer Western Europe. The United States, with its monopoly on nuclear weapons, could launch a nuclear strike from Europe on the Soviet homeland without exposing itself to nuclear retaliation. The two military capacities offset each other: the result was a stalemate, with each side effectively deterring the other.

Then, in 1957, the launch of Sputnik, the first Earth-orbiting satellite, foreshadowed a Soviet capacity to deliver strikes on targets in North America. This called into question the effectiveness of American deterrence. Was it credible that, in response to a Soviet attack on Western Europe, the United States would make war on the Soviet Union, thereby inviting a nuclear attack on its own territory? If the Soviet leaders became convinced that such an American response was not likely, they might be tempted to launch an attack in Europe, believing that they could conquer the continent without American resistance.

One logical response to the new problem was for the European countries the American nuclear guarantee was supposed to protect to obtain their own nuclear weapons, on the assumption that any country would be prepared to retaliate in nuclear fashion for a direct attack on itself, if not on other countries. President Charles de Gaulle of France invoked this logic to justify his country's nuclear weapons program, although he also had other reasons for wanting to join the nuclear club.

Through its participation in the American-led Manhattan Project, which produced the first atomic bombs during World War II, Great Britain already had its own nuclear weapons. By this logic, however, West Germany, too, needed a nuclear arsenal; and, given Germany's history during the first half of the twentieth century, no one, least of all the Germans themselves, desired this.

In the end, therefore, in response to the new circumstance, the United States opted to bolster rather than change the existing Western policy of deterrence in Europe. The American government sought to reinforce the credibility of that policy by stating, publicly and frequently, that it would indeed defend its European allies despite the risks of provoking a nuclear attack on its own territory. Washington backed up this stance by stationing nuclear weapons on the European continent and by putting its own troops on the front lines in Germany as a "trip-wire" designed to persuade the Soviet leaders that if they attacked they would trigger American participation in the war that would follow. The policy of reinforcement worked; or at least, the desired outcome came to pass. For whatever combination of reasons, the Soviet Union never launched a westward attack of any kind.[109]

In the post-Cold War period North Korea and the United States mutually deterred each other in roughly the way the United States and the Soviet Union did in Europe before Sputnik. American nuclear (and non-nuclear) weapons could devastate North Korea if the Pyongyang regime repeated its attack on South Korea of June 25, 1950. North Korea had, however, the non-nuclear means to prevent the United States and its allies from themselves initiating an attack: it had up to 12,000 artillery pieces deployed along the Demilitarized Zone (DMZ) that separated it from the South, weapons that, if launched, would inflict death and destruction—possibly on a large scale—on South Korea's capital, Seoul, with a population, counting the entire metropolitan area, of 25 million people. North Korea would certainly lose a second Korean War but the Kim regime might do devastating damage to South Korea as it expired, enough damage to deter an attack on Pyongyang by either South Korea or the United States or both.[110]

In the balance between the United States and its East Asian allies on one side, and the DPRK on the other, a North Korean capacity to reach North America with nuclear weapons would strengthen Pyongyang in a way that called into question the reliability of American protection for its East Asian allies within range of those weapons. The United States and its allies could choose to respond in one or more of four ways.

First, they could decide simply to live with nuclear-equipped, long-range North Korean ballistic missiles, as NATO lived with Soviet missiles, assuming that the result in post-Sputnik Europe would be repeated on the Korean peninsula. The Americans and their Asian allies might conclude that even with its enhanced military abilities, existing American deployments sufficed to ensure that North Korea, like the Soviet Union before it, would refrain from mounting a serious attack.

Second, the anti-DPRK coalition could also deploy active defenses against North Korean missiles. The United States considered such measures during the Cold War but ultimately decided against them, signing the 1972 Antiballistic Missile (ABM) Treaty that effectively banned them. The American government concluded that such defenses could never defeat a major attack by the large and growing fleet of Soviet missiles. The technologies of missile defense improved significantly over five decades, however, and North Korea would not be able to deploy anything like as much nuclear firepower as the Soviet Union did. The United States, having withdrawn from the ABM Treaty in 2002, announced in 2017 that it would install such a system in South Korea.[111]

Third, if they came to believe that the North Koreans no longer found the American nuclear threat credible, the East Asian allies of the United States could, like Charles de Gaulle's France, acquire nuclear weapons of their own. While no Western European country followed the French example, in East Asia nuclear proliferation would likely involve not only South Korea but also other countries. Despite the powerful anti-nuclear sentiment it has harbored since achieving, in August, 1945, the dubious distinction of being the only country to suffer a nuclear attack, Japan would likely be one such country. Taiwan might well be another. If a "cascade" of nuclear proliferation developed, the bomb could spread even farther across the region.

Finally, the United States, either in concert with some or all of its East Asian allies or unilaterally, could launch a preemptive strike to destroy North Korea's nuclear infrastructure, with an emphasis on its long-range missiles. In June, 2006, William Perry, a former American secretary of defense, and Ashton Carter, then a future one, argued in *The Washington Post* that if North Korea deployed, on its territory, a nuclear-armed missile capable of hitting the United States, the American president should order an attack to destroy it.[112]

None of the four courses available to the United States and its East Asian allies in response to North Korean development of long-range, nuclear-equipped missiles was free of dangers. Several had the potential to increase the risk of regional war, and to do so entirely apart from China's aggressive maritime policies.

Simply accepting a North Korean capacity to strike North America in the expectation that this would have no impact on East Asia would make the peace of the region, and the safety of millions of Americans, dependent on the prudence and rationality of Pyongyang's young, untested, evidently capricious if not irrational, vicious and possibly sadistic leader. It would risk, as well, more aggressive North Korean conduct in the region: the regime sponsored terrorism and carried out limited attacks on South Korea when it could only barrage Seoul with its non-nuclear artillery. What might it do with the presumably far more powerful protection afforded by the capacity to hold an American city hostage?

As for defenses against missile attack, while they could be expected to improve in sophistication, in response to a North Korean assault they would have to work perfectly to qualify as even minimally adequate. If North Korea launched, for example, five missiles at a city, and a defensive system intercepted four but the fifth reached its target, the result would likely be a catastrophe, with hundreds of thousands, perhaps millions of South Koreans or Japanese or Americans dead. As Pyongyang acquired more missiles, the chances of repelling completely a North Korean nuclear attack would fall.

In an East Asia in which a number of countries possess nuclear arsenals, the chances of their being used would rise. Unlike the United States and the Soviet Union in the Cold War, most of the new nuclear-weapon states would lack the capacity for "assured destruction"—that is, the ability to absorb a nuclear blow and still inflict devastating damage on its attacker. Without such a capacity a nuclear-armed country has a much greater incentive than the two Cold War nuclear superpowers did to strike first if it suspects that it will be attacked; and it is all too easy to imagine North Korea's suspicions rising to very great heights indeed, regardless of whether they were justified.

The shortcomings of the relatively peaceful alternatives to it made a preemptive strike to destroy a fleet of North Korean long-range missiles, if not attractive, at least a measure worthy of serious consideration. Such a strike would trigger, at the least, a shooting war on the Korean peninsula; and a second Korean War would, like all wars, surely bring with it unpleasant surprises. The surprises would be all the worse if China intervened on the side of North Korea, as it did in 1950. Even if China were to remain aloof from such a conflict, however, indeed even if no such war were ever to be fought, just as Vladimir Putin's assault on Russia's neighbors has transformed the international relations of Europe, so China's shift from a more or less placid to an assertive foreign policy transformed the environment of security in East Asia.

The New/Old Asia

With the post-Cold War peace at an end, East Asia, like Europe, reverted to a geopolitical alignment familiar from the Cold War era. Like Vladimir Putin's Russia in Europe, China aspired to dominate its home region at the expense of the other countries there, which motivated the others to band together in order to resist. In the 1950s and 1960s the threat to these countries had come from both the giant communist powers of day. It was common during the early Cold War period to refer to the "Sino-Soviet bloc."

By the middle of the second decade of the twenty-first century, China and Russia—the first no longer an orthodox communist country, the second not communist at all—were aligned again, but their relationship had undergone a reversal. In the earlier period the Soviet Union had been very much the senior partner: the more advanced economically and more powerful militarily of the two, it was also the original Marxist-Leninist state and promulgator and guarantor of that ideology's orthodoxy. By the twenty-first century, by contrast, China's three decades of double-digit economic growth had made it a rising power. Post-communist Russia had lost half the Soviet Union's population—now distributed among fourteen other independent states—had a stagnant economy heavily dependent on revenue from the sale of energy, and, as an international presence, was in decline.

While each country had revisionist ambitions, which gave them a common hostility to the American-led international order they sought to upend, the two also harbored suspicions of each other and competed for influence in the countries of Central Asia that were situated between them.[113] Moreover, in East Asia, aside from its ambivalent relationship with Russia and a few small countries that had become economic clients, notably Laos and Cambodia, China had few friends and no genuine allies.

Ranged against the People's Republic were the other countries of the region, which China's rapid growth and assertive maritime policies threatened.[114] The others increased their own military efforts, to the point that, in 2012, for the first time, Asian military expenditures exceeded the defense spending of the European members of NATO.[115] In Japan, the richest and potentially the strongest of them, Shinzo Abe, an advocate for larger Japanese military forces and a more active Japanese foreign policy, became prime minister in 2013.[116] In April, 2015, the United States and Japan announced an agreement to expand the reach of the Japanese armed forces.[117] Vietnam, a much poorer country than Japan, nonetheless equipped itself with submarines to counteract China's growing naval prowess.

The East Asians also moved to reinvigorate their hub-and-spokes alliance pattern with the United States. Those Cold-War arrangements had not disappeared during the peaceful years of the post-Cold War era but, because the need for protection had sharply declined, military cooperation with America had played a less important role in their foreign policies.[118] In 2014, the Philippines, having in the 1990s asked the United States to vacate the Cold-War-era American air and naval bases on its territory, signed a ten-year defense cooperation agreement with its former tenant that included renewed American access to those bases.[119] Vietnam, whose communist government had fought a bitter war against American troops in the 1960s and 1970s that cost an estimated one million Vietnamese lives, intensified its defense cooperation with its onetime adversary. For its part the United States announced a "pivot" to Asia, signaling the recognition that security competition had resumed there and that Washington would therefore have to devote more political attention and military resources to the region.

While strengthening their ties with the United States, the countries of East Asia began, in tentative fashion, to forge what had been conspicuous by its absence during the Cold War: a series of military connections with one another. Australia was particularly active in bringing together countries with common concerns about China, working, for example, to involve India, a country in South rather than East Asia that shared a disputed border with China, in the security affairs of the western Pacific.[120] Japanese naval forces conducted joint military exercises with the navy of the Philippines in the Pacific and with the Indian navy in the Indian Ocean.[121]

The renewal and strengthening of alliances and the increased investment in arms that China's aggressive maritime policies touched off in East Asia testified to the end of the post-Cold War peace in the region. Themselves forms of security competition, these measures were also preparations for the most costly and dangerous enterprise of all: war. With the end of the post-Cold War era, war in East Asia became a far more likely prospect than in the preceding quarter century. Certainly neither China nor the countries its ambitions threatened desired a war: the communist regime in Beijing hoped to achieve its revisionist goals without having to fight for them. Still, China's revisionism raised the chances of armed conflict.

It did so, in part, because it involved a substantial increase in Chinese military power on the high seas. In naval rivalry the goal is command of the sea. Only one country at a time can have it: dominance cannot be shared, and the country that achieves it has the navies of others at its mercy. That is what made the German bid for naval mastery before World War I so dangerous for Great Britain. Had its attempt succeeded, Germany would have gained the power to cut off the British from their trading partners and their imperial possessions, with both of which they communicated by sea.[122]

As long as the United States has the upper hand militarily in the Asia-Pacific region, China cannot fulfill its political aspirations there. If China should achieve military superiority, the other Asian countries would find their interests, and indeed what they—and international law—consider their own maritime territory to be in jeopardy. Because the stakes are so high, both China and the United States have very great incentives to do whatever is necessary to gain or retain maritime supremacy, including fighting for it.

China might at some point conclude that it had acquired such supremacy, or at least enough maritime power in all its forms—ships, supporting aircraft, and missiles capable of striking American ships and American bases in the region—to permit it to seize territory it claims but does not control: the most prominent candidates for seizure are the Senkakus and Taiwan. In such a scenario, China would count on using overwhelming local power for a swift, successful strike that its rival claimant—Japan or the democratic government of Taiwan—could not resist and that the United States could not, or would not, mobilize rapidly enough to contest. The Chinese government would portray such an attack, above all to the Chinese people, as a measure to repair an injustice rather than an act of aggression. Such a campaign, if successful, would tilt the balance of power decisively in China's favor. If other countries resisted, East Asia would be at war.

Even without a Chinese effort at an amphibious coup of this kind, a war pitting China against the United States could erupt in the western Pacific more or less accidentally. To enforce its broad maritime territorial claims, China has engaged in aggressive patrolling, which has the potential to lead to collisions of military forces that could in turn ignite outright hostilities. In the disputes with Japan over the Senkakus and with Vietnam and the Philippines over the status of the waters near the Paracel Islands in the South China Sea, the parties involved have sent military vessels to the locations in question and hinted at their willingness to use force. In response to China's claims, the United States began conducting "Freedom of Navigation Operations" (FONOPs) in the western Pacific. In October, 2015, an American destroyer sailed within 12 nautical miles of the Subi Reef near the Spratly Islands in the South China Sea, a site of Chinese military construction. This exercise was designed to demonstrate that the United States did not recognize China's claim to a 12-mile zone of sovereignty around the reef because it was uninhabited and therefore, by international law, not properly Chinese territory for this purpose.[123] For their part Chinese officials began to refer to the disputed waters as part of China's "core interests." In the regime's vocabulary the term denoted issues over which it was prepared to fight.[124]

Naval maneuvering could also provoke spontaneous, localized fighting, in which case the weight of the parties' wider political interests would prevent either China or the countries it threatens, including the United States, settling by compromise the issue in dispute. Having invested so heavily domestically in presenting itself to the Chinese people as the avenger of the historical wrongs done to their country, the communist regime would risk a serious loss of support at home if it were seen to be retreating from a confrontation over a territorial claim.[125]

For their part, the smaller Asian countries have their own nationalist reasons not to give way to China.[126] Where China confronted an ally or friend of the United States—Japan or Taiwan, for example—the American government would also have an incentive to lend its support, lest it gain a reputation in the region for unreliability. Such a reputation would shake the foundation of the security order in East Asia: especially with China's newly assertive foreign policy, the countries of the region will feel secure only to the extent that they believe that they can count on American military assistance when they need it.[127] Indeed, to allow China to prevail in such a confrontation would risk encouraging even more assertive Chinese maritime policies, the ultimate result of which would be the eviction of the United States Navy from the western Pacific.

In the worst case, each side might regard a minor clash, especially if either believed it portended a major one, as an occasion for striking the other preemptively. China, as the weaker party in military terms, might calculate that it could reduce its disadvantages by landing the first blow. On the other side, the plan the American military developed for war with China, called Air-Sea Battle, called for attacks on targets on the Chinese mainland, targets that would be easier to destroy or cripple if the United States were to initiate hostilities.[128]

Security competition need not, however, become outright warfare, as the history of the Cold War demonstrates. In the Soviet-American rivalry, nuclear weapons had a powerful restraining influence. In twenty-first-century East Asia the United States and China both have large stockpiles of such weapons, and these, too, induce restraint. A conflict in the region begun with non-nuclear munitions—ships firing at each other over one of the reefs or manmade islands that China claims, for example—could escalate to the point at which nuclear weapons were used. Such a war would surely do more damage than any political goals would conceivably be worth. A common awareness of the possible consequences of a direct military clash of any kind injects a large dose of caution into the international relations of the region.[129]

While nuclear weapons may suppress open warfare, they do not eliminate security competition. Of the three pillars of peace—defined as the absence of security competition—East Asia in the wake of the post-Cold War period lacked two, because of China. While the other countries of the region accepted, indeed welcomed, the hegemony of the United States, China sought to overthrow it; and whereas most of the other significant sovereign states had adopted democratic governance, the Chinese political system remained autocratic, with the Communist Party arrogating all political power to itself.

The third building block of peace, however—economic interdependence—was very much present in East Asia.[130] It, too, served to moderate, although it did not abolish, geopolitical rivalry there. As they did in Europe and indeed everywhere, the technology-driven advances of globalization made the volume of international trade and the cross-border flow of money greater in twenty-first-century East Asia than ever before.[131] China and the United States in particular came to depend heavily on each other. The United States borrowed extensively from China to finance its budget deficits;[132] China sold its manufactures to, and bought food from, the United States. For the other countries of the region, for which the United States had once been the main economic partner for their export-oriented economies, the twenty-first century saw the growth of intraregional trade, and especially trade with and investment in China.[133] In addition, China and the other Asian countries became part of supply chains, in which component parts of a single product are made in a number of different countries although they are usually assembled in just one, often China.[134] Involving as they do multiple countries, supply chains deepen the economic integration among them.[135]

Moreover, economic interdependence has considerable political weight in the twenty-first century because governments depend so heavily on economic growth as a source of legitimacy and popularity. The Chinese Communists believe that they must deliver a rising standard of living in order to remain in power, cross-border commerce makes a substantial contribution to rising living standards, and war would cut off commerce. The regime in Beijing thus has a powerful incentive to avoid war.[136] Nor is China's the only government in the region for which sustaining economic growth, and the trade and cross-border investment that nourish it, looms large.[137]

The fact of economic interdependence had the same effect in East Asia as did the fact of nuclear weapons. Both were universally understood underlying conditions that discouraged the pursuit of political aspirations through war. Like nuclear weapons, interdependence was seldom if ever mentioned in political discourse; but it did not have to be, any more than a driver who proceeds with care along a winding cliffside road has to remind himself of the existence of gravity.

As in Europe, however, the fact of economic interdependence did not always have a pacifying effect in East Asia. Like Russia, China sometimes attempted to use its economic relations with others coercively. As by far the largest country of the region, access to China's market was, almost by definition, more important to the other countries than access to any one of theirs was, individually, to China. Beijing sought on occasion to use this asymmetry as leverage to achieve its political aims.[138]

In response to the flare-up with the Japanese over ownership of the Senkakus in 2010, the Chinese government reduced, for a time, the export of rare earth minerals on which some Japanese industries depended.[139] When South Korea announced that it would deploy American antiballistic missile systems to protect itself against North Korea, China retaliated by boycotting some South Korean products with large sales to Chinese consumers.[140]

China's efforts at economic coercion did not achieve their goals: Japan did not retract its claim to the Senkakus nor did South Korea entirely forswear ballistic missile defense. In general, China had less economic leverage than the regime liked to believe.[141] Still, China's formidable economic importance did complicate efforts to check its ambitions. It made the members of the anti-Chinese coalition reluctant to adopt explicit policies of deterrence and containment. Whereas during the Cold War the United States and its allies publicly announced their determination to prevent the advance of communism in Europe, in

East Asia, even in the face of Chinese revisionism, the countervailing coalition refrained from clear, direct statements to that effect about the People's Republic.

In contrast to their public reticence, in their private counsels and their military planning the United States and the countries of East Asia were preoccupied with China's political aspirations and military capability.[142] Their public silence arose from China's immense economic importance. The members of the anti-Chinese coalition feared that an explicit, outspoken policy of deterrence would jeopardize their extensive, growing, and valuable commerce with China.[143] Even speaking openly about the possibility of war with China had the potential to be costly, by discouraging investment and raising insurance premiums for the shipping on which so much Asian trade depended.

Not surprisingly, the East Asian countries wanted the best of both worlds: flourishing trade and investment with China along with an American presence in the western Pacific robust enough to hold in check the Chinese ambitions that threatened their interests and their maritime territory. They were reluctant to take sides too openly in a confrontation between the United States and China,[144] although their security depended on the Americans being willing to engage in such a confrontation if they themselves were endangered.

Their approach to China resembled the sport of water polo: above the water's surface the players comport themselves with balletic grace; beneath it they are sometimes fiercely kicking one another. So it was with the international relations of East Asia in the second decade of the twenty-first century. Publicly the emphasis fell on the ever-expanding economic interdependence that had done so much to lift the economies of the region and that gave China and its neighbors powerful common interests. Privately, occasionally emerging into public view, a loose coalition was forming to oppose a China that seemed bent on regional domination.[145]

As did other countries' economic entanglements with China, so the tactics the People's Republic employed in pursuit of its ambition to dominate East Asia complicated the efforts of the other countries of the region, including the United States, to resist. China launched initiatives that were provocative but not sufficiently bellicose to warrant a major military response.[146] China's construction of artificial islands, its building of military facilities on them, and its military maneuvers around the Senkakus and other maritime territory it claimed, all chipped away at, but did not individually threaten to destroy, the political and military status quo in the region. China's strategy in Asia resembled Russia's in Europe, launching probes for the purpose of testing the opposing coalition's strength and resolve while making low-cost, if modest, strategic gains[147]—although with two differences: none of China's provocations undermined existing security arrangements or violated international law as egregiously as did the Russian attack on and occupation of neighboring Ukraine; and Russia was not powerful enough to aspire realistically to dominate Europe, while China could anticipate accumulating the economic and military strength to restore its historical supremacy in Asia.

China's campaign of revisionism presented its regional opponents, including the United States, with a dilemma. If the opponents reacted forcefully to any particular Chinese initiative, they risked setting in motion a sequence of events that would lead to war; and war in the region, given the availability of nuclear weapons, could have catastrophic consequences. On the other hand, when the partisans of the regional status quo did not react forcefully, but confined themselves to rhetorical protests, China scored a victory, the balance of power in East Asia tilted, if only slightly, in China's direction, and the People's Republic had no disincentive to taking further, similar steps. China, like Russia in Europe, employed "salami tactics."

Along with the ambivalence of its members about confronting a country with which their economic fates are entwined and the difficult choices China's calibrated military challenges pose, the coalition to defend the East Asian status quo that China's revisionist aspirations created had to operate under the burden of yet a third complicating feature: the role of the United States. Any effort to check China's revisionist aspirations would require active American participation, which was another source of fragility.

The countries of East Asia were connected to one another, in military terms, not directly but at one remove, through their parallel ties to the United States. They were not, that is, formal allies but rather had an ally in common. To remove the United States from the anti-Chinese coalition would cause its collapse.

Moreover, China possessed nuclear weapons. Containing a country with such weapons requires another country that also has them: in this case, like deters like. None of the other members of the coalition possessed such weapons: they relied on the nuclear arsenal of the United States. Without it, and all apart from the impact of a nuclear-armed North Korea, they would have to acquire nuclear arms of their own to stand up to China; and nuclear proliferation in Asia would bring with it a new set of dangers.[148]

Finally, China's most aggressive policies involved its maritime claims, which meant that the other countries required naval forces to cope with them. Among the members of the countervailing coalition only the United States had a navy large and powerful enough for the task. While Japan, South Korea, and Taiwan could equip themselves with nuclear arms quickly if they chose to do so, none could hope to build, in a short period of time, a navy of the size and with the firepower that America had and that China was on the way to having.

The persistence of the American foreign policy that lent itself to these necessary tasks in checking China could not be assumed. From the end of World War II through the post-Cold War era the United States maintained a commanding military and political presence in the Asia-Pacific region. By the time the post-Cold War peace came to an end, however, America's position there—and indeed elsewhere in the world—had come under political and economic pressure. In the first instance the pressure came in both cases not from other countries but from within the United States itself. The experience of two frustrating, costly, and at best only partly successful post-Cold War military interventions, in Afghanistan and Iraq, called into question among Americans the wisdom not simply of military expeditions to turbulent countries but also of America's overall foreign policy of global military, political, and economic leadership that had given rise to them.

At the same time, a decline in the American rate of economic growth, combined with an increase in economic inequality—both the result more of broad social and economic trends than of deliberate public policies and thus not amenable to short-term correction—reduced the national appetite for spending money outside the country's borders on projects that did not bring immediate gains to Americans. Both attitudes contributed to the election, in 2016, of Donald Trump as president of the United States.[149]

To add to the domestic obstacles to a globally engaged American foreign policy, beginning during the Cold War and carrying through the post-Cold War period, for reasons having little to do with its foreign policy, the United States ran annual budget deficits and accumulated a large and growing national debt. At some point the federal government would have to begin to reduce the deficits and bring the debt under control. Because the country's entitlement programs, Social Security and Medicare, rather than military spending, claimed the bulk of the American government's expenditures, deficit reduction would have to come from cutting back on these social welfare programs. Such cutbacks might well lead, however, to a retrenchment in the country's foreign policy; resenting the loss of direct benefits to themselves, American voters might well demand that the money spent on foreigners—which is how many of them regarded expenditures for the American naval power that checked Chinese ambitions in East Asia—be reduced as well.[150]

The claim of the American military deployments in the Asia-Pacific region on the public purse had to compete not only with programs providing direct benefits to American taxpayers and voters but also with similar military and diplomatic efforts in other parts of the world. The coalition that opposed Russia's revisionist aspirations in Europe depended on American military power, as did the one opposed to China's ambitions in Asia. Placing even greater strain on American foreign policy was a comparable role in yet a third region of the world. There, as in the other two, a revisionist power sought military and political supremacy at the expense of countries aligned with, and that depended on, the United States. That third region was the Middle East.

3

The Middle East

The Hegemonic Truce

Today, Iran has once again become an empire as it has been throughout history. This empire's capital is Baghdad, the center of our civilization, culture, and identity today as it was in the past . . . The entire Middle Eastern region is Iranian . . . we will defend all of the region's people because we consider them part of Iran.

— ALI YOUNIS, former Iranian minister of intelligence
and advisor to President Hassan Rouhani, March, 2015[1]

[In the Middle East] there are millions of people who now must reconfigure the way they see themselves and the world, not just through a political revolution, but through a cultural one. There is no way any outside power can deliberately accelerate or channel this transformation. And since we are much closer to the beginning of that process than the end, the region will remain a cauldron for years if not decades to come.

— MARTIN KRAMER[2]

Truce

In the wake of the post-Cold War era, Europe and East Asia were geopolitical twins,[3] with large, formerly communist countries seeking to overturn the existing political order confronting a broad but ambivalent opposing coalition with the United States at its center. The Middle East, to continue the metaphor, qualified as their cousin. It had some important features in common with them but also notable differences.

96

When the Cold War ended, the part of the world encompassing western Asia and northeast Africa and including Anatolia, Mesopotamia, the Levant, the Persian Gulf, and the Mahgreb, all with largely Muslim populations, became, compared with its recent past, more peaceful. Peace there came to an end, as in Europe and East Asia, through the efforts of a revisionist country to expand its own power and influence at the expense of its neighbors: Iran's aggressive policies corresponded to those of Russia and China. A quarter century after the collapse of communism in Europe, security competition had returned with a vengeance to the lands stretching from Marrakesh to Bangladesh.

In the Middle East, however, even at its most tranquil, peace had shallower roots and was more fragile than in Europe and East Asia. Indeed, the international relations of the region more closely resembled a temporary truce than a deep peace. Unlike in the other two regions, none of the major Middle Eastern countries ever considered security competition to be a thing of the past with only a minor place, or no place at all, on its government's agenda. Moreover, when the shaky peace came to an end, the Middle East became more violent, with considerably more death and destruction, than in Europe or the western Pacific.

It became less peaceful in the wake of the Cold War because the end of that conflict had a less powerful impact there than elsewhere. The conclusion of the Soviet-American rivalry did not leave in its wake the core of a security community, among whose members war had become unthinkable, as it did in Europe and East Asia. It failed to do so, among other reasons, because the contentious post-World War II political issues in the Middle East arose independently of the Cold War and so outlived it. Between 1945 and 1991 the region was the site of a number of wars but none of them grew out of the global struggle between international communism and the Western democracies. While the collapse of communism in Europe eliminated the principal causes of armed conflict in both Europe and East Asia, therefore, it did no such thing in the Middle East. A shaky truce rather than a full peace obtained there for yet another reason: while Europe had, for a time, each of the three pillars on which modern peace rests and East Asia had two of them, the Middle East had only one.

Democracy, the most popular form of government in the other two regions, had only a very modest presence in the Middle East. Of all the countries there, Israel had a solidly democratic political system and Turkey an intermittently democratic one, but the Arab heart of the Middle East had never produced a democracy.[4]

The absence of democratic government in the region had several causes. It stemmed from the local version of Islam, which emphasized the divine source of the law and so left no legitimate political space for the human legislation that is the business of democracy. It stemmed as well from the local bias against a political form associated with Islam's great historical rival, the Christian West. In addition, democracy was missing in the Arab Middle East because the region lacked the political foundation on which democracy rested in Europe and Asia: the modern nation-state.[5]

The nation is a modern political category. Most Middle Easterners, especially Arabs, remained resolutely non-modern—that is, traditional—in their political loyalties. Most Middle Eastern states therefore comprised not single, self-conscious, cohesive nations, like France, Japan, or Norway, but instead often mutually hostile clans, tribes, sects, and ethnic groups[6] that resisted sharing power among themselves, as democracy requires and as genuine nations do.[7] Nor did the states that governed these disparate groups, whose borders had often been drawn arbitrarily by foreign powers, have one of the defining features of the modern governance elsewhere: the rule of law. Instead, the whims of the rulers were supreme.

The rule of law, and in particular the security of property rights and the effective enforcement of contracts, are necessary for the establishment and successful operation of a prosperity-producing free-market economy. Because most of the countries of the Middle East also lacked this, the second modern pillar of peace, economic interdependence, was also absent from the region.

Having such economies, the countries of Europe and East Asia have traded with and invested in one another in large volume, which contributed to the post-Cold War peace in both regions. Except for Israel, the countries of the Middle East, by contrast, do not have vibrant, productive economies and conduct little intra-regional trade. Their economies do not produce much that their neighbors want or need. To be sure, a number of Middle Eastern countries do conduct trade on a massive scale, but not within the region and only in one commodity: oil.

Roughly two-thirds of the world's readily accessible reserves of oil are located in the Middle East, most near the Persian Gulf. The world's major economies, in Europe and Asia, depend on Middle Eastern oil, and the large sums they spend to purchase it fill the treasuries of the governments that control the commodity.

Oil presented another obstacle to the establishment of democracy. The huge revenues it generated gave the rulers who received them both the incentive to remain perpetually in power, in order to keep those revenues for themselves, and the resources to bribe and coerce the people they rule to accept this state of affairs. In this way the Saudi royal family and the other undemocratic governments of the oil-exporting domains resembled the Putin regime in Russia. Oil also gave those who controlled it the means to exercise influence beyond their borders: the distribution of petroleum reserves shaped the balance of power within the Middle East. Thus the local leaders of the two blocs contending for primacy in the region in the wake of the Cold War, Saudi Arabia among Sunni Muslims and Iran among the Shia, both harbored large reserves of oil.

Its oil made the Middle East important to powerful countries elsewhere at a time when familiar sources of geopolitical significance had disappeared. Great Britain maintained a robust military and political presence after World War I for strategic reasons, to control the Suez Canal and access to what truly mattered to the British: their Indian empire. With the end of that empire and the retreat of British power the United States stepped in, again for strategic purposes: to guard against the expansion of the power and influence of its great global rival, the Soviet Union. With the end of the Cold War, without its oil the Middle East would have held no more interest for the rest of the world than sub-Saharan Africa, another site of political turmoil and poor economic performance that largely disappeared from the international agenda in the post-Cold War era. Because the world needed its oil, however, the Middle East remained significant for Europe, Asia, and North America, and its significance formed the basis for a version of the third pillar of peace that, unlike democracy and economic interdependence, was present in the wake of the Cold War: hegemony.

For most of its history one or two powers, either on its periphery or more distant from the region, dominated the Middle East. The Turkish Ottoman Empire held sway over much of it from the fifteenth century through 1918. The British and French supplanted that Empire after it was defeated in World War I.[8] When Britain and France retreated from the Middle East in the 1960s the United States partially replaced them. Unlike the two European powers, the Americans did not seek to govern, directly or indirectly, any of the countries of the region. Concerned above all to prevent Soviet encroachment, the United States also opposed, during the Cold War era, local regimes that aspired to primacy, first—and after an initial period of friendship that ended in American disappointment[9]—Nasser's Egypt and then Saddam Hussein's Iraq.

Nasser's bid for mastery of the Middle East came to an end with Israel's decisive victory over Egypt's armed forces and those of Jordan and Syria, in June, 1967. In 1991 the United States organized a broad international coalition that, relying mainly on American military power, reversed the 1990 Iraqi occupation of neighboring Kuwait by expelling Saddam's army. The 1991 Gulf War coincided with the end of the Cold War: the Soviet Union sided with the United States, for the first time since World War II, in opposing Saddam. A few months later the Soviet Union itself collapsed, leaving the United States at the summit of world politics as the sole surviving superpower. Although the Americans had not deliberately sought hegemony in the Middle East, that is what the outcome of the Cold War and the Gulf War gave them.

During the post-Cold War era, American Middle East policy concentrated not on reinforcing the stability of the region but rather on trying to resolve one of the several political disputes there, the one between Israel and one of its Arab neighbors, the Palestinians. Historians of the twenty-second century will wonder at the obsession of successive American governments with promoting the relaxation of Israeli control over the tiny sliver of territory wedged between the cease-fire line of the Arab-Israeli war of 1948 (Israel's War of Independence) and the Jordan River, territory that the Israeli army had captured in the defensive war it waged in 1967, and establishing on that territory yet another independent Arab state. The Israeli-Palestinian conflict had only marginal significance for the Middle East as a whole.[10] It was not, in any case, susceptible to resolution because the Palestinian party to it, adamantly opposed as it was to Jewish sovereignty in any part of the Middle East, sought not peace with but rather the elimination of the state of Israel.[11]

Israel's strategic significance in Middle Eastern affairs and for American policy in the region lay elsewhere. It supplemented American hegemony because Israeli military prowess helped to keep in check countries hostile to the United States, to the regional status quo, and therefore to peace. As an effective regional ally, it lowered the cost of the American role in the Middle East. It helped to free the United States from the necessity of stationing military forces there on a large scale, as America had done in Europe and East Asia during the Cold War and continued to do, in reduced numbers, in those two regions after the Cold War ended.[12]

In several respects the post-Cold War American role in the Middle East more closely resembled classic imperial hegemony than it did the benign version of it in the other two regions. Unlike in Europe and East Asia, the United States did not, with the exception of Israel, share basic political values with its Middle Eastern allies. Nor, with the exception of its need for oil, did it have economic ties of any consequence with them. For friendly Middle Eastern governments the connection with the United States served the traditional purpose of protecting them from actual and potential adversaries (which included, in most cases, the people they undemocratically governed), not the modern one of forging a security community among whose members war had become unthinkable.

Moreover, while in Europe and East Asia for at least part of the post-Cold War period all major countries accepted the American role, this was never the case in the Middle East. One Middle Eastern country—Iran—resented and opposed the American presence and never abandoned the goal of expanding its own power at the expense of the United States. The clerical leaders of the Islamic Republic of Iran saw America not as a police force to be welcomed but rather as an occupying army to be evicted. The government of Iran considered American hegemony to be malignant, not benign, and wished to overthrow it, although for most of the period following the end of the Cold War it lacked the strength to attempt seriously to do so. For its part, the United States saw Iran not as a potential partner in a common security order but as an adversary. The American government adopted the same policy toward Iran that it had maintained against the Soviet Union during the Cold War: containment.[13]

After the fall of the Berlin Wall, Europe seemed to have been cured of the affliction of war, and East Asia appeared to be on the way to conquering it. In the Middle East, however, that dread disease was only in partial remission. While shakier even at its zenith than in the other two regions, and less the product of the consent of the local countries than the result of the power of the United States, the peace in the Middle East did share one important feature with its counterparts in Europe and East Asia: it ended.

It ended partly because of the weakening of the hegemonic power. The United States suffered simultaneous terrorist attacks on New York City and Washington D.C. on September 11, 2001, which killed almost 3,000 people and wounded more than 6,000 others. The attacks shocked the American government and the American public and propelled the country into two wars that, in the end, diminished its willingness to sustain its hegemonic post-Cold War role in the Middle East.

The attacks originated in Afghanistan. The American military proceeded to remove from power there the Islamic fundamentalist Taliban regime that had sheltered al Qaeda, the Arab terrorist group that had conducted the attacks. The United States then helped to install a new government in Afghanistan but ultimately found itself bogged down fighting an insurgency that the Taliban and other fundamentalist groups conducted from bases in neighboring Pakistan.

Eighteen months after the terrorist attacks the American government launched a second military campaign, in Iraq. American military forces easily dislodged Saddam Hussein's government but then became entangled in an insurgency even fiercer and deadlier than the ongoing one in Afghanistan. The Iraq War cost the United States, by official count, 4,487 dead and 32,226 wounded. The American public turned against both conflicts and its support for a robust military policy in the Middle East weakened.

The chief responsibility for bringing to an end such peace as the region enjoyed in the wake of the Cold War belonged elsewhere, however. As in Europe and East Asia, in the Middle East security competition returned not because of what the United States did or did not do but rather as the result of the decades-old revisionist aspirations of a local power. The principal disturber of the peace, the equivalent, for the Middle East, of Russia in Europe and China in East Asia, was Iran.

Iran

Contemporary Iran can trace its roots to antiquity, to the Persian kingdom of Cyrus the Great in the sixth century B.C. that grew into an empire that clashed with the Greeks of that era, from whom Western civilization is descended. The Achaemenid empire that Cyrus founded was succeeded, in due course, by the Parthian empire of the third century B.C. and that of the Sassanids in the third century A.D., both of them large Persian-dominated domains. Islam came to these lands in the seventh century, shortly after its founding, and in the sixteenth century the then-ruling Safavid dynasty proclaimed the Shia rather than the Sunni version of the religion to be the official faith—Islam having split into two generally hostile sects in a dispute over the proper succession to the Prophet Muhammad.

In the late nineteenth and early twentieth centuries Iran suffered from political instability and the incursions of outside powers. In 1907 Russia and Great Britain divided the country into three zones, with the Russians dominating the northernmost of them and the British holding sway in the south. During World War I, British, Russian, and Ottoman troops all occupied what was still known as Persia. The war, in combination with the influenza pandemic of 1918, led to a massive loss of life among its inhabitants.[14]

In 1921 an army officer named Reza Khan seized power and in 1925 proclaimed himself shah, the Persian term for emperor. He established what he called the Pahlavi dynasty, a name deliberately borrowed from antiquity to emphasize the country's long and distinguished history.[15] For the next two decades he maneuvered among the great powers, but in 1941 the British, unhappy with his affinity for Nazi Germany,[16] forced him to abdicate in favor of his son, Mohamed Reza.

The Iran over which the two Pahlavis presided lacked the geographic scope of the great Persian empires of the past[17] but it did include non-Persians—Azeris, Kurds, Baluchis, Arabs, and others—who comprised about half the country's population. Both shahs took it as their governing mission to modernize the country;[18] and under their rule Iran acquired a modest industrial economy, although it depended heavily on the export of the oil that was discovered within its borders in 1905. People moved from the countryside to the cities in considerable numbers and the state provided education on a large scale, including—and contrary to the practice of centuries—for women. The Pahlavi regime also reduced the power of the Shia clergy.[19]

On the basis of their long lineage and the glories of the ancient civilization from which they were descended, many Iranians regarded themselves, much as the Chinese did in East Asia, as culturally superior to their neighbors[20] and entitled, by reason of that lineage and superiority, to primacy in their region. Like the Chinese, they saw their country as a natural hegemon; and like the Chinese they lamented the fall from primacy that they had experienced over the centuries, in both cases mainly because of the rise of the West.

Throughout the Cold War, Iran, like China, lacked the power to impose itself upon its neighbors; and the shah faced two further obstacles to the role for which he believed his country was destined: Iran was Shia while much of the Middle East (and the overwhelming majority of Muslims elsewhere) adhered to the Sunni branch of the faith; and it was ethnically Persian, an Indo-European people, while most people in the region were Semitic Arabs. The second Pahlavi sought to expand his country's role in the Middle East not in opposition to but in partnership with the United States. Out of suspicion of the Soviet Union, with which Iran shared a border and that had withdrawn from the northern part of his country reluctantly after occupying it in World War II, the shah forged a close alignment with the Americans. They, in turn, favored him with political support, the sale of arms, and the promise, by President Richard M. Nixon, of a prominent regional role as the chief American surrogate there.[21]

In 1979 a broad movement drawn from diverse sectors of Iranian society came together to overthrow the shah. He fled into exile and died soon thereafter. A government headed by Shia Muslim clerics replaced him. The monarch's increasing and arbitrary personal power, his arrogance and isolation, the social strains of the modernizing trends over which he presided, and the inflationary pressures that the spike in the global price of oil in the first part of the decade had helped to generate, all combined to create widespread discontent with the regime.[22]

Millions of people took to the streets to demonstrate against it and strikes crippled the Iranian economy. The Pahlavi dynasty fell, as well, because the shah himself turned out to be a weak and irresolute leader, incapable of acting decisively either to reform his government or to repress his opponents. His chief foreign supporter, the United States, led by President Jimmy Carter, behaved in a similarly indecisive fashion in the face of the challenge to its ally.

The Iranian upheaval and change of government ranks with those that occurred in Russia in 1917 and China in 1949 as the three great revolutions of the twentieth century.[23] As in Russia and China, in Iran an entirely new cadre took control of the government while the members of the old elite either left the country or were killed. As on the two previous occasions, a shrewd, determined, ruthless, duplicitous, charismatic figure led the Iranian revolution: the Shia cleric Ruhollah Khomeini, operating initially from exile in France, played the role in Iran that V.I. Lenin and Mao Zedong did in Russia and China respectively.

As in the other two revolutions, the new regime in Iran brought to the task of governance a radical governing creed: the Iranian project of establishing a theocracy, a state governed according to the divine law as interpreted and enforced by the Shia Muslim clergy, differed from the precepts of the shah's rule as sharply as had Lenin's and Mao's dictatorship of the Communist Party and centrally planned and controlled economic order from what had gone before in Russia and China. As in those two countries, the revolutionaries seized and retained power through violence and repression.

As in Russia and China, finally, in Iran, too, war followed revolution. Even before consolidating power throughout the Russian empire Lenin ordered an attack on Poland. The year after the communist triumph in the Chinese civil war, Mao sent a Chinese army into battle against the United States in Korea. Iran, for its part, waged a bloody eight-year struggle with neighboring Iraq.

On September 22, 1980, the Iraqi dictator Saddam Hussein began the war by invading Iran. Confident that his army would achieve an easy victory, and thus gain territory he believed rightfully belonged to

his country, he sought to shock and perhaps dislodge the newly established clerical regime in Tehran that was fiercely hostile to him, and
make himself the undisputed leader of the Arab world. After initial
setbacks Iranian forces stopped the Iraqi advance and by July 1982 had
driven Iraq out of Iranian territory. At that point Khomeini decided to
continue the conflict in order to unseat Saddam, but the war turned
instead into a stalemate. On the defensive, Saddam's regime bombed
Iranian cities and used chemical weapons against Iranian combatants.
In July, 1988 the Iranian leader finally accepted a peace proposal and
the war ended.[24] It had killed as many as one million Iranians.

Devastating as the war had been for Iran, it did allow the regime
to portray itself as the champion of the nation, defending it against
a predatory foreign enemy. The conflict with Iraq thus helped to en-
trench Khomeini and his theocratic principles in power.[25]

The political order he created had an important feature in common
with Russian and Chinese communist rule: all three had systems of
power parallel, and indeed superior, to the formal government. Just as
the Communist Party controlled the Soviet and Chinese legislatures
and bureaucracies, so a clerical "Supreme Leader"—first Khomenei
himself and then, after his death, another cleric, Ali Khameini—
exercised ultimate authority in Iran. A Shia militia, the Revolutionary
Guard Corps, operated separately from the police and the army.
Organizations dominated by regime loyalists controlled much of the
country's economy.[26]

As the leader of the revolution Khomeini had promised to replace
the shah's autocracy with democracy.[27] Instead, the Islamic Republic
of Iran became a dictatorship, permitting neither liberty nor popular
sovereignty and governed, like communist Russia and China, by a self-
selected, self-perpetuating elite. It did have an elected president and
parliament; but each was subordinate to the unelected clerics and in
the elections to choose them the clerical establishment decided who
could and could not run.

Just as the communists justified their dictatorial rule on the basis
of their version of a sacred doctrine, Marxism-Leninism (in China
Marxism-Leninism-Maoism), so too did Iran's rulers assert that
Islamic law, and their authority to interpret and implement it, gave
them the right to exercise power over their fellow Iranians. Just as

the communists aspired to do with the Russian and Chinese people, the mullahs tried to control the everyday lives of individual Iranians, seeking to force them to conform to the regime's version of the norms of traditional Islam. They banned alcohol, for example, insisted that women practice modesty by covering themselves when appearing in public, and instituted stoning as a punishment for law-breaking.

Khomeini also transformed Iran's relations with its neighbors and with the rest of the world. The Islamic Republic's foreign policy continued the shah's quest for regional primacy, but went further: its leaders sought not only to revise the distribution of power in the Middle East but also to foment revolutions within the other countries there. The leaders of the Islamic Republic regarded the governments of the other Muslim-majority countries of the Middle East as insufficiently pious, indeed heretical and illegitimate, and advocated their overthrow.

Iran adopted an attitude of extreme hostility to the United States. On November 4, 1979 radical students, in defiance of international law and custom, seized fifty-two diplomatic personnel in the American embassy in Tehran and held them hostage for 444 days, making reconciliation between the American government and the new regime impossible. The estrangement between the two deepened with American support for Iraq in the Iran-Iraq War. The United States had already earned the mullahs' enmity through its close ties with their enemy, the shah.[28] More importantly, America epitomized the Western culture and secular values that Khomeini had made it his mission to purge from Iran.[29] The fact and example of the United States, even more than its military power, posed a mortal threat to the Islamic Republic. It was no accident that the clerics called it "the Great Satan." In scripture— Muslim as well as Jewish and Christian—Satan is the tempter who through his wiles persuades Adam and Eve to disobey God. Khomeini and his associates saw the American devil as attempting to do the same thing to the people of Iran.

Khomeini also reversed the shah's cordial relationship with Israel. The new policy had its roots in his and his clerical colleagues' genuine, religiously-based anti-Semitism;[30] but opposition to the Jewish state also served a strategic purpose. It put Iran on the side of the Arabs in a conflict that Arab leaders regularly (if cynically) proclaimed to be of surpassing importance to them. The Iranian mullahs hoped thereby to mitigate some of the Arabs' reflexive opposition to a Shia and Persian power, which stood as one of the principal obstacles to Iranian primacy in the Middle East.[31]

In the decades after 1979 the regime to which the Iranian revolution gave rise became oppressive and domestically unpopular. The fervor it had initially inspired among Iranians dissipated. In fact, government according to his interpretation of Islamic law had, in an important way, the opposite effect from the one Khomeini had intended. Iranians became far less religious. Attendance at the country's mosques plummeted.[32]

The Iranian revolution's original promise of democracy remained unfulfilled: Iranians enjoyed no more freedom than they had had under the shah. Indeed, in matters of personal behavior they had less, as their clerical overlords sought to impose on them what the clerics regarded as proper Islamic standards of conduct.

Revolutionary Iran also became poorer. The Islamic Republic did far worse in fostering economic growth than had the Pahlavi dynasty.[33] Khomeini expressed no regret for the regime's economic record. To the contrary, he dismissed economic considerations on the grounds that the revolution "was not about the price of watermelons." Failing to diversify the range of the country's economic activities, Iran continued to rely heavily on the sale of oil for its income. As it did in other countries, the government's extensive involvement in the operation of the economy discouraged entrepreneurship and innovation and retarded growth.[34] As in post-communist Russia and post-Mao China, government control of the economy in Iran paved the way for widespread corruption. Like them, the Islamic Republic of Iran was, among other things, a kleptocracy. Regime officials, members of the Revolutionary Guards, and their families amassed fortunes through their political connections even as the vast majority of their fellow countrymen struggled to get by, which only deepened public distaste for the ruling clerics.[35] In 2012 an estimated 40 percent of all Iranians lived in poverty.[36]

The regime's failure to provide either bread or freedom to those it governed produced widespread discontent, which led to attempts to reform Iran through the ballot box. Mohammed Khatami, a liberal cleric, won two terms as president, in 1997 and 2001. Despite reformist rhetoric, however, he proved unable to implement serious political or economic change. The clerical establishment, led by Supreme Leader Khamenei, thwarted him. In 2013 another putative reformer, Hassan Rouhani, won the presidency, but again, the principal political and economic structures of the Islamic Republic remained intact.[37] Between Khatami and Rouhani came the presidency of Mahmoud Ahmadinejad, an enthusiastic supporter of the regime, whose second election, in 2009, triggered a nation-wide uprising.

A moderate reformer, Mir Hossein Mousavi, ran against Ahmadinejad in his bid for a second term. The Mousavi candidacy inspired a record-high turnout on election day but the government declared Ahmadinejad the winner even before the polls had closed. Angry Iranians took to the streets to protest what was obviously a stolen election. The protests, which became known as the Green Movement, started in the capital, Tehran, and quickly spread across the country. They involved millions of people in Iran's largest cities, especially students, and professionals but not, in appreciable numbers, the clerics, small merchants (*bazaaris*) and workers who had joined the uprising that had brought down the shah in 1979. The protests continued in one form or another for 20 months but the authorities finally put an end to them, arresting, imprisoning, and in some cases murdering protesters.[38]

The spontaneous emergence of the Green Movement and the large number of Iranians who joined it demonstrated the breadth and depth of the internal opposition to the Islamic Republic. The Movement's ultimate fate, however, showed that the regime retained the determination, and the loyalty of the security services,[39] necessary to maintain its grip on power.[40]

While the government that the revolution of 1979 produced did not deliver what it had initially promised domestically, it did, true to Khomeini's ambition, engage in continuing and often successful efforts to expand its power and influence beyond its borders. It never wavered in its goals of changing the distribution of power in the Middle East in its own favor and subverting the governments of the other countries of the region.

As with Russia and China, Iran's history served, in the eyes of its rulers and at least some of the people they ruled, as a warrant for regional hegemony. Just as Russia was, for Vladimir Putin and his colleagues, historically destined to be a great European power and China, for its twenty-first-century communist leaders, had an historical vocation for primacy in East Asia, so Iranian domination of the Middle East would, in the eyes of the ruling elite and no doubt even some outside it, restore the natural political order there, one dating back to the great Persian monarchs of antiquity.[41] Like Russia and China, Iran's revisionist foreign policy, which ended the Middle Eastern version of a post-Cold War peace, stemmed as well from its domestic politics.

Like Russia after the fall in the price of oil, and like post-Cold War China anticipating the obsolescence of its formula for double-digit annual economic growth, Iran's economic performance—worse for longer than those of the other countries—did not fulfill the expectations of the Iranian people. As in Russia and China, economic stagnation deprived the regime of an important source of political support. Like the revisionist Russian and Chinese foreign policies, aggressive conduct beyond its borders by the Islamic Republic had the potential to bolster the government's standing by appealing to a public sentiment that resonated among Iranians as it did with Russians and Chinese: nationalism.[42] In Iran, nationalism had a sectarian tinge: the Islamic Republic depicted itself as standing up for Shia Muslims throughout the Middle East, whom the Sunnis had historically persecuted. This helped to compensate, the mullahs surely hoped, for their many failings at home.[43]

Although following the Russian and Chinese pattern in attempting to generate domestic legitimacy, however, the government of Iran differed from them as well. With the decline, actual or prospective, in economic growth, nationalism served as a particularly important resource for the regimes of Vladimir Putin and Xi Jinping because neither could rely on two long-established and historically reliable sources of short-term public support and long-term political legitimacy: tradition, and specifically the purportedly divinely-supplied legitimacy with which hereditary monarchies, including Russian tsars and Chinese emperors, had claimed for centuries; and modern ideology, according to which the laws of history rather than the laws of God, and the ruling group's superior understanding of them, made it fit to rule.

In the post-Cold War era the other two revisionist powers had left ideology behind. Russia had ceased to be communist and the Chinese had ceased to believe, or even hypocritically to profess belief, in orthodox Marxism-Leninism-Maoism. What remained of communism in China (although it was hardly an insignificant remnant) was the Communist Party's monopoly of political power.

In Iran, by contrast, ideology lived on. While the public demonstrated little allegiance to the founding theocratic principle of the Islamic Republic, namely that clerics should govern according to their interpretation of Islamic law, the political and economic elite remained committed to that principle. They did so, at the least, because ideology gave them the title to their power and wealth. This rendered negligible their incentives to abandon or question it.[44]

An aggressive foreign policy was built into the ruling ideology. If its founding precepts were true—and its rulers, as noted, had every incentive to believe them to be true—then the governing principles of other Middle Eastern countries were false and the governments following these heretical principles were unfit to hold power. If the ideological foundations of the Islamic Republic were sound, that is, Iran had a mission to dominate its region in order to spread them. A faltering economic performance and public discontent, although undoubtedly undesirable from the regime's point of view, mattered less to them than such developments did to Putin's kleptocratic clique in Russia or the ruling Communist Party in China: the Iranian political system rested, in the publicly expressed views of its leaders, on eternal, immutable truths that transcended the political and economic circumstances of any particular moment. As one cleric put it, "It is the government's duty to take the people to heaven even by force or whip."[45] For this reason the clerics worried less about public support—of which they enjoyed less and less as the years went on—than did their Russian and Chinese counterparts.

Iran had far less military power than Russia or China and did not use it directly, as did the other two, to seize territory. Instead, the Islamic Republic extended its reach through the use of proxies, in a way reminiscent of the Soviet Union and communist China. Those two revolutionary states had made use of communist movements or formally organized communist parties in other countries to do their bidding and spread their influence. Similarly, Iran relied on Shia Muslims in Arab countries and elsewhere for this purpose.

It stirred riots among the Shia in eastern Saudi Arabia and Bahrain in 1979, for example.[46] Its greatest success came in Lebanon, a country divided among Sunni and Shia Muslims and Maronite Christians. There it inspired, recruited, equipped, trained, and controlled a Shia militia called Hezbollah—Arabic for "the party of God." Hezbollah grew in strength from its beginnings in the early 1980s to become the most formidable military and political institution in the country, over-shadowing the Lebanese government and the Lebanese army. It served as an instrument of Iranian foreign policy, waging a war with neigh-boring Israel and fighting to protect the regime of Iran's client, Bashar Assad, in Syria. Through Hezbollah as well as other groups Iran be-came, by the assessment of the United States Department of State, the world's leading sponsor of terrorism.

The Islamic Republic conducted, directly and indirectly, terrorist operations against Israeli targets through support for Palestinian ter-rorism and against Jews who were not even Israeli citizens and who lived elsewhere—in Argentina, for example. It conducted such oper-ations, as well, against the country it designated as its principal ad-versary, the United States. Iranian agents bombed buildings housing multinational peacekeepers in Lebanon's capital, Beirut, in 1983, killing 241 Americans as well as fifty-eight French service personnel, and an apartment complex in Khobar, Saudi Arabia, in which Americans lived in 1996, resulting in 19 American deaths. From its inception the regime also kept up its campaign of rhetorical vilification against "the Great Satan."

The American government intermittently attempted to improve rela-tions with Iran but the Islamic Republic invariably rebuffed its overtures. During the post-Cold War period Russia and China had friendly rela-tions with the United States for extended periods of time. Revolutionary Iran never did. The American enemy helped to justify the repression that the regime practiced, but its anti-Americanism had deeper roots than that: hostility to American power and especially American values and cultural patterns was too deeply embedded in the regime's rationale for holding power to permit reconciliation of any kind.[47]

Ironically, much of the success that Iran enjoyed in expanding its power and eroding the post-Cold War security arrangements and dis-tribution of power in the Middle East came about because of the foreign policy of the United States. The two American wars that the September 11 terrorist attacks triggered removed regimes hostile to the Islamic

Republic. In 1998 Iran came close to war with the resolutely anti-Shia Taliban government of Afghanistan[48] and from 1980 to 1988 it waged the war with Saddam Hussein's Iraq. In the wake of September 11, and specifically in response to the attacks of that day, American military power deposed both regimes.

Because the two wars proved frustrating and costly for the United States, moreover, the American public developed a distaste for military measures in the Middle East, which redounded to the benefit of the country that aimed to reduce and ultimately eliminate American military hegemony there. The post-Cold War military initiatives of the United States thus inadvertently contributed to the revisionist program of the Islamic Republic. So, too, did an Iranian military initiative in which the United States became entangled: the regime's efforts to acquire nuclear weapons.

The Bomb

The shah began a program of nuclear power-generation, with American assistance, in the 1960s.[49] Upon seizing power the leaders of the Islamic Republic announced that they had no interest in using these facilities to produce nuclear weapons, the possession of which, they said, violated the laws of Islam. Nonetheless, they launched a clandestine program to build such weapons, investing heavily in mastering the most demanding step in the bomb-making process, the fabrication of the explosive material—either enriched uranium or purified plutonium. In 2002 it came to light that the regime was secretly building two additional nuclear installations: one for enrichment at Natanz; the other, at Arak, to produce plutonium.[50] The nuclear weapons program greatly accelerated during the Ahmadinejad presidency. At its outset Iran had only a few of the centrifuges that enrich uranium. During his second term it added thousands.[51]

The mullahs had good reasons to want the bomb. Nuclear weapons would serve a defensive purpose, providing insurance against the fate of the Taliban, Saddam Hussein, and the Libyan dictator Muammar Gaddafi: the armed forces of the United States had removed all three from power. If the Islamic Republic could threaten nuclear retaliation in response to an American attack, as those three had been unable to do—Saddam had lost his nuclear weapons program in the 1991 Gulf War and Gaddhafi had voluntarily relinquished his—the United States would surely not dare to launch one.

The weapons of mass destruction that Iran sought also had a more aggressive potential use. They could serve as a shield behind which the Islamic Republic could continue and even accelerate its pursuit of hegemony in the Middle East. An Iranian bomb might well reduce the American willingness to oppose Iran's regional initiatives, for fear that doing so would entangle the United States in a conflict that would provoke an Iranian nuclear attack.

Iran reportedly received assistance in developing ballistic missiles from the East Asian rogue state and disturber of the peace, North Korea, assistance that may have extended to the fabrication of nuclear explosives.[52] The countries an Iranian bomb would threaten, like those in the crosshairs of nuclear North Korea, would have four ways from which to choose in responding to one.[53] They could attempt to build systems of defense against it. Where nuclear weapons are concerned, however, the offense has a decided advantage over the defense because even one bomb penetrating a defensive system would do catastrophic damage to the target country. The more nuclear explosives an attacker can launch, therefore, the less effective a strategy of defense will be, giving Iran (and North Korea) the incentive to amass as many such explosives as possible.

In response to an Iranian bomb the Islamic Republic's adversaries could implement a strategy of deterrence.[54] Deterrence is effective to the extent that it is credible to the party being deterred. The deterrence of North Korea gained credibility from the fact that it was already well established: the United States had stationed a contingent of troops in South Korea for precisely that purpose since the end of the Korean War in 1953, more than half a century before the Pyongyang regime detonated its first nuclear explosion. During much of the Cold War the American force in Korea included short-range nuclear weapons. The Middle East, by contrast, had no similar history of the permanent presence in the region of American military personnel furnishing deterrence; and no country bordering on Iran was a good candidate to provide as hospitable a base for American soldiers and American weapons as South Korea.

Defense against and deterrence of a nuclear-armed Iran would depend chiefly on the United States. The countries of the region could also attempt to deter Iran without American help by acquiring nuclear weapons of their own. Nuclear proliferation is the third possible response to an Iranian bomb. Proliferation would bespeak a lack of confidence in American deterrence. America's Middle Eastern allies would want nuclear weapons of their own if they became convinced that the United States would not protect them.[55] If one such country obtained them,[56] others would likely follow. Such a proliferation "cascade" would bring new dangers to the region.

The nuclear standoff between the United States and the Soviet Union during the Cold War never turned into a shooting war in no small part because, for most of that period, each country had a nuclear arsenal large enough that the other could not hope to destroy it entirely even in a massive attack. Since some nuclear weapons would survive such an attack, the attacker would have to count on devastating retaliation in response to any attack it launched, which was a good reason that neither side ever launched one. By contrast, new nuclear powers in the Middle East, including Iran, would initially—and for some time—have small stockpiles of weapons. They would have to fear having them destroyed in a surprise attack; and since the distances among the countries of the region are small, unlike the distance between the two great Cold-War nuclear powers, all would have reason to believe that they would have virtually no warning of such an attack. This would in turn tempt each of them to launch their weapons in a preemptive attack, in order to prevent their own destruction. All would have, to borrow a phrase from popular culture, an itchy trigger finger. In a crisis, therefore—and the twenty-first-century Middle East is nothing if not a crisis-prone region—nuclear proliferation could bring catastrophe.

Those whom Iranian nuclear weapons threatened would have a fourth option: they could attempt to eliminate the threat by forcibly preventing the Islamic Republic from building such weapons. This option entails attacking and crippling the Iranian nuclear program. The American air force has the planes and the munitions necessary for this task. Those same military instruments could have devastated North Korea's nuclear infrastructure before it produced nuclear explosives; but because North Korea had the capacity to rain down destruction on South Korea with non-nuclear artillery in response, the American military did not do so. North Korea successfully deterred the United States.

Iran also had the ability to mount, directly or indirectly, punishing attacks on American allies in its region in response to an American military initiative to set back its weapons-building effort; but this potential did not, in and of itself, have the same deterrent effect as North Korea's. America's Arab allies in the Persian Gulf, within range of Iranian missiles and aircraft and susceptible to Iranian-inspired uprisings among their Shia population, and Israel, facing Hezbollah's large Iran-supplied fleet of rockets trained on its cities from neighboring Lebanon, were vulnerable, like South Korea, to deadly retaliation for an American attack. While South Korea firmly opposed such an attack on North Korea, however, Saudi Arabia and Israel actually *favored* American military action to keep nuclear weapons out of Iranian hands, despite the costs they themselves would likely incur. In fact, Israel, with a small but highly skilled and technologically advanced air force of its own, made clear its willingness to attack Iran's nuclear facilities itself. Unlike what happened in East Asia, in the Middle East the local allies of the United States did not veto an American anti-nuclear weapons campaign of aerial bombardment.[57]

The opponents of the Iranian nuclear program had another way of trying to block it: economic pressure, the goal of which was to inflict enough damage on Iran's economy to persuade its rulers to abandon their quest for the bomb in order to get relief from it. Countries in East Asia, and beyond, had carried out this strategy toward North Korea, but without notable success. Denying the communist regime in Pyongyang trade and investment did not deflect its drive for nuclear weapons for several reasons: acquiring these weapons was the regime's foremost goal; the country was already wretchedly poor and the government exercised such formidable powers of repression that further hardship, no matter how severe, would not generate pressure from the North Korean people to change course; and neighboring China was willing to supply the North Korean regime with the fuel and food it needed to avoid economic and social collapse.

Sanctions on Iran had greater success. The clerical regime relied heavily for its income on one commodity, oil. Reducing its sale of oil thus had the potential to create serious problems for it. The clerics had to fear that economic hardship would spark political rebellion because, dictatorial though it was, the Islamic Republic did not and could not impose the degree of repression on the people it governed that its North Korean counterpart did. Nor did Iran have the equivalent of China, a powerful neighbor prepared to counteract the effects of externally imposed economic punishment.

Beginning in 2006, acting through the United Nations Security Council[58] and led by the United States, the international community did place sanctions on Iran and strengthened them over time, resulting in an almost complete trade embargo.[59] The Iranian economy felt the effects: oil revenues fell by half and the country's currency lost two-thirds of its value.[60] The United States denied the Iranian government and Iranian businesses access to dollars, which sharply reduced their economic activity.[61] All this generated economic and political pressure that pushed the Iranian regime into negotiations about the status of its nuclear program.

The negotiations began in secret, with the United States, represented by the administration of President Barack Obama, taking the lead. They ultimately produced, in July, 2015, an agreement known as the Joint Comprehensive Plan of Action (JCPOA). Under the terms of the agreement Iran made a number of concessions. It agreed to reduce the number of uranium-enriching centrifuges it operated, closed down several nuclear-related facilities, and cut its stockpile of low-enriched uranium. The American government said that these terms put Iran at least a year away from building a bomb.

The Islamic Republic received, however, substantial concessions in return. For four decades the United States had made central to its nonproliferation policy the rule that countries such as Iran would not be permitted to have the means to enrich uranium. They would not, that is, be permitted to have the complete "nuclear fuel cycle."[62] Obama had reiterated this policy in his first term in office[63] but then abandoned it in the final agreement with Iran. In addition, the restrictions the JCPOA placed on the Iranian nuclear program all had expiration dates, from ten to fifteen years in the future, after which the Islamic Republic would be free to operate the program however it wished.

Arms control accords typically include provisions for inspection to ensure that all parties are observing its terms, but those in the JCPOA contained a number of serious weaknesses.[64] Furthermore, with the conclusion of the agreement all internationally-imposed sanctions on Iran were lifted.[65] Finally, while the agreement placed restrictions on Iran's direct bomb-making measures, it did no such thing for closely related activities such as the development and testing of ballistic missiles,[66] let alone the Islamic Republic's political and military initiatives to expand its power and influence at the expense of neighboring countries. If the JCPOA yielded a pause in Iran's effort to equip itself with the world's most powerful weapons, it did nothing to impede its revisionist campaign to achieve primacy in the Middle East.[67] As in Afghanistan and Iraq, American policy once again abetted Iran's hegemonic ambitions.

The outcome of an international negotiation normally reflects the balance of power between and among the parties to it. Contrary to this pattern, while the United States itself, not to mention the international coalition for which it spoke, far surpassed Iran in military might, and although the sanctions put considerable pressure on the regime to get them lifted lest they trigger a political explosion, in the negotiations over its nuclear program the Islamic Republic secured what was, from its standpoint, a very favorable agreement. Under ordinary circumstances the United States, being in so much stronger a position than Iran, would have extracted greater concessions. Because its terms favored a regime that had displayed resolute hostility to the United States for almost four decades, the Obama administration declined to put it to a vote of the Senate, as previous administrations had done with arms treaties. Instead, it designated the JCPOA an "executive agreement" and employed legislative maneuvers to ensure that a two-thirds majority in the Senate would be needed to overturn it.

The reasons that the accord departed from the historical norm in which the strong prevailed over the weak had to do with the personal agendas of the Americans responsible for conducting the negotiations. Secretary of State John Kerry, the principal negotiator, seemed to be eager to a fault for a concrete achievement that could serve as a capstone to his long public career. He was apparently all the more eager to make an accord with Iran that capstone because his previous effort to broker peace between Israel and the Palestinians had failed.

The ultimate responsibility on the American side rested with President Obama, who had several apparent motives for refraining from pressing Iran harder in order to get terms more favorable to the United States and its regional allies. He had, from the beginning of his presidency, made it a high priority to improve relations with Iran.[68] He believed that detente with the Islamic Republic was possible and that, once achieved, it would do a great deal to pacify the Middle East.[69] He had refrained from publicly supporting the Green Movement so as not to spoil the chances of a rapprochement with the dictatorship the Iranian protesters were challenging.[70] He and his colleagues hoped that the JCPOA would become the vehicle for a broader reconciliation with the Iranian clerics.

Obama also seemed particularly averse to making use of the immense American military advantage over Iran. To be sure, he more than once declared that, in the effort to keep the mullahs from getting the bomb, "all options" were "on the table," by implication including mounting an attack on the Iranian nuclear facilities. In every other way, however, he gave the impression of someone willing to go to any lengths to avoid the use of force.[71] He publicly and privately warned Israel against attacking Iran,[72] thereby weakening his own side's negotiating position since the threat of an Israeli strike would have given the American negotiators additional leverage. He forfeited this leverage, presumably, because he feared an Israeli attack would trigger a wider war in which the United States would become involved.

In general, Obama appeared more interested in finishing his term in office without having to confront Iran than in ensuring that his successors would be spared the need to do so. As they negotiated an end to American participation in the Vietnam War in the 1970s, President Nixon and his National Security Advisor and then Secretary of State Henry Kissinger privately described their goal as achieving "a decent interval" between the departure of American troops and a Communist conquest of the entire country. In concluding the JCPOA, Kerry and Obama seemed to be hoping, with respect to Iranian nuclear weapons, for a similar outcome.

In May, 2018, Donald Trump, Obama's successor as the American president, who had harshly criticized the JCPOA during his campaign for the office, announced that the United States was withdrawing from the accord. He had the power to do this by himself because his predecessor had chosen not to make it a treaty subject to Senate ratification. The United States began to reimpose economic sanctions, with the hope of generating enough pressure on the regime in Tehran to negotiate a new agreement, without the flaws of the 2015 version. Several Western European countries, however, which had also levied sanctions against Iran but had ended them when they, too, signed the nuclear accord, said that they would continue to observe it.

The clerical regime had good reason to wish to sustain the JCPOA. It gained from the agreement because its terms kept the Iranian nuclear program largely intact, accepting only a delay in carrying it forward. It also succeeded in escaping military action that could have crippled the program and might have harmed the regime itself. In exchange for modest concessions, furthermore, Iran broke free of what had become very costly economic sanctions.

Even before the agreement had been signed, however, an upheaval across its home region, in which the United States played no significant role, had created new opportunities for the Islamic Republic to pursue its campaign of revisionism in the Middle East.

The Arab Spring

On December 17, 2010, a street vendor named Mohamed Bouazizi in the Tunisian town of Sidi Bouazizi set himself on fire to protest unfair treatment at the hands of municipal authorities. His self-immolation touched off protests in his country that spread, over the next year, throughout the Middle East. The specific causes varied from place to place, but everywhere the corruption and cruelty of the rulers and the poverty and humiliation of those they ruled sent people into the streets and motivated them to take up arms.[73] They drove some long-standing regimes from power and mortally threatened others, not only in Tunisia but in Egypt, Libya, Syria, Bahrain, and Yemen as well.[74]

What became known as the Arab Spring at first aroused hopes for the creation of democratic governments where none had existed.[75] The upheavals brought, instead, chaos and violence, anarchy and civil war.[76]

With the breakdown of the established order, the people of the region embraced their most basic group identities. For the majority of them, their deepest allegiances were religious in nature and therefore, being Muslims, sectarian. In the midst of the violence, the fourteen-centuries-old cleavage between Sunnis and Shia came to the fore. Shia all over the Middle East gravitated to the protection and patronage of the leading Shia power, Iran. The Islamic Republic was able for this reason to take advantage of the Arab Spring and its consequences to expand its influence. Five years after Mohamed Bouazizi's death, officials of the Islamic Republic could boast, and Sunni leaders lament, that Iran, the erstwhile Persian interloper in the Arab Middle East, had gained effective control of four Arab capitals: Damascus in Syria, Beirut in Lebanon, Baghdad in Iraq, and Sana'a in Yemen.

The Iranian use of Shia proxies and allies to advance its hegemonic designs did not, of course, begin in 2011. The creation and exploitation of Hezbollah in Lebanon originated three decades earlier. The clerical regime had also pursued a similar strategy, again with considerable success, in Iraq. There, in 2003, the armed forces of the United States did in a few weeks what Iran had failed to accomplish over eight bloody years: remove Saddam Hussein from power. True to their own political values, the Americans insisted on choosing a successor government through free elections. Not surprisingly in a country 60 percent of whose population were Shia Muslims, the elections delivered power to Shia political parties.

Iran had close ties with several of these parties, having given them clandestine support and sheltered some of their leaders during the Saddam era.[77] The Islamic Republic also followed its Lebanese pattern of helping to organize, and supply with armaments, Shia militias, which came to exercise substantial influence in Shia-dominated Iraq.[78] In addition, Iranian-sponsored militants using Iranian-supplied munitions took part in attacks on American troops stationed in Iraq after Saddam's ouster.[79]

The upheavals of the Arab Spring had different consequences for the countries affected, and for Iran's project of regional hegemony, depending on the religious affiliations of their inhabitants. Those with overwhelmingly Sunni populations tended to divide between the adherents to a harsh, fundamentalist version of Islam—called in the West Islamism—and their coreligionists who did not, however devout they were, embrace the Islamist version of the faith. In Egypt, after the 2011 fall of Hosni Mubarak, the dictator who had held power for almost three decades, elections brought the fundamentalist Muslim Brotherhood to power the following year. In July 2013, after massive demonstrations in Cairo and other cities against the government, the military overthrew the Brotherhood. Abdel Fattah al-Sisi, a former officer like Mubarak and his predecessors, Anwar Sadat and Gamal Abdel Nasser, became president of Egypt. Iran benefitted from Egypt's turbulent politics, which turned the most populous Arab country inward: in more stable circumstances, the government in Cairo might have been more active in opposing the Iranian bid for dominance in the Middle East.

In Libya, resistance to Muammar Gaddafi, who had held power since 1969, turned into a civil war in which the Western countries, led by the United States, intervened on the side of the rebels. With Gaddafi deposed and killed, Libya descended into anarchy. Militias, some of them professing Islamism, others based on clans or regions, competed violently for power. Only Tunisia, where the Arab Spring had begun, managed to make a transition to a reasonably stable, reasonably democratic political system, one in which an Islamist political party held power and then relinquished it peacefully. However, as two small North African countries distant from the heart of the Middle East, Libya and Tunisia had little bearing on Iran's regional ambitions.

By contrast, in countries with substantial Shia populations the Arab Spring touched off sectarian conflicts leading in some cases to Iranian involvement. In the tiny oil state of Bahrain, where Shia outnumbered Sunnis but the Sunnis monopolized political power, the Shia mounted mass protests, demanding a change in their subordinate social and political status. The Sunni ruling family resisted, and neighboring, Sunni-ruled Saudi Arabia sent in 1,200 troops to suppress the Shia.

In Yemen, the Sunni ruler was driven from power and the Houthis, a Shia-affiliated group from the north of the country that received some support from Iran, succeeded in taking control of much of it, including the capital, Sana'a.

Saudi Arabia, alarmed at the prospect of what it anticipated would be a Shia, Persian satellite on its doorstep, intervened in what had become a civil war, conducting intense bombing against Houthi targets that caused considerable damage and displaced thousands of already wretchedly poor Yemenis. The war in Yemen thus enabled the Islamic Republic to distract, and to enmesh in a war that showed no sign of ending, the Saudi monarchy, which presided over the richest Sunni country and was adamantly opposed to Iranian hegemony in the Middle East. The fighting that the Arab Spring triggered to which Iran devoted the most attention and resources, however, and where it made the biggest strategic gains, took place in Syria.

In 2011 the Assad family, first the father Hafez and then his son Bashar, had ruled the country, in murderous fashion, for forty-one years. The Assads belonged to the Alawi sect, which Iran treated as an off-shoot of Shiism although many Sunnis did not consider it part of Islam at all,[80] and whose members comprised only 12 percent of the Syrian population. When the Arab Spring came to Syria, initially peaceful protests evoked brutal suppression, sending much of the Sunni population, three-quarters of all Syrians, into active rebellion against the regime.[81] The ensuing civil war took a higher toll than any of the other episodes of mass violence in the Middle East that Mohamed Bouazizi's suicide inspired. By 2017, by some estimates, 470,000 Syrians had died and fully 11 million had become refugees, 6 million of them internally displaced and the other 5 million living outside the country.

The resistance to Assad included many different and occasionally mutually hostile groups, including some with Islamist political orientations. In the early years of the civil war the rebels held the upper hand, evicting the regime from most of the country outside the heavily populated western strip along the Mediterranean and taking control of the country's second largest city, Aleppo.

Iran had a large stake in Syria. The Alawi regime had become an ally and client and the Iranian Revolutionary Guards used it as a transit corridor to supply and control Hezbollah in Lebanon. The clerics in

Tehran therefore decided to do all they could to save Bashar Assad, and in the end they succeeded.

The Islamic Republic provided the Assad regime with arms and military guidance. More importantly, it provided troops. Iran did not contribute many of its own soldiers;[82] rather, it ordered an estimated 8,000 Hezbollah fighters to the Syrian front. It recruited, trained, and equipped 7,000 to 10,000 more Shia from Iraq, Afghanistan, Saudi Arabia, Pakistan, and other places,[83] creating a kind of international Shia army to support its strategic ambitions in the Middle East.[84] Shia from outside Syria were not the only foreigners to become involved in that country's fighting. In fact, to a far greater extent than any of the other Arab-Spring-inspired Middle Eastern wars, the Syrian civil war became an international conflict. This, too, ultimately worked to Iran's advantage.

As part of their campaign to prevent Shia political gains and resist Iran's drive for hegemony in the Middle East, the Sunni oil-exporting countries of the Persian Gulf, above all Saudi Arabia, sent financial aid and weaponry to the groups opposing Assad, with much of their support going to Islamist factions. The most notable Islamist advance, however, came from a group that did not rely heavily on Gulf oil money but nonetheless achieved spectacular success.

The group was descended from al Qaeda in Iraq, which had fought against the United States after the fall of Saddam. In 2014 the successor organization seized large parts of southern Syria and northern Iraq, including Mosul, Iraq's second largest city, and proclaimed the establishment there of the Islamic State in Iraq and Syria (ISIS).[85] ISIS declared itself a caliphate, with religious descent from the Prophet Muhammad and authority over all Muslims. It imposed on the people it controlled a form of Islam even harsher and more brutal than the style of governance in Iran or Saudi Arabia.

ISIS was able to conquer a large tract of territory because of the retreat of the Assad regime in Syria and the weakness of the Shia-dominated post-Saddam government in Iraq. It received tacit and often active support from the people of the largely Sunni territories it subdued, who saw it as offering the most effective resistance to Shia domination. ISIS represented the revenge of the Sunnis.[86] Although adamantly hostile to Shia, Shiism, and Shia-dominated countries, ISIS proved ultimately to be an asset to Iran because its extreme form of Islamism alienated even Sunni-majority countries and its enthusiastic support for terrorism in the West drew the Western countries, particularly the United States, into active opposition to it.

The Obama administration had criticized Assad and provided modest, ineffective assistance to what it considered to be non-Islamist groups opposing the Syrian regime. In general, however, Obama, having withdrawn all American troops from Iraq during his first presidential term, displayed a pronounced aversion to renewed military engagement in the Middle East. This reluctance did a great deal to determine his policy toward the Iranian nuclear program. Even before the conclusion of the JCPOA, having declared in 2012 that the Syrian government's use of chemical weapons would provoke an American response, when presented with clear evidence of such use the following year he reneged on his earlier commitment.[87]

In response to the establishment of ISIS, however, American military personnel did return to Iraq—largely in an advisory capacity rather than in combat units—and with American air power provided crucial assistance in finally putting an end to the Islamic State in 2017. In confronting ISIS the United States aligned itself with the governments that the Islamists most bitterly opposed, those of Syria and Iran. The fall of ISIS left a vacuum that Shia forces friendly, and in some cases loyal, to Iran were well positioned to fill. Along with the Afghan Taliban and Saddam Hussein, therefore, ISIS joined the list of Iranian enemies that the Great Satan had defeated.

Russia also inserted itself into the Syrian civil war. In September, 2015, the Russian air force began a bombing campaign in support of the Assad regime. The Russian government portrayed the campaign as aimed at defending Syria's legitimate government and defeating Islamist terrorism, although its bombing concentrated more on the non-Islamist resistance to Assad than on ISIS. For Vladimir Putin and his regime, the military expedition to Syria served the same purposes as the invasion of Ukraine. It compensated for actual and potential domestic political weakness.[88] It gave the Russian president the opportunity to bolster his standing with the public by portraying himself as a staunch opponent of terrorism, a defender of a Russian ally—Russian ties with the Assad regime dated back to the Cold

War—and a leader who made his country once again a formidable international presence.

The Russian bombing campaign, which killed many civilians and destroyed non-military buildings on a large scale, did help Assad re-conquer the city of Aleppo and consolidate power in western Syria. The bombing had another, indirect benefit for Putin: it increased the flow of Syrian refugees, some of whom fled to Europe. Their arrival there, and the welcome some European leaders, in particular German Chancellor Angela Merkel, initially afforded them, provoked a political backlash across the continent. This counted as a gain for the Russian regime because it weakened the governments of Europe, another goal of Putin's.

Russia's ongoing military presence in the Middle East strengthened Iran, with which, because the two had common adversaries—above all the United States—Putin had made an informal alliance. The consequences of the Arab Spring—foremost among them the Syrian civil war—also worked to the Islamic Republic's advantage. They gave Iran the opportunity to carve out two land corridors running from the Persian Gulf to the Mediterranean, providing it, potentially, with a powerful military foothold in the heart of the region.[89]

By the middle of 2018, as a result of the JCPOA, the end of ISIS, and the preservation or restoration of Alawi rule in much of Syria, Iran held a stronger military and political position in the Middle East than it had had five years earlier. The surge in its power and influence completed the demise of the relatively peaceful post-Cold War order in the region.

The New/Old Middle East

In 1993 Shimon Peres, a former prime minister and future president of Israel, published a book entitled *The New Middle East*.[90] In it he predicted that the Cold War's end, the benign effects of which were al-ready visible in Europe and East Asia, would transform the Middle East as well. Beyond the demise of European communism he designated the recently begun peace talks between his country and the neighboring Palestinians as the development that would catalyze a host of welcome changes. The negotiations, he anticipated, would forge a lasting settle-ment between Israelis and Arabs that would usher in, as the book's dust jacket put it, "a reconstituted Middle East, free of the conflicts that plagued it in the past, set to take its place in a new era—an era that will not tolerate backwardness or ignorance. [Peres] sees a social revival, and an economic revival as well . . ."

A quarter century later, the Middle East had indeed been transformed, but not in the way that Peres had foreseen. The conflicts in the region had become more numerous and more violent, not less so. The Islamist apostles, both Sunni and Shia, of what Peres (and much of the rest of the world) regarded as backwardness and ignorance were in the ascendant. The falling price of oil had imposed economic hardship on some places and war had brought economic collapse to others.

Peres' vision proved inaccurate in one other way: he had made the premise of his analysis the belief, widely shared around the world, that the Arab-Israeli conflict was central to Middle Eastern affairs, that what happened in the Holy Land shaped the entire region and that resolving that conflict would begin a new, glorious chapter in the history of the region. Despite the negotiations the Israeli-Palestinian conflict continued, but the descent of the Middle East into severe repression and chaos within its countries and war between and among them had nothing to do with it.[91]

Up to a point, the Middle East in the wake of the Arab Spring resembled Europe and East Asia. The relative peace of the post-Cold War era—a shallower peace than in the other two regions but a deeper one than during the Cold War period—had come to an end. A revisionist power, with Iran's role in the Middle East replicating Russia's in Europe and China's in East Asia, had launched (or, more accurately in the Iranian case, intensified) a campaign to change the regional balance of power and influence in its favor. Like Russia and China, Iran engaged in probes—initiatives aggressive enough to strengthen its own position but not so provocative as to trigger a major response;[92] and, as in the other two regions, Iran's probes achieved some success.

Just as Russia annexed Crimea and extended its reach into eastern Ukraine, and China expanded its maritime presence while steadily improving its air and naval forces in the western Pacific, so the Islamic Republic helped maneuver its clients into commanding positions in Lebanon, Iraq, Syria, and Yemen. In all three cases the other countries of the region formed a coalition to resist the revisionist power, and all three of these coalitions revolved around the United States. The geopolitical map of each of the three regions thus had a common shape: all were divided in two.

In important respects, however, the Middle East differed from Europe and East Asia. Russia in Europe and China in East Asia, while formidable powers, had no allies.[93] They and they alone sought to overturn the post-Cold War military arrangements in their respective regions. Iran, by contrast, did not stand alone. A series of governments, political parties, and militias across the Middle East worked closely with it. The new security competition in the Middle East did not feature a single revisionist power being opposed by all the other countries: instead, it pitted the two main Islamic sects, the Sunni and the Shia, against each other. The Sunnis had dominated the region almost continuously since the beginnings of the sectarian schism in the seventh century; the previously-suppressed and downtrodden Shia were, with Iranian leadership, bidding to overturn the long-standing regional hierarchy. In no small part for that reason, some of the Sunni adversaries of the Islamic Republic sought to roll back its gains and, if possible, remove it from power in Tehran.

In Europe and East Asia the members of the anti-Russian and anti-Chinese coalitions had mixed feelings about the revisionist power, in neither case wanting to pursue a policy of unambiguous opposition because of economic ties with the aspiring hegemon. Europeans needed Russia's energy; East Asians wanted access to China's market. Iran's Sunni adversaries, however, had no comparable economics-based reservations about opposing it. An important fact of life in the other two parts of the world, economic interdependence was absent in the Middle East.

It did, however, surpass the other two regions in one respect: it was more violent. In Europe, eastern Ukraine, but nowhere else, was the site of ongoing fighting. In the western Pacific political and military tension reigned but the countries with maritime borders were not shooting at each other either on land or at sea. The Middle East, by contrast, included multiple theaters of war. Armies, armed militias, and terrorist bands clashed in Syria, Iraq, Yemen, and Libya.

Finally, Iran's revisionist motives differed from Russia's and China's. A genuine commitment to the revolutionary principles of Ruhollah

Khomeini's version of Shia Islam continued to animate the policies, including the foreign policies, of his political heirs. Formerly communist Russia and formally communist, but in important ways capitalist, China had abandoned Marxism-Leninism and its Maoist variant. It was old-fashioned nationalism, and especially the recourse to aggressive nationalism as a source of political support in the absence of either democratic legitimacy or economic success, that drove the regional revisionism of Vladimir Putin and Xi Jinping. The long-standing conviction that the Persian state should dominate the Middle East and the hope of compensating for the regime's pronounced economic failures no doubt affected the foreign policy calculations of the rulers of the Islamic Republic;[94] but those rulers also retained, even if in diluted form, what Russia and China had left behind: an ideology.

What bound Iran's regional coalition together, however, was not ideology but sectarian allegiance. A small minority—about 10 percent—of Muslims worldwide, the Shia made up almost half the Islamic population of the Middle East. Historically subordinate to the Sunnis in the Arab world, as the political structures of the region collapsed they gravitated to non-Arab Iran both for protection and as a way of asserting their own power.[95] In the sectarian civil war that the Arab Spring inspired, the Shia coalition more than held its own.

It did so because it had greater cohesion than its Sunni adversary. Accustomed to being beleaguered minorities in their respective countries, the Shia communities in Iraq, Lebanon, Syria, and (up to a point) Yemen accepted Iranian support and with it Iranian guidance and leadership. In war, secure supply lines count for a great deal and the Shia side benefitted from the geographic contiguity of Lebanon, Syria, Iraq, and Iran. It also managed to attract useful military assistance from beyond the region, specifically from Russia in the battle for Syria.

The 450,000 people it killed and the 11 million refugees it created in its campaign to keep the Alawite Bashar al-Assad in power in Damascus demonstrated that the Shia coalition was unburdened by moral scruples when it came to the use of force to advance its interests. Finally, beyond political solidarity, geographic coherence, and general ruthlessness, the Iran-led side in the security competition in the Middle East had one further advantage: the weaknesses of its adversary.

As in Europe and East Asia, that adversary, the counterhegemonic coalition, had the United States at its core. Lacking a regional security organization like NATO in Europe,[96] however, the coalition in the Middle East fit the hub-and-spokes East Asian pattern, with each country in the region having a closer security relationship with the United States than with its neighbors. Unlike in the other two regions, however, America's Arab coalition partners did not share its political values. Because none had a democratic political system[97] the anti-Iran coalition lacked one of the ties that bound the United States to its security partners in the other two regions.

Nor were the members of the anti-Iranian bloc necessarily willing or able to put troops in the field to block the advances of the Islamic Republic. The Gulf oil exporters, especially Saudi Arabia, brought money and anti-Iranian and anti-Shia zeal to the coalition but not much usable military force.[98] Israel, the most formidable military power in the region, shared the Saudi hostility to the Islamic Republic but would only commit troops or air power to battle when directly threatened, and had little to do with the Syrian civil war, although it did attack Iranian military installations in the country that were being established for the purpose of menacing Israel itself.[99]

The United States had far greater military resources than all the members of the Shia coalition combined, including Russia; but its commander-in-chief from 2009 to 2017, Barack Obama, made it his supreme goal in the Middle East to conciliate rather than to oppose the Islamic Republic, in no small part in order to negotiate a pause in the Iranian nuclear weapons program.[100] Obama offered no resistance to Iran's drive for regional hegemony and sometimes even seemed to encourage it.[101] Obama's successor as president, Donald Trump, had, at least rhetorically, a more forceful attitude toward Iranian revisionism; but he also made clear his distaste, in the wake of the American experiences in Afghanistan and Iraq, for military operations in that part of the world, a distaste that not only Obama but also many other Americans shared.

The distinction of being the most committed anti-Iranian and anti-Shia force in the Middle East, the one most willing to shed blood in opposing both, belonged to ISIS and the sundry Sunni Islamist groups across the region: it was their militance that drew volunteers from all over the world to their ranks. Most of the members of the

American-centered counterhegemonic coalition, however, emphatically including the United States, regarded such groups as adversaries rather than allies, and with good reason: like the Islamic Republic, the Sunni Islamists aspired to overthrow the incumbent Sunni governments and drive the United States from the Middle East, although the region they envisioned would be dominated by them rather than Iran.

The problematical role of ISIS illustrated yet another weakness in the anti-Iran coalition. Its members had different and sometimes conflicting priorities. Despite his aversion to placing American combat troops in the Middle East, Obama sent a contingent (albeit largely in an advisory role) back to Iraq and contributed American air power to help the Iraqi government defeat the Islamic State. While the American public maintained a deep distrust of the ruling clerics in Tehran, dating from the 1979 revolution and the ensuing hostage crisis,[102] the Islamic terrorist groups such as ISIS evoked even more powerful hostility in the United States because of a more recent and more costly episode, the September 11 attacks. This gave the American government greater political leeway to risk American lives to fight terrorist organizations than to oppose Iran.

Similarly, the chief concern of Turkey, an important Sunni country, was neither ISIS nor Iran but rather Kurdish nationalism, which, the government in Ankara feared, could encourage secessionist activity among the 14 million Kurds living in Turkey—about 18 percent of the country's population. When Kurds living in Syria proved effective in opposing ISIS, this pleased the United States, which supported them, but alarmed the Turks, who did not.[103] As for Egypt, its government counted the Muslim Brotherhood, the largest opposition group within its country, a greater threat than Shia Iran.

Thus the anti-Iran coalition suffered not only from differing priorities but also from internal divisions, sometimes sharp ones. Egypt had little use for Turkey, where the ruling political party, the AKP, identified with the Muslim Brotherhood.[104] ISIS so offended the United States that the Americans joined Iran in defeating it, thereby strengthening the Iranian regime, but America's Gulf allies were far more concerned about the balance of sectarian power in the region than with the Islamic State's oppressive governance or terrorism against the West. All this meant that while the Shia bloc was able to act decisively and in unified fashion, the American-led coalition opposing it, although larger and militarily far stronger, could not. Ironically, the only party to the anti-Iranian effort with which none of the Arab countries had any serious strategic problem was Israel, which had served as the target of official Arab public hostility since its establishment in 1948.

The Middle East after the post-Cold War peace differed from Europe and East Asia in yet another way: the extent to which countries outside the region became involved in its affairs. The United States was active in all three; but despite the budding Sino-Russian friendship China had little impact on the international relations of Europe, and Russia had virtually none on East Asia, although, like the other countries of the region, it bordered on the Pacific Ocean. By intervening in the Syrian civil war Russia inserted itself into the Middle East, and China had major economic interests there, even without a military presence, because of the region's oil and because Beijing hoped to include Iran in its "One Belt One Road" project.[105]

In the nineteenth century and for much of the twentieth Europeans had had the greatest impact from abroad on the Middle East. Britain and France established empires there and Germany sought influence before both world wars. While in the past Europe had affected the internal politics of the Middle East, in the twenty-first century the reverse occurred: the wars of the region helped to generate a flood of refugees to Europe and the decision by European governments to welcome them caused a political backlash across the European Union.

One final feature of the Middle East distinguished it, in the wake of the relatively peaceful post-Cold War era, from the other two regions. Because it had its roots in the cultural disorder caused by the encounter between the Muslim societies of the region and the powerful twenty-first-century forces of modernity, the upheaval within the countries of the Middle East and the intense and closely related security competition between and among them seemed destined to continue indefinitely.

Less peaceful than Europe and East Asia during the post-Cold War era, the region had very poor prospects of regaining even the modest tranquility it had enjoyed then. In the other two regions, by contrast, it was possible to envision circumstances in which the post-Cold War peace would ultimately return.

4

Peace Regained?

Don't it always seem to go
That you don't know what you've got til it's gone . . .
—JONI MITCHELL, "Big Yellow Taxi"

Accident or Precedent?

The world in the wake of the post-Cold War era bore a marked resemblance to the world before that unusually peaceful twenty-five-year period. It resembled, that is, the world of the Cold War itself. In Europe, East Asia, and the Middle East, as during the Cold War, a revisionist country seeking to upend the existing political arrangements in order to enhance its power and influence confronted a broad but not always tightly knit opposing coalition led by the United States. As during the Cold War, the opposing sides had different political systems: dictatorship dominated the revisionist camp while the members of the opposing coalition were generally democracies, except in the Middle East. In none of the three parts of the world where the status quo was under challenge did the challenger appear to be plotting to begin a major war—as, for example, Nazi Germany had done in 1939—to achieve its goals. Rather, as in the Cold War, it launched probes to test the resistance the opposing coalition would mount as well as to advance, where possible, its own power and influence.

International relations after the post-Cold War era do differ from those of the Cold War in three important ways. First, whereas in the earlier period the challenge to the status quo in all three regions came from a single source—the Soviet Union—in the later one three different revisionist countries pursued hegemonic ambitions in their respective regions: post-Soviet Russia in Europe, China in East Asia, and Iran in the Middle East. Second, the Cold War pitted competing ideologies with universal claims against each other, with the Soviet Union seeking to spread Marxist-Leninist political and economic systems all over the world and the American-led coalition defending, with some exceptions, while being committed to the advance of democratic politics and free-market economics. By contrast, none of the revisionists after the end of the Cold War was campaigning to convert the world to its own ideological principles. Russia and China had little in the way of genuine ideology and both touted non-interference in the internal affairs of other countries as an important principle of international relations. The Islamic Republic of Iran, which did have a theocratic creed, worked to bring other Muslims under its sway but not, realistically, the rest of the world. Third, and finally, whereas during the Cold War the communist bloc practiced economic self-sufficiency and had few economic ties beyond the bloc's borders, the three revisionists all traded with and courted investment from other countries, even including those that opposed their regional ambitions.

Amid the similarities and differences one basic continuity between the world of the Cold War and the world after the post-Cold War era stands out: in both periods all major countries had to conduct their policies toward one another under the threat of war. All had to gear their foreign policies to the possibility of armed conflict. In both eras, security competition pervaded international politics.

The resumption of security competition might seem to demonstrate that the intervening post-Cold War era did not differ fundamentally from the centuries that came before, that while international relations were unusually peaceful during those twenty-five years they had undergone no major change. The relative tranquility of that quarter century, it might be argued, stemmed from the particular circumstances that the end of the Cold War produced, especially the distribution of power within the international system.

Following the fall of the Berlin Wall and the collapse of the Soviet Union, the United States temporarily enjoyed enormous power in comparison with all other countries. Post-Soviet Russia, stripped of half its population and one quarter of its territory, was both weakened and traumatized; China, little more than a decade into the free-market reforms that turned it into the world's fastest growing and second largest economy, still lagged well behind America; and Iran was temporarily intimidated by the swift American-led military victory over Iraq in the Gulf War of 1991. When the global distribution of power changed, as it always does, and when the United States, for that reason and because of its own missteps, came to look less formidable than it had in the immediate aftermath of the Cold War, the normal pattern of international politics—competition and the struggle for primacy— resumed in earnest, as it always does.

On this account the post-Cold War peace was like the play of a slot machine that rewards the player with a jackpot: a rare event, but one produced by the normal working of the machine and, because of the way the machine works, very unlikely to be repeated any time soon. To use another metaphor, the age-old game of nations produced an unusually peaceful period between 1989 and 2014 but the rules of the game did not change, and as the game continued, it yielded a different, more familiar, more conflict-ridden international order.

In interpreting the provenance and the significance of the peaceful quarter century following the end of the Cold War, the case for continuity is therefore plausible. The contrary argument, however, that that period represents something new and different in international history, that it saw the establishment of peace on Earth for the first time and that it counts not as an accident but as a precedent, has crucial and compelling evidence in its favor.

The decisive piece of evidence that the post-Cold War period differed fundamentally from the past is the absence of security competition. In Europe for a time, and in East Asia as well, not only did the major countries not fight each other, war itself dropped off their agendas. They ceased to feel the need to prepare for war, to plan for war, to gear their foreign policies to the possibility of war, as governments had done since time immemorial. They achieved—or at any rate enjoyed—a deeper peace than in the past.

By itself the absence of a shooting war among the major countries did not break new ground. That had happened before. It happened during the Cold War itself. The United States and the Soviet Union never fought each other directly. The peaceful episodes of the past were usually due, however, to the existence of security competition rather than to its absence. During the Cold War, and in some previous eras such as the years following the defeat of Napoleon in 1815, a balance of power—that is, a relatively even distribution of military might among the major countries—dampened the impulse to wage war. The absence of armed conflict stemmed from their calculations that none was strong enough to gain from fighting.

Similarly, when the vicissitudes of security competition gave one power a major military advantage over its neighbors, it sometimes imposed peace through hegemony. The others refrained from fighting because they couldn't win, the hegemon behaved peacefully because it had already won. In the post-Cold War era, by contrast, peace came from the absence of the *intention* to fight, not from the perceived lack of the capability to prevail.

This was a new and different condition of international politics. In human affairs new and different conditions come about not by accident but through the impact of new and different forces. An effect, that is, requires a cause, and often more than one. The unprecedentedly deep peace of the post-Cold War era had three causes.

The benign hegemony of the United States contributed to the peace. This condition reversed a familiar pattern in international politics. Hegemony—the supremacy of one particular state—has a very long history and hegemons have often brought peace through domination. Whereas the hegemons of the past imposed themselves on the countries and the regions to which they ultimately brought peace, however, and in fact usually encountered active resistance, in the post-Cold War period the countries of Europe and East Asia valued, welcomed, and supported the American military presence.

This broke with precedent. The Europeans and Asians were like law-abiding citizens who are happy to have a policeman patrol their neighborhood to guard against crimes that none of them has any intention of committing but who are not entirely certain about the peaceful intentions of others. The Europeans and Asians did not *expect* aggression from their neighbors, however. They did not resemble citizens who desire a police force because they are confident that their neighbors will engage in criminal acts without a police presence. This distinguished the post-Cold War era from the Cold War. The United States had deployed forces in the two regions after 1945 precisely to forestall the international political equivalent of criminal acts. What began at the outset of the Cold War as a system of alliances to protect some countries against others turned, with the end of that conflict, into a confidence-building measure to ease the insecurities of all. Originally stationed in Europe and Asia to deter would-be aggressors, the American forces remained after the Cold War to reassure all the countries of each region that none had any interest in aggression.

Benign American hegemony reflected as much as it caused the deep post-Cold War peace. The Europeans and East Asians approved of the American presence in their regions because two other features of the world of the late twentieth century had already made their attitudes toward one another unprecedentedly peaceful.

Like hegemony, trade has a very long history, going back several thousand years. Trade on a very large scale, however—large enough to foster economic interdependence, in which exchange with other countries has a significant economic and political impact on those engaging in it—is recent. It dates from the Industrial Revolution. The post-Cold War period coincided with the third great surge in trade since the nineteenth century—the third era of globalization. The expanding volume of trade, combined with the rapid increase in cross-border investment, meant that armed conflict, by interrupting them, would impose very high costs on the countries waging it even if they emerged victorious from the conflict. The greater the level of economic interdependence, the more costly war became; and with the end of the Cold War that level, and thus its attendant costs, had risen to very great heights indeed. This powerfully discouraged war.

Similarly, democracy, the final cause of the deep post-Cold War peace, has a long history, going back to ancient Greece. Only in the last quarter of the twentieth century, however, did democracy spread widely beyond northern Europe and North America to become the most common of all political systems.[1] Democracy reduces the capacity for war by giving the public the means to check the sometimes bellicose ambitions of their rulers. It also fosters a political culture of peaceful compromise that, when extended beyond a democracy's borders, curtails warlike intentions. Economic interdependence and democracy, both more widely practiced than ever before in the post-Cold War era, made that period a uniquely peaceful time.

An unusual feature of the early post-Cold War years illustrates their singularly peaceful character. The Cold War was the fourth great global conflict of the modern era, after the Napoleonic Wars of the late eighteenth and early nineteenth centuries and the two world wars of the first half of the twentieth. Formal peace conferences followed the first three: in Vienna in 1815, in Paris in 1918-1919, and at Yalta and Potsdam in 1945. No such meeting convened, however, at the conclusion of the Cold War.

Some of the work of the earlier peace conferences—apportioning the territories of the losers among the winners, and extracting reparations from, while putting suitable governments in charge of, the vanquished powers—had gone out of fashion, discredited as unwarranted intrusions on sovereignty. Indeed, because they had nourished revanchist sentiments in Germany after World War I, these practices had come to be seen as counterproductive. That was one reason that no peace conference convened. There was another: peace had already been effectively established. It had been incubated during the Cold War itself, as the American-centered military alliances in Europe and East Asia turned into communities in which security competition was absent. What was needed after 1989, certainly in Europe, was to consolidate and expand the already existing peace,[2] not to devise it in the first place.

After the first three global conflicts peace had to be constructed by officials of the members of the winning coalitions out of the political ruins that the fighting had created. The spread of economic interdependence and democracy, by contrast, had already created the foundations of peace even as the Cold War was still under way. Diplomats devised the first three peace settlements. Long-running, deeply rooted processes of political and economic change gave birth to the fourth. With the end of the fourth conflict peace emerged, like a butterfly from a chrysalis. It was the product less of human design than of historical metamorphosis. It was, therefore, a different creature— a different kind of peace—than the arrangements the conquerors of Napoleon, of the German kaiser, and of Hitler managed to fashion.

Like the peaceful periods of the past, however, the post-Cold War peace came to an end. If its existence demonstrates that deep peace, peace without security competition, is possible, its fate shows that such a peace, like the truces of the past, is perishable. This raises the question of whether the kind of peace the post-Cold War era enjoyed can be restored. The circumstances in which it ended suggest that restoration is possible.

Perpetual Peace?

The post-Cold War peace did not end because of countries' fears that their neighbors would dominate them if they did not achieve dominance first. Security competition did not resume, that is, because the insecurity that the age-old anarchic structure of international politics generates, which some identify as the fundamental reason for conflict,[3] overrode the pacific intentions of the sovereign states of that system. Nor did peace end because governments resorted to force in order to enrich themselves, over the span of human history probably the most common proximate cause of armed conflict.

The post-Cold War peace ended because three countries brought security competition back to their regions by adopting foreign policies of aggressive nationalism. Yet nationalism by itself does not explain the end of peace. In the modern era, and indeed in the second decade of the twenty-first century, other countries have harbored significant nationalist sentiment without engaging in aggressive foreign policies. Nor did Russia and China, at least, pursue such policies for all of the post-Cold War period. In its early years they took part in the unprecedentedly peaceful international relations of Europe and East Asia.

Their abandonment of peaceful policies, leading to the destruction of the post-Cold War peace, coincided with the rise of a serious domestic problem for their governments: the loss, both actual and prospective, of public support for the ruling regime. The power-holders in post-communist Russia, partly communist China, and the Islamic Republic of Iran all had more than one motive for embarking on campaigns to overturn the political arrangements and the distribution of power in Europe, East Asia, and the Middle East respectively; but they had in common the desire to enhance their standing with the people they ruled by, in effect, wrapping themselves in the flag: that is, by presenting themselves as the defenders of the nation against predatory enemies and the architects of an expansion of the power, influence, and respect it commanded in the world.

Governments have always needed legitimacy—that is, the sense among the members of the public that rulers have in some sense the right to rule. It has become more important than ever before in the twenty-first century, when governments no longer preside, as they did for most of history, over largely illiterate peasants with no acquaintance with the world beyond their villages, but must instead try to govern urban, literate, increasingly sophisticated and often politically active populations. In the present century, moreover, a tool that regimes from Genghis Khan through Stalin and Mao used to suppress active opposition—large-scale repression, including mass murder—is not easy to employ. Legitimacy does have several sources that are currently available, but Russia and China, and to a lesser extent Iran, could not draw on them.

In traditional societies, the divine right of kings proved a durable and, on the whole, effective doctrine over the centuries; but by the twenty-first it had died out everywhere except in a few corners of the Middle East. In the twentieth century a number of governments rested their claims to hold power on ideologies, sets of ideas that purported to make sense of, and furnish optimal ways of ordering, the basic features of social, economic, and political life. By the post-Cold War period, however, Russia's rulers had abandoned Marxism entirely[4] while China's had jettisoned most of it, retaining only the axiom that the Communist Party should monopolize political power. The governing creed of the Islamic Republic combined the traditional appeal to the divinity with features of modern ideology; but since fewer and fewer Iranians beyond the ruling clerical establishment subscribed to it, the mullahs in Tehran, like their counterparts in Moscow and Beijing, found themselves in need of other sources of legitimacy.

Post-communist Russia and post-Maoist China initially found that source in economic performance. They earned if not the enthusiastic support then at least the tolerant indulgence of the people they ruled by delivering—or, in the Russian case, taking unwarranted credit for delivering—economic growth. By the second decade of the twenty-first century, however, growth in Russia had ended with the collapse of the global price of oil, China faced the imminent exhaustion of the model of economic growth that had produced impressive results for more than three decades, and the Islamic Republic had not managed a creditable economic performance since its establishment.

By the twenty-first century the most common, most popular, and most successful basis for political legitimacy around the world was democracy. While populist challenges to the political status quo arose throughout the Western world during the century's second decade, they did not eliminate the capacity of the Western political systems to generate public support for governments chosen, and abiding, by the rules of democracy. Democratic governments were legitimate because of the way they were selected—through free and fair elections—and because of the way they governed—protecting economic, religious, and political liberty. None of the revisionist regimes, however, could solve its legitimacy problem through democracy because democracy was incompatible with their remaining in power and governing as they did. The rulers of Iran would certainly not survive a free election, and even if the Putin and Xi regimes in Russia and China managed to do so the transparency, protection for property rights, and rule of law that democratic governance brings with it would make impossible their common central activity, which had become, over the years, their main reason for being: stealing their countries' wealth.

Lacking recourse to tradition, ideology, economic success and democracy, the revisionist regimes turned to aggressive nationalism to ensure their continuation in power. Seeking success abroad as a way to reinforce a political position at home is a venerable tactic, one that certainly did not originate with twenty-first-century Russia, China, or Iran.[5] Governments have periodically started wars they believed they could win in order to make themselves more popular. In no other period, however, did this tactic loom as large in international politics as in the post-Cold War era. Its relative importance in promoting security competition, compared with other historical periods, stemmed partly from the decline in the other causes of international conflict and partly from the unavailability to the governments of the three revisionist countries of other sources of political legitimacy.

The prominence of international success as a way to preserve their grip on power meant that, of the four potential sources of legitimacy, the last of them, democracy, played a particularly large role in twenty-first-century politics and foreign policy. Democracy also had an outsized importance for the prospects of restoring the kind of deep peace that the world had enjoyed in the quarter century after the end of the Cold War. The specter of democracy haunted the Russian, Chinese, and Iranian dictatorships, and they adopted revisionist foreign policies in order, among other reasons, to keep it at bay. Indeed, nothing better illustrates the attraction of popular sovereignty and liberty everywhere in the twenty-first century, and the threat that this posed to the revisionist autocracies, than the efforts of Vladimir Putin, Xi Jinping, and the Iranian mullahs to resist and discredit the political system that incorporates them.

Each experienced public protests on a large scale, with the protestors expressing democratic themes: Russia in 2011,[6] China in 1989, Iran in 2009 and again on a smaller but still impressive scale in 2018. In response, the three revisionist regimes jailed and sometimes killed people actively promoting democracy. They censored democratic ideas wherever and however they could.[7] All three made it a point of trying to persuade those they governed that efforts to promote democracy were merely disguises for foreign campaigns to subdue and dominate their own countries.[8] They asserted, as well, that democratic practices were alien, indeed poisonous, to the proud and robust traditions of Russia, China, and Iran.[9]

The Putin government claimed that its system of "sovereign democracy"—that is, its actual lack of democratic governance—was in keeping with, and necessary for, Russia's resistance to Western and American dominance. The Chinese communists warned its cadres to be vigilant against Western constitutional democracy, universal values, and civil society.[10] The Iranian theocrats made it clear that they considered Western social and political ideas and practices the deadly enemy of everything that was good, true, and genuinely Islamic and Persian.

If democracy had not held such a broad twenty-first-century appeal it is likely that the three revisionists would have conducted less aggressive policies in their respective regions: certainly they would have felt their hold on power to be less threatened. If, however, the three actually had had democratic governments, their relations with their neighbors would also surely have been less contentious. For of the three modern forces making for peaceful international relations, democracy has the strongest effect.

The first of them, the benign hegemony of the United States, was as much a consequence as a cause of the deep post-Cold War peace. The countries of Europe and East Asia welcomed the American military presence because it helped to solidify the peace to which they were already committed; and they regarded American military forces as useful for reinforcing peace because these forces answered to a democratic government. An undemocratic United States would not have reassured them. Democracy in America is the reason that counterhegemonic coalitions did not form against the United States, as took place in opposition to other countries that had become supremely powerful. As for economic interdependence, while it provides incentives for peaceful relations among trading partners, they do not necessarily have a decisive impact, as the first world war, waged among European countries that had extensive prewar economic connections, demonstrated.[11]

Democracy is a particularly powerful antidote to armed conflict because it suppresses both warlike conduct and warlike impulses in several ways: by giving the public the means to control its leaders who may have bellicose intentions; by mandating the transparent conduct of public affairs, which reduces suspicion and therefore insecurity on the part of other countries; and by fostering—indeed requiring—peaceful relations among citizens, which, when carried over to the realm of foreign policy, encourages peaceful international relations. Democracy does more to promote deep peace than does economic interdependence in another way, because of a key difference between them. Interdependence has a prudential effect: it makes war seem an unprofitable proposition. Democracy has a principled impact: to the democratic outlook war is morally wrong, which provides an additional layer of protection against it. This sentiment makes democrats reluctant even to contemplate war seriously, at least against other democracies, which suppresses not only actual fighting but also preparations to fight—that is, security competition.

Peace and democracy, in fact, have important features in common. Both require the appropriate social and political underpinnings to take hold. Without such foundations, peace treaties and democratic constitutions are merely pieces of paper: the signatories to the Kellogg-Briand pact of 1928 promised to eschew war; those signatories included

Germany but Adolf Hitler, a bellicose figure if ever there was one, came to power in 1933 and ignored the treaty. In the same way, the Soviet constitution of 1977 guaranteed a panoply of civil and political rights but the ruling Communist Party never intended to honor these guarantees and did not do so.

Democracy and peace are similar, as well, in that neither abolishes all conflict. Indeed, democracy presumes that citizens will have different and sometimes opposing ideas, opinions, and preferences, often strongly held ones. Nor has the innate capacity for aggression vanished from the human gene pool.[12] A democratic political system offers a way of resolving the inevitable disputes without violence. The well-known 1839 American painting by Edward Hicks, "The Peaceable Kingdom," depicts a variety of animals sitting placidly together, predators side by side with their prey. In a similar picture of a "Peaceable Democracy," they would be arguing with one another.[13]

In the same way, peace, even a deep peace without security competition, does not and cannot do away with all sources of contention between and among countries. Rather, it involves the deeply felt and broadly shared proscription against going to war over these disputes. The members of the European Union differed among themselves on a wide variety of issues during the post-Cold War period and afterward, but war among them had become, by the end of the Cold War, unthinkable.

The prominence of democracy in fostering nonviolent international relations vindicates Immanuel Kant's 1795 essay "Perpetual Peace," which identified the spread of what he called republican government—which is close to modern-day democracy—as a necessary condition for the end of warfare.[14] If Russia, China, and Iran were to adopt, by whatever route, fully democratic political systems including both popular sovereignty and the protection of economic, religious, and political liberty, the need for nationalist assertion as a source of legitimacy would shrivel.

To be sure, even in that event the sense of Russian, Chinese, and Persian destiny would not disappear, just as the capacity for aggression has not vanished from the supply of inborn capacities that every member of the human species possesses; but, as with human aggressiveness, nationalism would find economic and political outlets other than the military drive for domination. Democratic Europe and Asia, at least, would welcome expanded regional roles for democratic Russia and China. The United States would be happy for the two, were they to become democracies, to act as major global "stakeholders," assuming major responsibilities around the world.[15]

A democratic Russia would not devote itself to carving out an old-fashioned sphere of influence on the territory of the former Soviet Union against the wishes and at the expense of the now-independent countries there. It would remove the forces it has dispatched to and sponsored in eastern Ukraine and would agree to hold an honest plebiscite on the Crimean Peninsula to determine whether Crimea's inhabitants wish to belong to Ukraine or Russia. (They might well opt for Russia.) A democratic Russia would resume compliance with the arms treaties that the Putin regime abandoned and cooperate with NATO to reinforce the structures of common security. In response, the United States and its allies would remove all economic sanctions on Russia, and, if they had learned anything from their past mistakes, would either admit Russia to NATO as a full member or devise an entirely new system of pan-European security in which Russia would participate on an equal basis with all the other member countries.

A democratic China would adhere to the widely accepted international laws and customs governing the western Pacific rather than disregarding them and claiming virtually all of the East and South China Seas as its sovereign territory. Such a China would negotiate measures of military cooperation with the United States and its East Asian allies, perhaps including joint naval patrols of vital locations such as the Straits of Malacca.

On North Korea a democratic China would at least refrain from supporting the communist regime there, although any Chinese government might consider more active forms of pressure on an unpredictable, nuclear-armed neighbor to be excessively risky. Dropping its assertion that Taiwan must be governed from Beijing would be difficult even for a Chinese government with democratic legitimacy, given the political capital that the communist regime has invested over the decades in insisting on this. Renouncing that claim would, however, pay dividends for all Asians, not least the Chinese themselves. It would reassure the others in the region of China's peaceful intentions and dispose them to welcome rather than oppose the expansion of Chinese influence in the region.

An Iran in which a democratically-elected, rights-protecting government had replaced the rule of the clerics would not be attempting to subvert other Middle Eastern governments or sponsoring terrorism across the region and around the world. It would cease its genocidal threats against the state of Israel and restore the diplomatic relationship the two countries maintained in the time of the shah. A democratic Iranian government would not live in fear of being overthrown, and so one of its motives for acquiring nuclear weapons would fade in importance. At the same time, the world would find facilities for enriching uranium less threatening in a democratic Iran than it does in the Islamic Republic.

While democracy in Iran would remove one of the causes of conflict in the Middle East, however, it would not make that region peaceful. It would not restore stability to Syria. It would not put an end to the multiple causes of conflict in the region.[16] One of them in particular, the great sectarian divide in Islam between Sunnis and Shia, would continue to engage Iran under whatever government it had: Iran would continue to be a predominantly Shia country that would have difficulty remaining indifferent to the fate of other Shia, some of whom suffer from discrimination or even persecution in majority-Sunni Middle Eastern countries. Indeed, a democratically-elected Iranian government would be more susceptible to domestic pressure to interest itself in the conditions of Shia elsewhere than was the autocratic shah, who maintained decent relations with governments that mistreated the Shia within their borders.

Prediction is hazardous—especially, in the adage sometimes attributed to the American sage and baseball player Yogi Berra, about the future—but it seems safe to predict that the political transformations of Russia, China, and Iran into stable democracies would do more to make Europe, East Asia, and the Middle East zones of peace, with security competition either abolished or dramatically reduced, than any other single development. Democracy in Russia would lead to the restoration of the deep European peace of the early years of the post-Cold War era. Democracy in China would make it possible to construct something like the European peace in East Asia. Democracy in Iran would not have the same impact on the Middle East: the region has too many sources of conflict and too many obstacles to the establishment of democracy in Iran's neighbors. Still, Iranian democracy would remove one of the principal causes of Middle Eastern conflict.

The road to peace on Earth therefore runs through popular sovereignty and liberty. What, then, are the chances that the three peace-disturbing revisionist powers will adopt them?

Universal Democracy?

An ongoing struggle takes place within each of the revisionist powers between the forces of democracy and the government's efforts to suppress them. It takes place, for the most part, beneath the surface of events, since each government punishes open displays of democratic advocacy. It occasionally breaks through to public awareness, however, as with the protests against Vladimir Putin's rigged elections in Russia in 2011, the large demonstrations in Tiananmen Square in Beijing and in other Chinese cities in 1989, and the Green Movement in Iran in 2009. Historically, the rise of democracy has received a substantial assist from external events, but these have very limited utility for democratic progress in the second decade of the twenty-first century: in those ongoing subterranean struggles, the partisans of democracy cannot count on them.

European empires, and especially the British Empire, brought the idea of democracy to much of the world beyond Europe. Many former British imperial possessions, not the least of them the United States of America, became democracies after their imperial masters returned home. This did not, to be sure, occur because the British were trying to bring popular sovereignty and liberty to the places they ruled: in most cases economic gain and strategic advantage motivated British imperial expansion. Nor did all former British possessions adopt and retain democracy. While India did, its fraternal twin Pakistan, where the British imprint was, if anything, heavier, did not. Nor, in any event, will empires return, at least not empires controlled by democracies.

The great global conflicts of the twentieth century—the two world wars and the Cold War—also advanced the democratic cause because democratic countries won them, conferring power on the winners and prestige on their political system. Still, another such conflict would seem to be a prohibitively high price to pay for spreading democracy even if any country or coalition could win it in any meaningful sense of the word. Moreover, empire and war by themselves could not and did not produce democratic governance. Even in countries with the experience of British rule, or impressed by democracy's successes in war, or both, it could only be established if the people of these countries chose to adopt it.

The greatest source of strength for democracy is therefore the power of the democratic example.[17] The availability of liberty and the practice of having the people choose the government are, for many people, valuable in and of themselves; and the prosperity of the countries that hold free elections and protect rights has added to their appeal, especially for people deprived of all three. That category includes many Russians, Chinese, and Iranians, who are well aware that their own countries suffer from much higher levels of corruption than democracy permits. As the number of democracies has increased, its advantages have, on the whole, become increasingly apparent and attractive to an ever-larger segment of the world's population. For this reason, the twenty-first century is a democratic age and remains so even in the face of the populist political revolts in the West. In the great flowing river of history, and despite the travails of democratic governments around the world, democracy has become the most powerful political current, as the Russian, Chinese, and Iranian governments, with their revisionist foreign policies undertaken with the aim of preventing that current from sweeping them away, know all too well. Just as hypocrisy is the tribute that vice pays to virtue, so aggressive nationalism is the tribute that dictatorship pays, in the twenty-first century, to democracy.

Economic considerations contribute to the appeal of the democratic model, but they also promote democracy independently in two ways. First, economic growth, the goal of virtually every government since the end of the Cold War, makes people wealthy, and the wealthier are, the more inclined they become to want, work for, support and participate in democratic politics. A 1996 article entitled "China's Short Road to Democracy"[18] began as follows: "When will China become a democracy? The answer is around the year 2015." The prediction proved inaccurate (or at least the date was premature) but the logic underlying it rested on an impressive body of evidence. Virtually every country with a per capita income above a certain level has a democratic government,[19] and China seemed destined to reach that level in the designated year. Second, almost all countries that have surpassed this level have done so through the working of a free-market economy, and free markets act as a school for political democracy because some of the standard practices they involve are similar to those that, in the political context, democracy entails.[20]

The course of modern history,[21] the prevailing global trends of the present, and important features of the world's economy thus promote, both individually and together, democratic governance where it does not exist, including in Russia, China, and Iran. Pro-democracy forces are formidable. They are not necessarily destined to prevail everywhere, however. They must contend with global realities and national policies that push against the expansion of popular sovereignty and liberty.

To be sure, in the twenty-first century the democratic example has lost some of its luster. The American-centered financial crisis of 2008 in particular and the deep global recession that it triggered tarnished democracy's good name, and its appeal.[22] Surely not entirely coincidentally, in the first decade of the new millennium the number of additional countries embracing democratic politics stopped rising. Democracy's global momentum came to a halt. By some assessments a "democratic recession" began.[23]

The progress of democracy confronted another major obstacle, especially in the three revisionist countries: the determined and resourceful opposition of undemocratic governments, which employed a variety of strategies beyond assertive nationalism to keep themselves in power. They engaged in repression, censoring democratic ideas and arresting those who protested against their autocratic rule. They subjected those they governed to barrages of anti-democratic propaganda. They employed carrots in addition to sticks, bribery as well as repression. The Putin regime in Russia and the ruling clerics of Iran used revenues from the sale of energy to try to pacify the Russian and Iranian populations, and enjoyed some success. The communist government in Beijing presided over rapid economic growth that lifted hundreds of millions of their fellow Chinese out of poverty, earning it credit with the beneficiaries of that growth.

In addition, the regimes' campaigns to enhance their countries' power and influence in their home regions, undertaken in no small part to divert attention from the oppression and corruption all three practiced, did have this effect. Russians, Chinese, and Iranians supported what their governments were seeking to do abroad while accepting, or overlooking, what these rulers were doing at home.

No matter how powerful the world's democracies, moreover, they could not use their power directly to create democratic governments beyond their borders. The United States, during the administration of George W. Bush, announced its intention to do this, but failed. It occupied Iraq, supported the country's adoption of a democratic constitution, and presided over free, fair, nation-wide elections. When the American troops went home, however, it slipped back into authoritarian rule and indeed civil war without the stabilizing presence of those forces.

Champions of an American policy of worldwide democracy promotion, and of its application to Iraq, sometimes invoked the post-1945 experiences of Germany and Japan as encouraging precedents. After being conquered and occupied by the United States and, in Germany, by America's democratic allies, these two countries, the dictatorial aggressors in World War II, turned into peaceful democracies. Germany and Japan, however, both had had some previous experience with democratic institutions and practices and after the war had revived their prewar free-market economies. The two countries possessed, that is, the social and economic bases of democratic government.[24] Iraq did not. One of America's first democratic evangelists, Thomas Jefferson, observed that "Some preparation seems necessary to qualify the body of a nation for self-government."[25] That observation is as valid in the twenty-first century as it was in the eighteenth, and no country or group of countries, mighty, wealthy, and self-confident though they may be, can endow another with the necessary preconditions for democracy.[26] It follows that the demise of a dictatorship does not necessarily pave the way for the establishment of democratic government.

Of course many countries have acquired the necessary prerequisites— the habits, customs, values, and institutions necessary for democratic government;[27] but this has happened over time, through gradually rising levels of income and education, occasionally by means of spells of democracy followed by reversions to autocracy as in Germany and Japan, and by transferring some of the practices associated with free-market economies to the realm of politics.

The subterranean struggle over democracy in Russia, China, and Iran therefore pitted the long-term trends that lay the basis for it against the determined efforts of the regimes in power to forestall these trends and, to the extent that they could not forestall them, to prevent people from acting on the resulting impulse for democracy. In addition, the battle over democracy within each of the three revisionist powers had its own particular features.

Russian leaders from Peter the Great in the seventeenth century through Stalin and his communist successors in the twentieth attempted to incorporate the material advances of the West—its military technology above all—while keeping out the Western ideas that threatened their rule. They sought, that is, the hardware of the West without its software; and in this effort they enjoyed considerable success, building powerful armed forces while maintaining autocratic political systems. Vladimir Putin seems to have the same goal, but fending off Western ideas, particularly the idea of democracy, is far more difficult in the twenty-first century than before. In the twentieth century the ruling Communist Party effectively sealed off the Soviet Union from the rest of the world: with the exception of communist officials Soviet citizens could not travel or read Western political writings, nor were they allowed to listen to Western broadcasting, although some managed to do so.

Putin cannot do any of this and has not seriously tried. In fact, his country has deep connections with the West: the elite keeps what it values most there—its money and its children. The ineluctable intrusion of Western culture, with its political ideas, assists the forces for democracy in Russia's internal, underground political struggle.[28] So, too, does the fact that Russia has now had some experience, however brief, with economic, religious, and political liberty and more or less free elections. The emergence of a Russian middle class, the group historically associated with democracy, also weighs on the side of a democratic future, although many of its members are employed by the state, which can therefore exercise a measure of control over them, rather than, as in the West, by the private sector.

The Putin regime's failure to develop a source of economic growth other than the sale of energy inevitably increases public dissatisfaction with its kleptocratic rule. Its unpopularity weakens the current government, which in turn weakens its anti-democratic campaign, although that alone does not guarantee its replacement by a rights-protecting political system with leaders chosen in free elections. Indeed, public discontent gives Putin an incentive to seek opportunities for foreign adventures to compensate for, and divert attention from, his regime's economic shortcomings.

Working against the forces of democracy within Russia is, first and foremost, the country's autocratic history. Throughout the centuries, almost until the end of the twentieth century, it never had anything approaching democratic politics. It also did not have democracy's economic counterpart, free-market economics. Tsarist Russia's "patrimonial state" lacked the quintessential free-market institution, private property.[29]

During the brief period of liberty and popular sovereignty in the 1990s, moreover, most Russians experienced sharp declines in their economic fortunes and witnessed corruption on a grand scale, giving them a jaundiced view of democracy, with which they came to associate these years.[30] In addition, the Putin political order's "vertical of power," in which the leader has ultimate authority over all political and economic matters, has stunted the growth of one of democracy's essential components, working institutions. Finally, the regime has a safety valve through which to relieve pressure for democracy—emigration. Some of the most talented citizens, the very people capable of building a modern, prosperous, democratic Russia, have availed themselves of the opportunity, which the Soviet Union did not permit, of living and working abroad in freer, richer—and democratic—countries.[31]

In China, surging economic growth has generated pockets of the kind of affluence in which democracy has historically flourished. Despite the system of censorship of the Internet, moreover, information from the democratic West flows into the country, as do Westerners themselves; and the hundreds of thousands of Chinese studying in Europe, North America, Australia, and New Zealand marinate in Western culture. Closer to home, despite censorship the Chinese people are aware of a functioning Chinese democracy on Taiwan and a freer society than theirs in Hong Kong.

The post-Mao history of the Chinese Communist party also gives reason for optimism about democracy's prospects. The authorities have, since the early 1980s, steadily relaxed their grip on the country's economy—shifting from government-imposed central planning to the extensive use of extra-governmental free-market mechanisms—in order to elevate and sustain the rate of economic growth. To continue that growth, on which the regime's political legitimacy has come to depend, even growth at a lower level than the double-digit annual rate of the three decades after 1979, will require further loosening communist control of Chinese society. To escape the "middle income trap," in which a country's cheap products are undercut by competition from lower-wage countries while its expensive ones do not match the quality of comparable goods made in the West,[32] Beijing will have to allow the financial system to operate more freely and foster greater innovation by providing more freedom to innovate.[33]

On the other hand, the country's economic success has furnished China's communist government with a reserve of political support from the hundreds of millions of Chinese who have shared in that success. The regime draws staying power, as well, from the hundreds of thousands of officials who have a stake in its perpetuation, including its vast corruption. The Chinese autocracy has a wider base than Russia's Putin-centered dictatorship. Furthermore, the members of the growing middle class that China's remarkable economic performance has created not only appreciate the Party's role in their good fortune, they also worry about whether a popularly-chosen government would do as well for the country as a whole and for themselves in particular.[34]

Would a more democratic Chinese government, one inevitably under the influence of the hundreds of millions of Chinese who remained very poor and who might well resent the gains of the middle class, protect those gains? Chinese either have personal memories or have heard personal recollections of the Cultural Revolution of the 1960s, when youthful mobs inspired by Mao assaulted the country's elite. They will not want to run the risk of suffering the wrath of the less fortunate themselves, which may incline them to support the communist dictatorship.[35] Fear of the future as well as dissatisfaction with Communist

Party rule has also driven the emigration of many of China's wealth-iest and many of its most talented citizens, who, if they had remained, might have worked for more democratic governance.[36]

Chinese democracy faces yet another obstacle. People who are not Han Chinese live within the country's borders in significant num-bers. Their proportion of the overall population is not large—about 8 percent—but Tibetan Buddhists and Uighur Muslims are concen-trated in the sparsely populated western part of China rather than being scattered among the far more numerous Han, and would secede if they could.[37] The advent of democracy could give them the opportu-nity to do so. Even Chinese who place a high value on liberty and free elections might well opt to forgo them to prevent the partial dismem-berment of their country.

In Iran the forces pressing for democracy are probably stronger, in relation to the opposition mounted by the regime, than in Russia and China. After four decades of existence, the government of the Islamic Republic commands, by all accounts, very little public support, and its anti-Western propaganda has little impact.[38] Iran is better endowed with the preconditions for democratic government—a middle class, a "civil society" of independent groups, a large Western diaspora in reg-ular contact with friends and family within the country—than any Arab country. Democracy has come to some sovereign states through the military defeat of its dictatorship and this path lies open to Iran as it does not to nuclear-armed Russia and China. Finally, Iran does have a history of intermittent constitutional government, going back to 1909. The regime's economic mismanagement and corruption have brought economic hardship to the majority of Iranians, making the ruling mullahs increasingly unpopular. Expressed in protest demonstrations at the beginning of 2018, that unpopularity had the potential to fuel a mass movement to overthrow them, although the end of the Islamic Republic would not, by itself, guarantee the advent of a genuinely Iranian democratic government. Furthermore, the more beleaguered the clerics become at home, the more aggressive they might become abroad.

On the other side of the ledger, the mullahs' resistance to democ-racy can draw on a source of energy and resolution unavailable to the Russian and Chinese autocrats: ideological commitment. True believers in Ayatollah Khomeini's vision for the country do remain, although they are fewer in number than at the time of the revolution, and many of them hold positions of power. Moreover, while Russians and Chinese live in regions where democracy has made major inroads, Iranians do not. The democratic current runs far more weakly in the Middle East than in Europe and East Asia.

In Iran, as in Russia and China, the one certainty about the tug-of-war over democracy is that it will continue. In a world in which democracy is the most common form of government, and when the richest parts of that world are democratic, no country can avoid pressure to follow their example. The rulers of Russia, China, and Iran, all three presiding over large countries with long histories of autocracy, are counting on being forceful and shrewd enough to resist the global democratic current instead of being swept away by it. Whether they will succeed only the future will tell.

Whether they succeed or fail, however, the quarter century after the opening of the Berlin Wall teaches, in retrospect, an important lesson: peace—deep peace, peace lacking not only the occasional war but constant security competition as well; peace not as the end of the conflict but as the end of security competition—is possible. It is not a mythical beast, the unicorn of international history. It has been sighted, in its mature form in Europe in the early 1990s and in a less fully developed version in East Asia at the same time. By the middle of the second decade of the twenty-first century it had vanished from sight but had not necessarily, to continue the metaphor, become extinct.

The post-Cold War quarter century of peace revealed the formula for reviving it, a formula first sketched out by Immanuel Kant 194 years before the unexpected collapse of communism in Europe put it into practice: peace comes, above all, from democracy. Yet an irony accompanies the formula: the world may know what that formula is but cannot act upon that knowledge to implement it. It has the recipe but lacks the ingredients. The world knows what must be done but cannot do it. Peace comes from democracy, but democracy cannot be installed from the outside. Countries do become democracies; but they cannot be made so by others.

The rest of the world has a great deal at stake in whether the three revisionist powers that ended the peace in their respective regions acquire political systems that would lead to its restoration; but beyond working to make their own democratic political systems attractive models, other countries can do very little to assist the forces of democracy in Russia, China, and Iran. The democratic world can, and does, *hope* that freedom will one day ring within their borders; but hope is not a strategy. Whether that hope will be fulfilled will depend on the choices of Russians, Chinese, and Iranians, in combination with the unpredictable vagaries of history.

NOTES

Chapter 1

1. Quoted in James Kitfield, "Martin Dempsey's World Is Falling Apart," https://www.politico.com/magazine/story/2015/09/martin-dempsey-retiring-213194

2. Arkady Ostrovsky, *The Invention of Russia: From Gorbachev's Freedom to Putin's War*, New York: Viking, 2016, p. 323.

3. "Men living together according to reason, without a common Superior on Earth, with Authority to judge between them, is *properly the State of Nature*. But force, or a declared design of force upon the Person of another, where there is no common Superior on Earth to appeal for relief, *is the State of War*." John Locke, *Second Treatise on Civil Government*, quoted in Michael Doyle, *Ways of War and Peace*, New York: W.W. Norton, 1997, p. 213.

   "International politics is a 'state of war'—a competition of units in the kind of state of nature that knows no restraints other than those which the changing necessities of the game and the shallow conveniences of the players impose." Stanley Hoffmann, *The State of War: Essays on the Theory and Practice of International Politics*, New York: Frederick A. Praeger, 1965, p. vii.

   "It is the state of mutual apprehension and armed surveillance—more than the spates of active fighting which, of course, establish this pattern of relations—that is the norm among human groups." Azar Gat, *War in Human Civilization*, Oxford: Oxford University Press, 2008 paperback, p. 66.

4. Azar Gat, *The Causes of War and the Spread of Peace*, New York: Oxford University Press, 2017, Chapters 1–3.

5. "Violent competition, alias conflict—including intraspecific conflict— is the rule throughout nature, as organisms vie among themselves to survive and reproduce under ever-prevalent conditions of acute scarcity, conditions accentuated by their own process of propagation." Gat, *War in Human Civilization*, p. 663. The discussion here of the biological basis of warfare is based on *Ibid.*, Part I.

6. Michael Mandelbaum, *The Road to Global Prosperity*, New York: Simon & Schuster, 2014, pp. 15–21.

7. France was a partial exception. The French withdrew from the integrated military command of NATO and charted a course in foreign policy that diverged in some ways from that of the United States. France remained, however, a member of NATO.

8. In 1819, the English economist David Ricardo showed trade to be an infallible mechanism for enrichment. He demonstrated that all trade between two countries benefited both of them—although not necessarily in equal measure. He proved that trade was, to use terminology not in use until almost two centuries later, a "win-win" proposition, which meant that maximizing trade with others served every country's economic interest. Not all countries, of course, then or since, have geared their international economic policies to Ricardo's findings.

9. According to one study, when a country expects trade to expand it tends toward peaceful conduct, but the expectation that trade will decrease can be a cause of war. Dale C. Copeland, *Economic Interdependence and War*, Princeton, New Jersey: Princeton University Press, 2015.

10. Thus China has attempted to use access to its huge market as a source of political leverage. Russia has done the same thing and has tried to make political gains by limiting the sale of its energy. The United States and the international community have organized economic embargoes on Iran and North Korea in order to stop those two countries' ongoing efforts to obtain nuclear weapons. See below, chapters 2, 3, and 4.

11. The idea that the people would not vote themselves into war first gained currency in the eighteenth century. The most articulate elaboration of the idea came from the German philosopher Immanuel Kant, who made it central to his 1795 essay *Perpetual Peace*:

    If the consent of the citizens is required in order to decide that war should be declared . . . nothing is more natural than that they would be very cautious in commencing such a poor game, decreeing for themselves all the calamities of war. Among the latter would be: having to fight, having to pay the costs of war from their own resources, having painfully to repair the devastation war leaves behind, and, to fill up the measure of evils, load themselves with a heavy national debt that

would embitter peace itself and that can never be liquidated
on account of constant wars in the future." Immanuel Kant,
Perpetual Peace, Indianapolis: Bobbs-Merrill, 1957, pp. 5–6.

12. Michael Mandelbaum, *Democracy's Good Name: The Rise and Risks of the World's Most Popular Form of Government*, New York: PublicAffairs, 2007, pp. 151–159.

13. Gat, *War in Human Civilization*, pp. 593–594; Gat, *The Causes of War*, p. 171.

14. In international politics "suspicion and insecurity are difficult to overcome because it is difficult to verify that the other side does not harbour offensive intentions." Gat, *The Causes of War*, p. 53.

15. Ancient Athens fought frequently, including against similarly-governed Greek states. More recently, in fact in the post-Cold War period itself, countries trying to make the transition from authoritarian to democratic governance, and without well-established traditions of liberty, have been prone to large-scale violence. In free elections, especially in places with no history of them, aspirants to political power have sometimes sought to win electoral popularity by presenting themselves as staunch opponents of presumed enemies within and without, which can precipitate violence. This happened in the Balkans in the 1990s when Yugoslavia fell apart. This is the theme of Jack Snyder, *From Voting to Violence: Democratization and Nationalist Conflict*, Princeton, New Jersey: Princeton University Press, 2000.

16. Robert J. Lieber, *Retreat and Its Consequences: American Foreign Policy and the Problem of World Order*, New York: Cambridge University Press, 2016, p. 24.

17. The middle period of the Cold War did produce two genuinely significant treaties: the Soviet-American Anti-ballistic Missile (ABM) Treaty of 1972, which forestalled a competition in systems of ballistic missile defense that would certainly have been expensive and might have proven dangerous; and the Nonproliferation Treaty (NPT) of 1968, by the terms of which those countries that had nuclear weapons at the time they signed it could keep them but other signatories had to forswear them. By 2017 the NPT had 190 signatories, five as nuclear-weapon states and the rest as non-nuclear-weapon states.

18. The agreements in question included the 1988 treaty eliminating intermediate-range nuclear-equipped missiles (INF) from Europe, the 1990 accord substantially reducing tanks, planes, and other non-nuclear—that is, "conventional"—forces on the continent (CFE) and the agreements of 1991 and 1993 cutting the number of long-range—strategic—missiles on both sides (START I and START II).

19. During the Cold War, beginning in the 1960s the United States and the Soviet Union had each been able to monitor the other's military forces and activities through reconnaissance by satellites. The later, transformative accords stipulated that each country had to allow foreign

observers into its country to check at ground level on weapons too small to be photographed accurately from space. This marked a political breakthrough: previously, the Soviet Union had resisted such "on-site" inspection.

20. For nuclear weapons the START treaties reinforced the relationship of mutual assured destruction, by which each nuclear power had the capacity to inflict catastrophic damage on the other even after absorbing a nuclear attack. Because neither side could hope to escape crushing damage after launching an attack, neither had an incentive to launch one: the arrangement favored the defense. The CFE Treaty made the non-nuclear forces on each side more or less equal in size, which discouraged an attack by either because, by standard military reckoning, a successful attack requires substantial numerical superiority on the part of the attacker. See Michael Mandelbaum, *The Dawn of Peace in Europe*, New York: The Twentieth Century Fund, 1996, pp. 84, 90–92.

21. The new EU countries included Poland, Hungary, the Czech Republic, Bulgaria and Romania. What had been the independent communist country of East Germany—the German Democratic Republic—merged into West Germany—the Federal Republic of Germany. Three small former union republics of the Soviet Union on the Baltic Sea—Estonia, Latvia, and Lithuania—also adopted democratic political systems and joined the EU.

22. Russia's cultural inheritance also worked against the acceptance of American hegemony in Europe, with Russia simply another European country under its protection. "Russians have always had an abiding sense of living in a providential country with a special mission—an attitude often traced to Byzantium, which Russia claims as an inheritance." Stephen Kotkin, "Russia's Perpetual Geopolitics: Putin Returns to the Historical Pattern," *Foreign Affairs*, May/June 2016, p. 3.

23. Martin Malia, *Russia Under Western Eyes: From the Bronze Horseman to the Lenin Mausoleum*, Cambridge, Massachusetts: Harvard University Press, 1999, pp. 13, 35.

24. Expansion took place in three stages: in 1999 Poland, Hungary, and the Czech Republic joined (the United States Senate had voted in favor of adding them in 1997); in 2004 Bulgaria, Estonia, Latvia, Lithuania, Romania and Slovakia became members; and in 2009 Albania and Croatia were included.

25. Michael Mandelbaum, *Mission Failure: America and the World in the Post-Cold War Era*, New York: Oxford University Press, 2016, p. 68; Timothy J. Colton, *Russia: What Everyone Needs to Know*, New York: Oxford University Press, 2016, p. 122.

26. Michael Mandelbaum, *NATO Expansion: A Bridge to the Nineteenth Century*, Washington, D.C. Center for Political and Strategic Studies, 1997, p. 4.

27. Nor did NATO membership prevent the erosion of some democratic practices in Hungary and Poland in the second decade of the twenty-first century.

28. Mandelbaum, *NATO Expansion*, p. 18; Mandelbaum, *Mission Failure*, pp. 71–72. The initial new members were Poland, Hungary, and the Czech Republic.

29. Russian opposition did play a major part in preventing Georgia and Ukraine from being invited to join NATO.

30. "With post-Cold War triumphalism increasingly seeping into conventional wisdom, most assumed that when the United States and major European powers wanted to do something in the international arena, they could impose their will without significant costs. Though this new NATO assertiveness was not deliberately directed against Russia, few within the alliance took seriously Moscow's concerns—which were met by most with either indifference or contemptuous disregard. Rarely if ever did U.S. leaders critically assess how they themselves would react if a powerful (and not even necessarily hostile) alliance sought to add Canada and Mexico to its ranks while excluding the United States." Dimitri K. Simes, "Destined for Conflict?" http://nationalinterest.orgint/feature/russia-america-destined-conflict

31. Charles Clover, *Black Wind, White Snow: The Rise of Russia's New Nationalism*, New Haven, Connecticut: Yale University Press, 2016, p. 232.

32. On the post-Napoleonic period see Henry Kissinger, *A World Restored: The Politics of Conservatism in a Revolutionary Age*, New York: The Universal Library, Grosset and Dunlap, 1964; and Paul W. Schroeder, *The Transformation of European Politics, 1763–1848*, Oxford: Oxford University Press, 1994, Part II. After World War II Germany was divided and the United States and the Soviet Union each incorporated into its own sphere the part it had occupied in the course of the war.

33. James Sherr, "A War of Narrative and Nerves," in *The Russian Challenge: Chatham House Report*, London: Royal Institute of International Affairs, 2015, p. 30.

34. "On March 24, 1999, Russian Prime Minister Yevgeny Primakov was on his way to Washington when he got word that NATO had begun bombing Kosovo. He ordered his plane turned around. A few hours later, he landed in a Moscow that was reeling from the insult of not being consulted." Masha Gessen, "Crimea Is Putin's Revenge," *Slate*, March 21, 2014, www.slate.com/articles/news_and_politics/foreigners/20014/03/21. See also Ostrovsky, *op. cit.*, p. 233.

35. Russia was particularly sensitive about this subject because of the secessionist aspirations of many in the rebellious Russian province of Chechnya.

36. Clover, *op. cit.*, pp. 265, 276.

37. On the Russian attitude toward the American war in Iraq see Mikhail Zygar, *All the Kremlin's Men: Inside the Court of Vladimir Putin*, New York: PublicAffairs, 2016, pp. 35–37.

38. Mandelbaum, *Mission Failure*, p. 73.

39. "Out of area or out of business" became the new NATO slogan. The alliance turned not to be neither particularly active nor particularly effective beyond the area of its Cold-War focus.

40. See Chapter 3.

41. Ostrovsky, *op. cit.*, p. 181; Clover, *op. cit.*, p. 245.

42. Boris Yeltsin was blamed by Russians for putting the country through radical economic "shock therapy," an effort to create a free-market system as quickly as possible, which his critics claimed was responsible for the hard times that followed. In fact, the opposite was the case: Russia, unlike some formerly communist countries such as Poland, did *not* undergo shock therapy, and the countries that did undergo it performed better economically than did Russia. Mandelbaum, *Mission Failure*, p. 61.

43. Ostrovsky, *op. cit.*, p. 235. ". . . just as the shortages of the 1980s discredited communism, so the crash of 1998 was a most spectacular demonstration that the market democracy model promoted by Yeltsin in the 1990s had failed as well." Clover, *op. cit.*, p. 246.

44. "Corruption in both its sense of bribes and kickbacks, and the fundamental distortion of society by a culture of rule by personal favours coupled with blackmail, has grown . . . into a fundamental system of government." Andrew Wood, "Russian and Western Expectations," in *The Russia Challenge*, p. 55.

45. Karen Dawisha, Putin's Kleptocracy, New York: Simon & Schuster, 2014, p. 1.

46. See David E. Hoffman, *The Oligarchs: Wealth and Power in the New Russia*, New York: PublicAffairs, 2002, Chapter 13 and Chrystia Freeland, *Sale of the Century: Russia's Wild Ride from Communism to Capitalism*, New York: Crown Books, 2000, Chapter 8.

47. On Putin's personality, personal history, and world-view see Fiona Hill and Clifford G. Gaddy, *Mr. Putin: Operative in the Kremlin*, Washington, D.C. Brookings Institution Press, 2015, and Steven Lee Meyers, *The New Tsar: Rise and Reign of Vladimir Putin*, New York: Vintage, 2016.

48. Colton, *op. cit.*, p. 181. "The two main pillars of the Soviet state, propaganda and the threat of repression, have been restored. The KGB, which was humiliated and broken up in the aftermath of the [1991] coup, has been rebuilt as the main vehicle for political and economic power. The secret police is once again jailing protesters and harassing civil activists." Arkady Ostrovsky, "Inside the bear," *The Economist*, October 22, 2016, p. 4.

49. Putin did not effectively control everything, especially outside the capital. Evgeny Gontmacher, "Russian Federalism: Myth or Reality?" in Leon Aron, editor, Putin's Russia, Washington, D.C. AEI, 2015.

50. Ostrovsky, *op. cit.*, pp. 266–267; Stephen Kotkin, "The Remarkable Rise of Vladimir Putin," *Foreign Affairs*, March/April 2015, p. 144.

51. "The state sector comprises, according to the IMF, more than 70 percent of the Russian economy. State-owned enterprises take up 80 percent of the country's top-ten firms' shareholder capital." Maxim Trudolyubov, "Russia Won't Recover Unless It Reforms Its State," www.wilsoncenter .org/articles/russia-wont-recover-unless-it-reforms-its-state

52. Mandelbaum, *The Road to Global Prosperity*, pp. 139–140; Colton, *op. cit.*, pp. 160–161.

53. Walter Laqueur, *Putinism: Russia and Its Future With the West*, New York: St. Martin's Press, 2015, pp. 47, 60; Clover, *op. cit.*, pp. 252–253.

54. "[Putin aide Vladislav] Surkov invented the phrase 'sovereign democracy' to express his master's orientation. It meant 'that the state should exert robust controls over a nominally democratic political system, one that was free of any foreign influence whatsoever.'" John Lloyd, "Action man," *TLS*, March 21, 2014, p. 11.

55. Ostrovsky, *op. cit.*, p. 306.

56. "Behind these political games was not a vision of Russia's future or an ambition to restore its empire but something far more primitive: a desire for personal enrichment, comforts, and power. Money was the only ideology the Kremlin subscribed to." *Ibid.*

57. "As Vladislav Inozemtsev pointed out in a recent essay on Russia's decline, 'the Russian elite actually owns the country, but formally cannot turn it into its property; therefore, its major aim is to plunder the national wealth rather than to increase it.'" Kirk Bennett, "The Perils of Putin's 'Manual Controls,'" www.the-american-interest.com/2016/10/05/ the-perils-of-putins-manual-controls

58. Zygar, *op. cit.*, p. 208.

59. Colton, *op. cit.*, p. 163.

60. Dawisha, *op cit.*

61. Malia, *op. cit.*, p. 29; Boris Makarenko, "The Difficult Birth of Civic Culture," in Aron, editor, *op. cit.*, p. 109. In 1985 Alexander Yakovlev, a principal architect of the reforms of the last Soviet leader, Mikhail Gorbachev, wrote to Gorbachev as follows: "For a thousand years we have been ruled by people and not by laws . . . What we are talking about is not the dismantling of Stalinism but a replacement of 1,000-year old model of statehood." Quoted in Ostrovsky, "Inside the Bear," p. 15.

62. "Russia's autocratic turn fell back on Muscovite, imperial, and Soviet patterns of thought and behavior." Colton, *op. cit.*, p. 149.

63. See above, p. 11.

64. Dawisha, *op. cit.*, p. 6.

65. Ostrovsky, *op. cit.*, p. 1.

66. Colton, *op. cit.*, p. 130; Mandelbaum, *Mission Failure*, pp. 60–61.

67. Zygar, *op. cit.*, p. xx. "For all his authoritarianism, Putin derived his legitimacy from popular support, and while he did not believe in fair elections, he paid careful attention to public opinion." Ostrovsky, *op. cit.*, p. 307. "Putin understood that to rule Russia he had to stay genuinely popular with 'the masses' and from time to time crack his whip at the elites: a 'good tsar' reining in the greedy 'boyars.' Popularity ratings are important: to rule effectively, one needs at least 60% support; to rule comfortably, 70%. Approaching 50%, however, which is totally fine in the west, is fraught with the dangers of civil strife in Russia." Dmitri Trenin, "Russia is the house that Vladimir Putin built—and he'll never abandon it," *The Guardian*, March 27, 2017. https://www.theguardian.com/commentisfree/2017/mar/27/russia-house-vladimir-putin-built-never-abandon

68. Kathryn Stoner and Michael McFaul, "Who Lost Russia (This Time)? Vladimir Putin," *The Washington Quarterly*, Summer, 2015, p. 175; Sergei Guriev, "Russia's Constrained Economy," *Foreign Affairs*, May/June, 2016, p. 18.

69. Lev Gudkov, "Resources of Putin's Conservatism," in Aron, editor, *op. cit.*, p. 58.

70. Clifford G. Gaddy and Barry W. Ickes, *Caught in the Bear Trap*, London: The Legatum Institute, 2013, especially pp. 6, 13, 16.

71. Colton, *op. cit.*, p. 150.

72. "The Putin regime owes its survival and success to one factor and one factor only—the export of oil and gas . . ." Laqueur, *op. cit.*, p. 21.

73. Bobo Lo, *Russia and the New World Order*, Washington, D.C. Brookings Institution Press, 2015, p. 85.

74. Undercurrents of nationalism had existed, however, even in the resolutely internationalist Soviet era. Clover, *op. cit.*, p. 7. See also John B. Dunlop, *The Rise of Russia and the Fall of the Soviet Union*, Princeton, New Jersey: Princeton University Press, 1993.

75. See Michael Mandelbaum, editor, *The New European Diasporas: National Minorities and Conflict in Eastern Europe*, New York: The Council on Foreign Relations, 2000.

76. Lo, *op. cit.*, pp. 96, 107. "According to witnesses, at a meeting behind closed doors [with President George W. Bush] Putin flew into a rage on the topic of Ukraine. 'Ukraine is not even a country,' he told Bush. 'Part of it lies in Eastern Europe, and the other, more significant part, was given by us as a gift!' He finished his short speech with these words: 'If Ukraine joins NATO, it will do so without Crimea and the eastern regions. It will simply fall apart.'" Zygar, *op. cit.*, pp. 153–154.

77. "To this day there is still no entirely plausible explanation as to why Crimea was handed over to the Ukrainian SSR. The most convincing theory seems to be agricultural: [Soviet leader Nikita] Khrushchev wanted to irrigate the Crimean steppe with water from the Dnieper, which

flows through Ukraine, and planned to make the Ukrainian leadership responsible for farming the peninsula." Ibid., p. 281.

78.   Steven Pifer, "The Ukraine Crisis and the West's Response: Diplomatic, Economic and Military Options," in *The U.S. Response to Russia's Assertiveness: Economic, Military and Diplomatic Challenges*, Washington, D.C. The Aspen Institute, 2015, p. 21.

79.   "Putin's numbers showed 82 percent of Crimeans voting for the annexation, while his own Human Rights Council's results showed only 22.5 percent voting in favor." Dawisha, *op. cit.*, p. 319.

80.   "Nine thousand four hundred were known dead in the Donbass by May 2016 and twenty-two thousand injured." Colton, *op. cit.*, p. 190.

81.   Zygar, *op. cit.*, p. 141.

82.   Niklas Nilsson, "Georgia's Rose Revolution: The Break with the Past," in Svante E. Cornell and S. Frederick Starr, editors, *The Guns of August 2008: Russia's War in Georgia*, Armonk, New York: M.E. Sharpe, 2009, pp. 91–101.

83.   Lo, *op. cit.*, p. 118. "The report, issued in 2009, stated categorically that 'it was Georgia which triggered off the war when it attacked Tskhinvali with heavy artillery on the night of 7/8 August 2008. However, the report also established that Russian military units had been operating in South Ossetia before the Georgian invasion: 'While the onus of having actually triggered off the war lies with the Georgian side, the Russian side, too, carries the blame for a substantial number of violations of international law.'" Clover, *op. cit.*, p. 310.

84.   By 2016 "Russia's defence spending will have tripled in nominal terms since 2007, and it will be halfway through a ten-year, 20 trillion rouble ($300 billion) programme to modernise its weapons. New types of missiles, bombers and submarines are being readied for deployment over the next few years. Spending on defence and security is expected to climb by 30% this year and swallow more than a third of the federal budget." "From cold war to hot war," *The Economist*, February 14, 2015, p. 20. ". . . two months after its war in Georgia, the Kremlin embarked on an ambitious program of defense modernization and military restructuring. These efforts, which Russian officials have projected will cost some $700 billion by 2020, are intended to transform the Russian military from a massive standing force designed for global great-power war into a lighter, more mobile force suited for local and regional conflicts." Dmitri Trenin, "The Revival of the Russian Military," *Foreign Affairs*, May/June 2016, p. 25. "According to the Stockholm International Peace Research Institute, Russian defense spending in 2015 increased by 7.5 percent to reach $66.4 billion. That makes Russia the largest military spender in Europe and one of the largest spenders on a per capita basis in the world—Moscow spends 4.5 percent of GDP on defense, compared to 3.5 percent for the United States." Max Boot, "Under Russia's Shadow," *The Weekly Standard*, June 27, 2016, pp. 25–26.

85. Clover, *op. cit.*, p. 310. "At the center [of Russia's grand strategy] is an effort to reassert Russia's preeminence in the former Soviet space . . . If Moscow cannot lure or force Ukraine into a Russian-dominated structure, then at a minimum it has to keep it out of an association— such as NATO or the European Union—beyond Moscow's control." Thomas Graham, "The Sources of Russian Conduct," https:// nationalinterest.org/feature/the-sources-russian-conduct-17462. Russia did not, however, formally annex eastern Ukraine and the assault against that country did not seem to be part of a systematic plan to expand Russia's border along the lines of the past. Daniel Treisman, "Why Putin Took Crimea," *Foreign Affairs*, May/June 2016, p. 53.

86. Zygar, *op. cit.*, p. 292; Clover, *op. cit.*, p. 320. In March, 2014, Putin defended the invasion of Ukraine by accusing the West of responsibility for it: "They're incessantly painting us into a corner because we have an independent position, because we stick to it and call things like they are without hypocrisy. But everything has its limit. In Ukraine, our Western partners crossed a line . . . Russia found itself in a position from which it could not retreat. If you compress a spring as far as it will go, it will snap back hard." Quoted in Colton, *op. cit.*, p. 186.

87. Colton, *op. cit.*, p. 185.

88. Zygar, *op. cit.*, pp. xx, 263, 272.

89. "Viewers [of Russian television] were hammered with literally non-stop images of radical youth accompanied with emotional commentary and historical parallels with the Second World War." Vitaly Sych, "The Moment of Truth: Ukraine has a Historic Chance to Transform if it Survives the War on the Eastern Front," in *The U.S. Response to Russia's Assertiveness*, Washington, D.C. The Aspen Institute, 2015, p. 28. See also Rajan Menon and Eugene Rumer, *Conflict in Ukraine: The Unwinding of the Post-Cold War Order*, Cambridge, Massachusetts: The MIT Press, 2015, p. 84.

90. ". . . the Russian leadership has encouraged the idea that the Soviet disintegration was merely the first step in a long Western campaign to achieve total dominance . . . which will perhaps culminate in a future attempt to pursue regime change in Russia itself." Fyodor Lukyanov, "Putin's Foreign Policy," *Foreign Affairs*, May/June 2016, p. 36. "Putin is not popular domestically because he has brainwashed his citizenry, but because his narrative about a humiliated but resurgent Russia—great, respected, and unbowed—resonates with Russians." Kirk Bennett, "The Perils of Putin's 'Manual Controls,'" *The American Interest*, October 5, 2016, www.the-american-interest.com/2016-10-05/ the-perils-of-putins-manual-controls/

91. Ostrovsky, *op. cit.*, p. 315; Menon and Rumer, *op. cit.*, pp. 87–88.

92. "The Kremlin was forced to spend $200 billion of its hard currency reserves bailing out its worst-hit industries and banks . . . the rouble fell

by a third against the dollar, and Russia was to end 2009 with a 7.9 per cent fall in GDP." Clover, *op. cit.*, p. 311.

93. Gudkov, *op. cit.*, p. 58.

94. Sergei Guriev, "Russia's Constrained Economy," *Foreign Affairs*, May/June 2016, p. 19.

95. According to an analysis of Russian polls, between 2010 and 2011 "disapproval of the country's economic course was associated with a large drop in Putin's ratings." Daniel Treisman, "Putin's popularity: Why did support for the Kremlin plunge, then stabilize?" Unpublished paper, February 1, 2014, p. 20.

96. Zygar, *op. cit.*, pp. 213, 217.

97. "The Kremlin is afraid that Kiev, as a capital that managed to topple a corrupt corporation of power, may set a precedent for Moscow to follow." Dmitry Oreshkin, "Moscow to Swallow Putin: The Rise of Civil Society in Russia's Capital," in Aron, editor, *op. cit.*, pp. 137–138.

98. "A study commissioned by Alexei Kudrin, a former finance minister, and conducted by a group of Russian sociologists . . . suggests that the roots of Mr. Putin's actions in Ukraine lie in the Kremlin's need to solidify its legitimacy after the growing discontent that erupted into street protests during the winter of 2011-12." "How Vladimir Putin tries to stay strong," *The Economist*, April 18, 2015, p. 45. ". . . incumbent Kremlin strategists believe that the annexation of Crimea, suppression of internal opposition, and relapse of a limited Cold War should guarantee Putin a decade of new 'stability' based on the threat of domestic and foreign enemies and Putin's willingness to confront them." Kirill Rogov, "Triumphs and Crises of Plebiscitary Presidentialism," in Aron, editor, *op. cit.*, p. 84. "Once economic growth was gone . . . [Putin] had to come up with a new ideology or, at least, a reason to support the government that failed to produce economic growth. Annexing Crimea, and the accompanying imperialistic and nationalistic discourse, are certainly a convenient distraction from Russia's economic problems." Guriev, *op. cit.*, p. 20. "In the Kremlin's quest to consolidate power, nothing has served it so well as the annexation of Crimea." Maria Lipman, "How Putin Silences Dissent," *Foreign Affairs*, May/June 2016, p. 44. ". . . with his popularity sliding inexorably downward in 2012-13, Mr. Putin shifted the foundation of his regime's legitimacy from steady economic progress and the growth of personal incomes to patriotic mobilization." Leon Aron, quoted in Lilia Shevtsova, "How the West Misjudged Russia, Part 4: Mad about Medvedev," *The American Interest*, February 3, 2016, www.the-american-interest.com/2016/02/03/how-the-west-misjudged-russia-part-4-made-about-medvedev/. ". . . there was a qualitative shift in the regime's character after 2014. Now, it draws its legitimacy from military action, rather than the ballot box." Nikolay Petrov, "Putin's Downfall: The Coming Crisis of the Russian Regime," *The European*

Council on Foreign Relations, ecfr.eu. ". . . Russia's economy is wilting under the weight of low oil prices, bad policies, and corrupt government. Rather than trying to address these problems, President Vladimir Putin is promoting military adventures designed to increase his personal support, unify his country, and distract attention from the plummeting ruble." Robert Cottrell, "Russia, NATO, Trump: The Shadow World," *The New York Review of Books*, December 22, 2016, p. 97.

99.   Arthur M. Schlesinger, Jr., "What Would He Have Done?" *The New York Times*, March 29, 1992, http://www.nytimes.com/books/00/11/26/specials/schlesinger-newman.html

100. Nor, historically, has the tactic been limited to Russia. ". . . Louis [XIV of France] knew that the European standing of the king was also a crucial factor in underpinning support for the monarchy at home. Even in remote Languedoc, for example, the dynasty's claim to defend France against Protestantism at home and abroad, and to frustrate 'the pernicious designs' of the Habsburgs, was central to its legitimacy." Brendan Simms, *Europe: The Struggle for Supremacy from 1453 to the Present*, New York: Basic Books, 2013, p. 50.

101. See above, p. 11.

102. Malia, *op. cit.*, p. 83.

103. ". . . after 1815 Russia's whole policy toward Europe, like her Polish policy, was one long holding operation against liberal nationalism . . ." *Ibid.*, p. 152.

104. *Ibid.*, pp. 92–93.

105. *Ibid.*, p. 170.

106. *Ibid.*, p. 241.

107. The Soviet government also feared that liberalization in Czechoslovakia would lead to that country leaving the Soviet-dominated military organization, the Warsaw Pact. In 1989, after the end of communist rule there, that is indeed what happened.

108. Putin demanded autonomous status (the details were not specified) for the eastern provinces of Ukraine, presumably as a way for Russia to exert influence there. "[Putin] wants the separatist Donbas to remain inside Ukraine, but as an open sore which Russia can prod when needed to control the country." "Alternative reality," *The Economist*, May 30, 2015. See also Lo, *op. cit.*, pp. 108, 110.

109. Zygar, *op. cit.*, p. 222.

110. "Facing an unmistakable decline in Putin's popularity (which, given the across-the-board negative ratings of the authorities is the regime's only claim to legitimacy), the government has responded with policies of social conservatism, repression, 'sterilization of politics,' and 'a war on civil society.'" Gudkov, "Resources of Putin's Conservatism," in Aron, editor, *op. cit.*, p. 70.

111. Colton, *op. cit.*, p. 235.

112. Lipman, *op. cit.*, p. 42; Colton, *op. cit.*, p. 193; Clover, *op. cit.*, p. 4; Ostrovsky, *op. cit.*, p. 2.

113. "Europe's militaries are once again training in earnest for war in their own backyard. Generations of soldiers who were trained to fight insurgencies in far-flung corners of the globe are now learning how to defend their native towns and cities." Sam Jones, "European war games," *Financial Times*, July 2/3, 2016, p. 18.

114. This geographical and political anomaly stemmed from the terms on which World War II had ended, according to which all the victorious powers—the Soviet Union, the United States, France, and Great Britain—had occupation rights in the once and future German capital. Soon after the war the Soviet Union ceased to be an ally, and indeed became a bitter adversary, of the other three countries, who merged their respective zones in the city into a single, unified, democratically governed one, thereby dividing the city between democratic and communist parts that were separated, after August, 1961, by a concrete and barbed wire wall. This made Berlin a small-scale version of Europe as a whole.

115. Michael Mandelbaum, *The Nuclear Question: The United States and Nuclear Weapons, 1946-1976*, New York: Cambridge University Press, 1979, Chapter 5.

116. ". . . it's not an actual Russian invasion that [Estonian foreign minister Sven] Mikser is worried about; he's more concerned about 'hybrid' threats, possibly exploiting Estonia's Russian-speaking minority . . ." Benjamin Oreskes, "Why Trump Makes This Small Country So Nervous," *Politico*, December 10, 2016, https://www.politico.com/magazine/story/2016/12/trump-russia-worries-estonia-214511

117. "In 2014 alone, Moscow repeatedly threatened the Baltic and Nordic states and civilian airliners, heightened intelligence penetration, deployed unprecedented military forces against those states, intensified overflights and submarine reconnaissance, mobilized nuclear forces and threats . . ." Stephen J. Blank, "Imperial Ambitions: Russia's Military Buildup," *World Affairs Journal*, June 22, 2015, www.worldaffairsjournal.org/print/96721. See also Keir Giles, "Russia's Toolkit," in *The Russian Challenge*, p. 43. By 2007 neutral Sweden, also a Baltic country, had begun to cooperate with NATO against Russia. Charles Duxbury, "Sweden Draws Closer to NATO as Russia Tensions Rise," *The Wall Street Journal*, October 27, 2016, https://www.wsj.com/articles/sweden-draws-closer-to-nato-as-russia-tensions-rise-1477570256?mg=prod/accounts-wsj

118. Quoted in Alan W. Dowd, "Answer the Baltics' S.O.S.," *The American Interest*, May 29, 2015, www.the-american-interest.com/2015/05/29/answer-the-baltics-sos.

119. "A report by the Rand Corporation, a think tank, earlier this year concluded after a series of war games that without a new big NATO

presence in the Baltics, a Russian invasion force could reach Tallinn (the capital of Estonia) and Riga (the capital of Latvia) within 60 hours. That would leave NATO to choose between escalating the conflict and accepting a fait accompli that would destroy the alliance." "Trip-wire deterrence," *The Economist*, July 2, 2016, p. 44. See also "Mr. Putin flexes his muscles," *The Economist*, August 12, 2017, p. 39, and "Outgunned," *The Economist*, March 10, 2018, p. 54. NATO did agree to create a rapid response force of 5,000 troops able to deploy within 48 hours of an order to do so. Pifer, *op. cit.*, p. 24. For an argument that the Russian threat to the Baltic countries is less dire than generally portrayed see Kirk Bennett, "Can NATO Defend the Baltics?" *The American Interest*, July 13, 2016. www.the-american-interest.com/2016/16/07/13/can-nato-defend-the-baltics/

120.   ". . . only five out of the twenty-eight members of NATO have reached the two percent of GDP threshold for defense spending recommended by the alliance." Lo, *op. cit.*, p. 228. See also the chart in Menon and Rumer, *op. cit.*, p. 142.

121.   ". . . in comparative dollar-denominated terms, Russia's economy amounts to a mere 1.5 percent of global GDP and is just one-15th the size of the U.S. economy." Kotkin, "Russia's Perpetual Geopolitics," p. 3.

122.   "Kremlin ideologists claim that, since the West is spiritually attacking Russia and Orthodoxy with feminist and LGBT propaganda, all of Moscow's responses—including aggressive military moves—are therefore defensive." John R. Schindler, "Why Vladimir Putin Hates Us," *Observer*, November 22, 2016. http://observer.com/2016/11/why-vladimir-putin-hates-us/

123.   Clover, *op. cit.*, pp. 14, 324.

124.   "Putin's domestic ideology, based on Orthodox Christianity and imperial patriotism, is skin-deep and inconsistent. Only 4 percent of Russians regularly attend church, even though 72 percent consider themselves Orthodox Christians. It's difficult to impose fundamentalist values on a society that is used to the Soviet Union's hostility to religion, has three times the abortion rate of the U.S. and contains large and autonomous Muslim and Buddhist populations." Leonid Bershidsky, "I'm an Anti-Putin Russian and Clinton Makes Me Nervous," *Bloomberg View*, October 11, 2016. www.bloomberg.com/view/articles/2016/10/11/i-m-an-anti-putin-russian-and-clinton-makes-me-nervous

125.   Evidence of the purely instrumental character of Putin's view that Russia differed from, and thus could never be part of, the West was the fact that he came to it well after he had assumed power. In the early years of his presidency he expressed interest in joining NATO. Zygar, *op. cit.*, pp. 110, 335. In 2003 he told a Scottish audience that "Russia is undoubtedly a part of Europe." *Ibid.*, p. 43.

126. "Of the roughly 771,000-strong Russian military, fewer than a hundred thousand fight in elite formations. Of these, the number on par with NATO's best is in the tens of thousands. Over the summer of 2014, Russia demonstrated the ability to draw as many as forty thousand troops to the Ukrainian border, including elite units. While this number was sufficient to menace Ukraine, it hardly represented a conventional threat to NATO forces in Eastern and Central Europe." Leslie H. Gelb, "Russia and America: Toward a New Detente," *The National Interest*, June 9, 2015.

127. "The purpose of probing is threefold. First, a probing state aims to check whether the rumors of its rival's weakening are true. A probe is a test, meant to elicit a response from the targeted power. Second, the revisionist state that engages in probing behavior wants to avoid a direct military clash with the existing great power. The risks of being wrong about the rival's resolve and capability are simply too big. Third, the state's objective is to achieve, if possible, low-cost revision of the existing regional order." Jakub J. Grygiel and A. Wess Mitchell, *The Unquiet Frontier: Rising Rivals, Vulnerable Allies, and the Crisis of American Power,* Princeton, New Jersey: Princeton University Press, 2016, p. 48.

128. "Close encounters between Russian and Western military aircraft have spiked. NATO fighter planes have made many hundreds of intercepts of Russian warplanes over the past year. Russian warplanes have stepped up provocative overflights of foreign airspace, and also are engaged in muscular interdiction." Bruce Blair, "Could U.S.-Russian Tensions Go Nuclear?" *Politico*, November 27, 2015. https://www.politico.com/magazine/story/2015/11/russia-us-tensions-nuclear-cold-war-213395

129. "If there is no sharp qualitative division between a minor transgression and a major affront, but a continuous gradation of activity, one can begin his intrusion on a scale too small to provoke a reaction, and increase it by imperceptible degrees, never quite presenting a sudden dramatic challenge that would invoke the committed response." Grygiel and Mitchell, *op. cit.*, p. 66.

130. Adam Segal, *Hacked: How Nations Fight, Trade, Maneuver and Manipulate in the Digital Age*, New York: PublicAffairs, 2016, pp. 16, 34.

131. *Ibid.*, pp. 60–66.

132. *Ibid.*, pp. 66–74. In both cases Russia's cyber tactics were part of what came to be called "hybrid warfare." The Putin regime hid its intentions until the last minute, disguised its soldiers, and relied on propaganda to rally support among Russians and sow confusion among Europeans. Sherr, *op. cit.*, pp. 26–27, and Giles, *op. cit.*, pp. 46–48.

133. Segal, *op. cit.*, p. 184.

134. On European defense spending see Barry R. Posen, *Restraint: A New Foundation for U.S. Grand Strategy*, Ithaca, New York: Cornell University Press, 2014, pp. 35–36.

135. Some European countries were internally divided about Russia, with political parties that felt some affinity for the Putin regime. Giles, *op. cit.*, p. 45; Lo, *op. cit.*, pp. 192–193; Anne Applebaum, "Russia and the Great Forgetting," *Commentary*, December, 2015, p. 26.

136. Grygiel and Mitchell, *op. cit.*, pp. 110, 175.

137. Max Fisher, "This chart should terrify Russia's neighbors," *Vox*, June 11, 2015. www.vox.com/2015/6/11/8764887/nato-russia-chart; Lieber, *op. cit.*, p. 30. Personalities and partisan affiliations made a difference in Germany's official policies toward Russia. "While [Christian Democratic] Chancellor Angela Merkel is a fluent Russian speaker, she has been much less compliant [toward Russia] than her predecessor, [Social Democrat] Gerhard Schroeder, who fitted the Kremlin's ideal of a European leader—partial toward Russia and dismissive of the concerns of smaller neighbors." Lo, *op. cit.*, p. 186. Public opinion in other NATO countries shared the Germans' reservations about defending their fellow alliance members. Eliot Cohen, *The Big Stick: The Limits of Soft Power & the Necessity of Military Force*, New York: Basic Books, 2016, p. 155.

138. See Michael Mandelbaum, "Pay Up, Europe," *Foreign Affairs*, September/October, 2017.

139. "'The risk is that [Russia] will test us unwisely and get more of a reaction than they expect and begin to lose control of the process,' says a US official. 'That is the way serious wars that were never intended begin. And that danger exists now.'" Neil Buckley, Sam Jones, and Kathrin Hille, "Return of an existential threat," *Financial Times*, November 16, 2016, p. 7.

140. "Since the end of the Cold War, Russia has moved nuclear weapons to the center of its national security strategy and military doctrine, in part to compensate for its conventional military inferiority to NATO." Matthew Kroenig, "Nuclear Trash Talk," *The Weekly Standard*, October 24, 2016, p. 18.

141. Ostrovsky, *op. cit.*, p. 308.

142. "Sanctions, like trade and investment, have traditionally been a story about the perks of size. While most countries have practiced some form of sanctions, their effectiveness turns on two basic variables: domestic market size (the loss of America as a potential market versus, say, Lichtenstein) and global market share (some countries have a near monopoly on the production of certain goods)." Robert D. Blackwill and Jennifer M. Harris, *War by Other Means: Geoeconomics and Statecraft*, Cambridge, Massachusetts: Harvard University Press, 2016, p. 58.

143. *Ibid.*, p. 11; Zygar, *op. cit.*, p. 142.

144. Marshall I. Goldman, *Petrostate: Putin, Power, and the New Russia*, New York: Oxford University Press, 2008, pp. 144–145.

145. Scherr, *op. cit.*, p. 31; Zygar, *op. cit.*, p. 282.

146.   Colton, *op. cit.*, p. 191. German Chancellor Angela Merkel played a major role in establishing a political consensus in favor of sanctions in Germany and in other European countries as well. Elizabeth Pond, "Germany's Role in the Ukraine Crisis," *Foreign Affairs*, March/April, 2015, p. 174.

147.   Cohen, *op. cit.*, p. 17.

148.   "The sector-targeted sanctions that were imposed on the Russian oil industry did not touch the gas sector at all, as Russian gas is vitally important for the European market. And as became evident soon after the announcement, sanctions on the oil industry applied only to Arctic deep-sea and shale exploration. The majority of the reserves of Russian oil companies are located in far distant regions, and cannot be developed without the use of the Western technologies that are under sanctions. But those projects are currently in the earliest stages of geological study, and none of them will enter the development stage within the next five years. Moreover, with the current level of oil prices, all those projects are economically nonviable. As a result, Western sanctions have no impact on the current volume of Russian hydrocarbon production." Sergy Aleksashenko, "Is Russia's Economy Doomed to Collapse?" *The National Interest*, http://nationalinterest.org/print/feature/russias-economy-doomed-collapse

149.   Guriev, "Russia's Constrained Economy," p. 19; Pond, *op. cit.*, p. 175.

150.   "Caught in the pincers of weak demand and rising supply from U.S. shale fields, crude oil on world markets cheapened from $111.87 per barrel in June 2014 (Brent monthly index) to less than $50 in January of 2015 and less than $40 in December." Colton, *op. cit.*, p. 192.

151.   ". . . why [has] . . . Russia not already used its unquestioned military predominance to obliterate Ukraine, either in 2014 or at any point thereafter, as Russian nationalists have pleaded [?] The reason is that Russian military escalation has the potential to trigger a host of dire consequences for Moscow. Among them are the perils of fighting a protracted guerrilla war in occupied Ukraine, the enormous financial cost of occupying and rebuilding a country devastated by conquest, the probability of driving Russia's post-Soviet neighbors into NATO's embrace, and the likelihood of crippling Western sanctions targeting Russia's overseas assets, energy and financial sectors, and state budget." Kirk Bennett, "Thinking Long-Term About Ukraine's Defense," *The American Interest*, September 25, 2017, https://www.the-american-interest.com/2017/09/25/thinking-long-term-ukraines-defense/

152.   The Shanghai Cooperation Organization included as well Kazakhstan, Kyrgyzstan, Tajikistan, and Uzbekistan. In July, 2015, it was decided to admit India and Pakistan as full members.

153.   Jack Farchy, "In Russia's backyard," *Financial Times*, October 15, 2016, p. 9. "In 1993, the economy of the two countries was about equal. Today,

the Chinese economy is four times larger [than Russia's]." Laqueur, *op. cit.*, p. 198.

Chapter 2

1. Quoted in George Walden, *China: A Wolf in the World?* London: Gibson Square, 2008, p. 265.
2. Quoted in Geoff Dyer, "US naval hawk urges sharper eye on Beijing," *Financial Times*, May 26, 2016, p. 3.
3. The countries of East Asia—China, Japan, Korea, and the Southeast Asian members of the Association of Southeast Asian Nations (ASEAN): Brunei, Cambodia, Indonesia, Laos, Malaysia, Myanmar, the Philippines, Singapore, Thailand, and Vietnam—form a less coherent political, economic, and cultural unit than do the countries of Europe. The Asians have less in common and fewer connections among themselves. Rather than a continuous land mass, like Europe, East Asia consists of both continental and island countries, some separated from others by hundreds of miles of water. It lacks the history of intensive interaction, the kind of common heritage that Christianity supplies, and the region-wide institutions that Europe has. Still, like Europe, East Asia qualifies as a distinct region of the world. All of its member countries, including the United States (which, for many practical purposes is a part of Asia as it is also part of Europe), touch on the Pacific Ocean. Each country's security depends far more heavily on the policies of the others than on what countries beyond East Asia do.
4. See p. 7.
5. The Sino-Soviet split had several causes: differences over territory—specifically land the Russian tsars had taken from a weakened China in the nineteenth century, disagreements about communist orthodoxy, Chinese resentment at what they regarded as insufficient support from Moscow, including Moscow's refusal to furnish China with atomic weapons, and rivalry for primacy within the international communist movement.
6. "Virtually all U.S. officials and many Asian leaders believe that American military predominance in the maritime realm has provided the foundation for a 70-year period of relative peace and prosperity throughout most of the Asia-Pacific region, forestalling arms races and militarized disputes and permitting a sustained focus on peaceful economic development." Michael Swaine, "The Real Challenge in the Pacific: A Response to 'How to Deter China,'" *Foreign Affairs*, May/June, 2015, pp. 145–146.
7. While not opposing the American military presence in East Asia, the government in Beijing did oppose the American alliance with Taiwan, which was first an explicit and then, after 1979, a tacit one.
8. The value of the trade across the Pacific came to exceed that of trans-Atlantic trade.

9. See Michael Mandelbaum, *The Ideas That Conquered the World: Peace, Democracy, and Free Markets in the Twenty-first Century*, New York: PublicAffairs, 2002, pp. 280–286, and Michael Mandelbaum, *The Road to Global Prosperity*, New York: Simon & Schuster, 2014, p. xiv.

10. On the connections between free markets and democracy see Michael Mandelbaum, *Democracy's Good Name: The Rise and Risks of the World's Most Popular Form of Government*, New York: PublicAffairs, 2007, Chapter 3.

11. Michael Pillsbury, *The Hundred-Year Marathon: China's Secret Strategy to Replace America as the Global Superpower*, New York: Henry Holt and Company, 2015, p. 159; Karl W. Eikenberry, "China's Place in U.S. Foreign Policy," *The American Interest*, June 9, 2015, www.the-american-interest.com/2015/06/09/chinas-place-in-us-foreign-policy

12. In 1976 the per capita income of China was $163. That of Bangladesh was $140. Howard W. French, *Everything Under the Heavens: How the Past Helps Shape China's Push for Global Power*, New York: Alfred A. Knopf, 2017, p. 248.

13. David Shambaugh, *China's Future*, Cambridge, Massachusetts: Polity Press, 2016, pp. 22–23; Richard Baldwin, *The Great Convergence: Information Technology and the New Globalization*, Cambridge, Massachusetts: The Belknap Press of Harvard University Press, 2017, p. 3.

14. See Graham T. Allison, *Destined for War: Can America and China Escape Thucydides's Trap?* Boston: Houghton, Mifflin, Harcourt, 2017. For the argument that no "Thucydides Trap" exists see Arthur Waldron, "There Is No Thucydides Trap," http://supchina.com/2017/06/12/no-thucydides-trap/

15. See Richard N. Rosecrance and Steven E. Miller, editors, *The Next Great War? The Roots of World War I and the Risks of a U.S.-China Conflict*, Cambridge, Massachusetts: MIT Press, 2015.

16. See Michael Mandelbaum, *The Fate of Nations: The Search for National Security in the Nineteenth and Twentieth Centuries*, New York: Cambridge University Press, 1988, pp. 136–137.

17. This was to be accomplished by the denial to Beijing of normal—that is "most favored nation"—trading status rather than through formal tariffs.

18. See Mandelbaum, *The Ideas that Conquered the World*, Part III. See also Shambaugh, *op. cit.*, p. 153.

19. This is the subject of Samuel P. Huntington, *The Third Wave: Democratization in the Late Twentieth Century*, Norman, Oklahoma and London: The University of Oklahoma Press, 1991. See also Mandelbaum, *Democracy's Good Name*, pp. 1–7.

20. North Korea and Cuba resisted markets in principle, but their communist governments allowed them in practice.

21. Mandelbaum, *Democracy's Good Name*, Chapter 3. According to President George H. W. Bush, "As people have commercial incentives, whether

it's in China or in other totalitarian countries, the move to democracy becomes inexorable." Quoted in John Pomfret, *The Beautiful Country and the Middle Kingdom: America and China, 1776 to the Present*, New York: Henry Holt and Company, 2017, p. 518. Robert Rubin, secretary of the treasury in the Clinton administration, asserted that China's accession to the World Trade Organization, with its free-market rules, would "sow the seeds of freedom for China's 1.2 billion citizens." *Ibid.*, pp. 569–570. President George W. Bush said that "trade will promote freedom. Freedom is not easily contained. Once a measure of economic freedom is permitted, a measure of political freedom will follow." Quoted in Bruce J. Dickson, *The Dictator's Dilemma: The Chinese Communist Party's Strategy for Survival*, New York: Oxford University Press, 2016, pp. 25–26. See also Joshua Kurlantzick, *Democracy in Retreat: The Revolt of the Middle Class and the Worldwide Decline of Representative Government*, New Haven, Connecticut: Yale University Press, 2013, pp. 59–60.

22. Mandelbaum, *Democracy's Good Name*, Chapter 4.
23. "The absence of war between democracies, Jack Levy concludes, 'comes as close as anything we have to an empirical law in international relations.' Another recent article notes that when all the interacting states are democracies, that is 'a near-perfect sufficient condition for peace.' " Charles Lipson, *Reliable Partners: How Democracies Have Made a Separate Peace*, Princeton, New Jersey: Princeton University Press, 2003, p. 1. See also Azar Gat, *War in Human Civilization*, Oxford: Oxford University Press, 2008, pp. 570–597. A list of studies connecting democracy with peace appears in Azar Gat, *The Causes of War & The Spread of Peace*, Oxford: Oxford University Press, 2017, p. 278 note 35.
24. Heavy repression by the Chinese government continued against the Muslim Uighurs in the Xinjiang autonomous region, presumably because they posed the threat of secession from China as Christians did not.
25. The Chinese phrase has also been translated as "Hide one's capacities and bide one's time" (Edward Luttwak, *The Rise of China vs. the Logic of Strategy*, Cambridge, Massachusetts: Harvard University Press, 2012, p. 87) and "keeping a low profile" (Willy Wo-Lap Lam, *Chinese Politics in the Era of Xi Jinping*, New York: Routledge, 2015, p. 190).
26. This is a theme of Pomfret, *op. cit.* See, for example, pp. 6, 41, 64, 93, and 152.
27. For a prescient prediction that China would not become steadily more democratic, see James Mann, *The China Fantasy: Why Capitalism Will Not Bring Democracy to China*, New York: Penguin Books, 2008.
28. French, *op. cit.*, pp. 3, 102, 116.
29. "The difference between Russia and China, I decided after decades of involvement with each, is that the first is suffering from an inferiority complex and the second from the opposite—both of them with reason."

George Walden, "Through the Mist," *The American Interest*, https://www
.the-american-interest.com/2017/05/19/through-the-mist/

30. Bobo Lo and Lilia Shevtsova, "A 21st Century Myth—Authoritarian
     Modernization in Russia and China," Moscow: Carnegie Moscow Center,
     2012, p. 48.

31. Stephen R. Platt, *Autumn in the Heavenly Kingdom: China, the West, and
     the Epic Story of the Taiping Civil War*, New York: Knopf, 2012

32. Pomfret, *op. cit.*, pp. 147–148. Mao Zedong claimed the May 4 Movement
     as one of the forerunners of the Chinese Communist Party.

33. French, *op. cit.*, pp. 72 and 249. The powerful, enduring Chinese drive
     to resume its rightful place in the world is a theme of Orville Schell and
     John deLury, *Wealth and Power: China's Long March to the Twenty-first
     Century*, New York: Random House, 2013.

34. Upon winning control of China, the communists "took a slogan first used
     by Chinese intellectuals in 1915 and have popularized it ever since: 'never
     forget national humiliation' (*wuwang guochi*)." Tom Miller, *China's Asian
     Dream: Empire Building Along the New Silk Road*, London: Zed Books,
     2017, p. 7.

35. He is widely believed to have made the declaration in his victory speech
     at the Gate of Heavenly Peace in the heart of Beijing on October 1, 1949.
     There is, however, no reliable record of his having done so. The phrase
     nonetheless became a popular one thereafter.

36. Lam, *op. cit.*, p. 214. "From local schoolroom to national museum the
     leadership has worked to instil the notion that China's modern history
     was shameful until the Party took over." Bill Hayton, *The South China
     Sea: The Struggle for Power in Asia*, New Haven, Connecticut: Yale
     University Press, 2014, p. 177. Mao used what he portrayed as imminent
     foreign threats to generate support for domestic programs. Thomas
     J. Christensen, *Useful Adversaries: Grand Strategy, Domestic Mobilization,
     and Sino-American Conflict, 1947-1958*, Princeton, New Jersey: Princeton
     University Press, 1996, pp. 6, 9.

37. Pomfret, *op. cit.*, pp. 4, 223. See also Jung Chang and Jon Halliday,
     Mao: The Unknown Story, New York: Random House, 2005, Chapter 20.
     In World War II "it was in fact the armies of the anti-imperialist, fiercely
     nationalist KMT that offered the chief resistance to Japan's army, drawing
     it ever deeper into the mire. It was they who shared in the suffering,
     hardship and endurance on the part of hundreds of millions of Chinese
     civilians that marked the eight wartime years beyond the relatively small
     and secure Communist base areas. It is quite possible that, had the KMT
     not spent so much of its force in that struggle, Chiang would have won
     the subsequent civil war." "The unquiet past," *The Economist*, August 15,
     2015, p. 36.

38. French, *op. cit.*, pp. 228–229.

39. *Ibid.*, p. 203.

40. Pomfret, *op. cit.*, pp. 5, 206, 362, 373, 494.

41. In depicting the United States as an aggressive adversary the communist regime received occasional unintended assistance from the American government. In May, 1999, as part of its war against Serbia over Kosovo, the American air force accidentally bombed the Chinese embassy in Belgrade, triggering anti-American demonstrations in Beijing. Pomfret, *op. cit.*, p. 564.

42. Michael Auslin, *The End of the Asian Century: War, Stagnation, and the Risks to the World's Most Dynamic Region*, New Haven, Connecticut: Yale University Press, 2017, p. 200.

43. Pomfret, *op. cit.*, pp. 404–405, 409.

44. ". . . from 1945 to 1965 the United States gave Taiwan more than $4 billion, the largest military and economic infusion per capita at the time. But, unlike many other countries, Taiwan did not waste the aid. It resulted in the creation of a global exporting giant. From 1952 to 1982, Taiwan's economy grew an average of 9 percent a year. An island that had but a few paved roads in 1950 became the Taiwan Miracle." *Ibid.*, p. 412. "In 1979, the island's per capita income was $1869; in 2015 it was estimated at $46,500, higher than that of the United Kingdom." Arthur Waldron, "Legacy Problems: China's Taiwan Dilemma," *Orbis*, Fall, 2016, p. 612.

45. Mandelbaum, *Mission Failure*, p. 34.

46. Shambaugh, *op. cit.*, p. 139.

47. Taiwanese independence "would be particularly dangerous for the Chinese Communist Party, given the role that the defense of national honor plays in the regime's legitimacy." Christensen, *The China Challenge*, New York: W.W. Norton, 2015, p. 176. The Communist authorities had another, related reason for insisting that Taiwan could not be permanently or formally independent of their control: the democratic political system established on the island in the 1990s. "Beneath Beijing's bluster, Taiwan terrifies China because the small island represents a magnificent vision of what the mainland could be and what the Communist Party is not." John Lee, "Why Does China Fear Taiwan?" *The American Interest*, November 6, 2015, www.the-american-interest .com/2015/11/06/why-does-china-fear-taiwan/

48. Robert Zoellick, the American deputy secretary of state, used the term in 2005.

49. For details see Shuaihua Wallace Cheng, "China's New Silk Road: Implications for the US," *YaleGlobal*, May 28, 2015, http:/yale .global.yale.edu/print/9911. The Chinese government undoubtedly anticipated that the lion's share of the economic benefits would flow to China. It also hoped that the economic interdependence OBOR fostered would furnish it with political leverage.

50. Other, similar initiatives included the Asian Bond Fund Initiative, the New Development Bank associated with the BRICs countries, and

the Chiang Mai Initiative involving currency swaps. George Soros, "A Partnership with China to Avoid World War," *The New York Review of Books*, July 9, 2015, p. 6. China was also part of negotiations for an Asian trade agreement separate from the Trans-Pacific Partnership, known as the RCEP (Regional Comprehensive Economic Partnership). See also Shambaugh, *op. cit.*, pp. 154, 162, and Auslin, *op. cit.*, p. 146.

51. Upon taking office in 2017 the American president Donald Trump announced that he would not submit the Trans-Pacific Partnership for congressional ratification.

52. The AIIB "represents more fully than anything else China's will to emerge, its bold coming-out and a demonstration of its resolve to become a powerful, across-the-board geopolitical actor." French, *op. cit.*, p. 187.

53. "More than three years after [its] unveiling . . . OBOR remains ill-defined and underfunded, and faces an uphill battle against many constraints like geography, Eurasian instability and current trade patterns." Jacob L. Shapiro, "One Belt, One Road, No Dice," *Geopolitical Futures*, January 12, 2017. https://geopoliticalfutures.com/one-belt-one-road-no-dice/. As for China's monetary ambitions, in order to promote the rmb to a position comparable to that of the dollar the Chinese government would have to reform the country's financial system in ways that the Western countries favored: making the system's workings more transparent, reducing the role of the government in setting the currency's value, and enlarging the scope for market activity. Moreover, if the Chinese currency were to reach international parity with the dollar, this would not necessarily weaken the global economy. It might well, instead, strengthen it, to the benefit of all countries—including the United States. See Barry Eichengreen, *Exorbitant Privilege: The Rise and Fall of the Dollar and the Future of the International Monetary System*, New York: Oxford University Press, 2011, pp. 142–152.

54. "By financing roads, railways, ports and power lines in underdeveloped parts of Asia, the Belt and Road Initiative aims to draw China's neighbours ever tighter into Beijing's economic embrace." Miller, *op. cit.*, p. 12.

55. China had last had a powerful maritime force in the fifteenth century, during the Ming Dynasty. Hayton, *op. cit.*, p. 25; French, *op. cit.*, pp. 96–98.

56. French, *op. cit.*, pp. 55, 184. China's fourteen land neighbors are North Korea, Russia, Mongolia, Kazakhstan, Kyrgyzstan, Tajikistan, Afghanistan, Pakistan, India, Nepal, Bhutan, Myanmar, Laos, and Vietnam.

57. Sheila Smith, *Intimate Rivals: Japanese Domestic Politics and a Rising China*, New York: Columbia University Press, 2015, pp. 1–8, 189–190, 193; French, *op. cit.*, p. 18.

58. "More than half the world's merchant tonnage passes through the South China Sea." Dominic Ziegler, "Disorder under heaven," *The Economist*, April 22, 2017, p. 8.
59. Hayton, *op. cit.*, p. 59; French, *op. cit.*, p. 189. " . . . Chinese passports issued from 2009 onward have carried a map of the South China Sea complete with a nine-dash line map." *Ibid.*
60. French, *op. cit.*, pp. 78–80.
61. *Ibid.*, p. 247. The artificial islands "are likely to be equipped with airstrips and military facilities, to reinforce Beijing's claim to territorial waters thousands of miles from the Chinese mainland." Gideon Rachman, "Militarism is a risky temptation for Beijing," *Financial Times*, September 1, 2015, p. 11. China was not alone in creating artificial islands. "Five of the six countries with claims to all or some of the reefs and islets in the South China Sea have built structures on them, often after reclaiming land. China, however, has taken this to unprecedented lengths . . . America's defense secretary, Ash Carter, said China had filled in over 2000 acres (810 hectares), 'more than all other claimants combined . . . and more than in the entire history of the region . . .'" "Whose splendid isolation?" *The Economist*, June 6, 2015, p. 34. During World War II, the American military tactic of capturing and building military bases on many small atolls in the Pacific on the way to the ultimate occupation of Japan came to be known as "island-hopping." To assert its twenty-first-century maritime authority in the South China Sea, China practiced "island-plopping."
62. "Recognized possession of an island gives the owner rights to the sea, to the fish swimming around it, and to the minerals that may lie on or below the seabed." Hayton, *op. cit.*, p. xiii. ". . . UNCLOS (United Nations Convention on the Law of the Sea) established the EEZ (Exclusive Economic Zone) concept which gave coastal nations exclusive rights over natural resources within a 200 nautical-mile limit but allowed for free navigation and overflights outside territorial waters extending to 12 nautical miles . . . But China's interpretation (and that of a small group of large developing countries such as India and Brazil) differs from that of most states: it requires naval vessels to seek its permission before entering its EEZ." Henry Tricks, "The Pacific Age," *The Economist*, November 15, 2014, p. 11. The United States and its East Asian allies did not accept this Chinese interpretation, which, if enforced, could exclude non-Chinese military vessels from waters stretching from the Strait of Malacca to Japan. *Ibid.*
63. After the Chinese declaration the United States sent two B-52 airplanes through the disputed space to demonstrate that America would not be bound by the Chinese position. Pillsbury, *op. cit.*, p. 204.
64. The test of his conviction, the Korean War, yielded mixed results. China's "human wave" attacks stunned American forces at the outset of the Chinese intervention, in late 1950, but thereafter superior American

firepower took a fearsome toll on the People's Liberation Army, killing an estimated 400,000 Chinese troops and wounding 486,000.

65. The four were first announced by Prime Minister Zhou Enlai in 1963.

66. Christensen, *The China Challenge*, pp. 28–30; Lam, *op. cit.*, p. xiv. "The real Chinese buildup began in the 1990s and accelerated in the 2000s, with one expert observer suggesting that year-on-year increases reached nearly 16 percent a year growth—well ahead of even the remarkable growth of the Chinese economy. The upshot is a defense budget that now amounts to $165 billion in 2014 and perhaps $180 billion in 2015—still between a quarter and a third that of the United States, but the second largest in the world nonetheless, and still growing." Eliot Cohen, *The Big Stick: The Limits of Soft Power & the Necessity of Military Force*, New York: Basic Books, 2016, p. 100. "In 2000, Japan's defense budget was 63 percent larger than China's. By 2012, though, it was spending barely a third of what China did." French, *op. cit.*, p. 224. China increased its share of global military spending from 2.2 percent to 12.2 percent between 1994 and 2015. Hal Brands and Eric S. Edelman, "Why Is the World So Unsettled? The End of the Post-Cold War Era and the Crisis of Global Order," Washington, D.C Center for Strategic and Budgetary Assessments, 2017, p. 10.

67. Christensen, *The China Challenge*, pp. 29–31, 97. "By 2030 it is quite possible that China's navy could include five aircraft carriers. It already possesses the largest number of surface ships in the world (370)." Shambaugh, *op. cit.*, p. 143. The Chinese also worked on developing anti-satellite capabilities, to interfere with American surveillance and communications. Robert Haddick, "Five Ways War with China Could Be Started . . . or Avoided," *The National Interest*, December 12, 2015, https://nationalinterest.org/feature/five-ways-war-china-could-be-started%E2%80%A6-or-avoided-14597

68. Pillsbury, *op. cit.*, pp. 134–142. Hayton, *op. cit.*, p. 215.

69. ". . . China is establishing a series of port-access arrangements all along the Indian Ocean littoral to east Africa." Shambaugh, *op. cit.*, p. 143. The regime's ultimate goal, according to one Chinese observer, was "to give [China] a dominant role in Asia and the Western Pacific—at the cost of the U.S.'s ascendancy." Quoted in French, *op. cit.*, p. 11. In 2017 China conducted joint naval maneuvers with Russia far from the Pacific, in the Baltic Sea. "Unlikely partners," *The Economist*, July 29, 2017, p. 35.

70. Pomfret, *op. cit.*, p. 628.

71. "Whatever the needs of the moment, the ideological foundations of China's move to take over its near seas were bound up in the concept of *tian xia*, namely that it was China's manifest destiny to once again reign preponderant over a wide sphere of Asia—the old 'known world'—much as it supposedly had in a half-idealized, half-mythologized past. Only by doing so could the country realize its dreams; only in this way could its dignity be restored." French, *op. cit.*, pp. 248–249.

72. China's more assertive foreign policies arose, as well, from a change in the way the country's government operated. Different parts of the vast bureaucratic apparatus over which the Party presided began to function as interest groups, pressing for more authority and more resources. See David M. Lampton, "How China is Ruled," *Foreign Affairs*, January/February 2014. Those departments and agencies that favored expanding Chinese power abroad, including but not limited to the People's Liberation Army, made their wishes known and their influence felt. Lam, *op. cit.*, pp. 227–228; Luttwak, *op. cit.*, pp. 9–10, 101–103. See also French, *op. cit.*, p. 87.

73. Christensen, *The China Challenge*, p. xvii; Lam, *op. cit.*, p. 4.

74. "According to my Chinese interlocutors, large segments of the Chinese public and elites feel that China's global power has risen quickly since the financial collapse of 2008 . . . The American 'hegemon' had taken a mighty blow when Wall Street collapsed. China, by comparison, seemed stable and strong . . ." Christensen, *The China Challenge*, p. 242. See also pp. 3, 260, Luttwak, *op. cit.*, pp. 8, 257, Pillsbury, *op. cit.*, pp. 16, 208–209, Pomfret, *op. cit.*, p. 599, and Shambaugh, *op. cit.*, p. 7.

75. Charles Clover, "Command and control," *Financial Times*, July 27, 2016, p. 7.

76. "Mr. Xi has used his power to reassert the dominance of the Communist Party and of his own position within it. As part of a campaign against corruption, he has purged potential rivals. He has executed a sweeping reorganisation of the People's Liberation Army (PLA), partly to ensure its loyalty to the party, and to him personally. He has imprisoned free-thinking lawyers and stamped out criticism of the party and the government and online. Though people's personal lives remain relatively free, he is creating a surveillance state to monitor discontent and deviance." "What the West got wrong," *The Economist*, March 3, 2018, p. 9.

77. "As developed in speeches, and Party interpretations, the Chinese Dream means a national renaissance, building a nation of prosperity, ethnic harmony, and strength and influence internationally. It harkens back to Chinese national goals laid out by 19th century reformers at the time of national weakness and humiliation . . ." Jeffrey A. Bader, "How Xi Jinping Sees the World . . . and Why," Washington, D.C., Brookings Institution Asia Working Group Paper 2, February 2016, p. 9. This slogan contrasted with the one propagated by Xi's predecessor, Hu Jintao: " 'harmonious society', *(hexie shihui)* which was usually taken to mean that China should get its domestic house in order, building a more livable, less conflict-ridden country. This slogan had a counterpart in foreign policy as well, albeit invoked somewhat less, called 'harmonious world' *(hexie shijie)*, which was itself a spin-off of an earlier slogan under

Hu, since dropped, that invoked China's 'peaceful rise.'" French, *op. cit.*, p. 206.

78. "China's leaders have created another demographic problem through the Communist Party's infamous one-child policy, promulgated in 1979 . . . the policy has prevented as many as 400 million births . . . China still projects that its population will begin to slide downward around 2030." Michael Auslin, "Asia's Precarious Rise, Review," *The Wall Street Journal*, March 4–5, 2017, p. 2.

79. "As demographer Wang Feng of the University of California-Irvine aptly describes the situation, 'The aging of China's population represents a *crisis* (emphasis added) because its arrival is imminent and inevitable, because its ramifications are huge, and long-lasting, and because its effects will be hard to reverse.'" Shambaugh, *op. cit.*, p. 78. ". . . between now [2017] and 2050 the number of men between twenty and twenty-five, that is, of prime military recruitment age, will fall by half." French, *op. cit.*, p. 280. "According to UN projections, by 2050 China will have 500 million people over the age of 60 out of a total population of some 1.35 billion . . ." Azar Gat, *The Causes of War & The Spread of Peace*, p. 229.

80. French, *op. cit.*, pp. 75, 185. "I believe that [demographic] factors help to explain why Xi has made his dramatic break with the famous Deng Xiaoping strategy of biding one's time. Xi has decided that China must seize whatever advantages it can now before its window of opportunity slams shut within the next ten or, at best, twenty years." *Ibid.*, p. 282.

81. Christensen, *The China Challenge*, pp. 242, 258. In July, 2016, Xi warned that without the appropriate discipline, "Our party will sooner or later lose its qualifications to govern and will unavoidably be consigned to history." "Master of nothing," *The Economist*, October 22, 2016, p. 37.

82. Auslin, *op. cit.*, p. 88. "The vast majority of these protests are triggered by disputes over land seizures and forced demolitions of homes by local governments and developers, arbitrary fees imposed on farmers by local officials, and wage arrears—although a growing number have to do with environmental degradation, corruption, and ethnic conflict." Shambaugh, *op. cit.*, p. 63. See also Minxin Pei, *China's Crony Capitalism: The Dynamics of Regime Decay*, Cambridge, Massachusetts: Harvard University Press, 2016, p. 145.

83. Auslin, *op. cit.*, p. 18.

84. Shambaugh, *op. cit.*, p. 128.

85. *Ibid.*, pp. 116–118. "The regime's repression is symptomatic of its deep and profound *insecurity*." *Ibid.*, p. 120. See also Orville Schell, "Crackdown in China: Worse and Worse," *The New York Review of Books*, April 21, 2016.

86. Shambaugh, *op. cit.*, p. 63.

87. Pomfret, *op. cit.*, pp. 535–536.

88. Shambaugh, *op. cit.*, pp. 119–120. Xi's anti-corruption campaign "resulted in about 750,000 people being charged with graft over the last three years." "The constrained dictator," *The Economist*, March 4, 2017, p. 34. Corruption as a basic and virtually unavoidable feature of the Chinese political system is the theme of Pei, *op. cit.* See, for example, p. 24.

89. ". . . the party's own legitimacy is dependent on constant growth." Shambaugh, *op. cit.*, p. 39.

90. "Since jettisoning Maoist Communist ideology in the reform period, the nominally Communist CCP has legitimized itself through fast-paced economic growth and by nationalism." Christensen, *The China Challenge,* p. 109.

91. "In 2007, former Premier Wen Jiabao bluntly described the nation's economy as characterized by the 'four 'uns': 'unstable, unbalanced, uncoordinated, and unsustainable.'" Shambaugh, *op. cit.*, p. 1. ". . . at the end of 2014 . . . an official from the Development Research Center, the State Council's main internal think tank . . . said that they had done studies projecting a progressive decline to around 3 percent [growth] by 2020–2025, and then hoped to sustain that rate for a number of years." *Ibid.*, pp. 30–31.

92. Michael Mandelbaum, *The Road to Global Prosperity*, New York: Simon & Schuster, 2014, pp. 156–166.

93. Shambaugh, *op. cit.*, p. 7; Keith Bradsher, "Beijing's Addiction to Debt Now Puts Its Growth at Risk," *The New York Times*, May 25, 2017, p. A1.

94. Shambaugh, *op. cit.*, pp. 28–29.

95. *Ibid.*, pp. 9–10.

96. Increasing China's consumption also faced an obstacle. The Chinese people had a very high savings rate because the country lacked a generous social safety net, prompting them to save for health care and retirement.

97. French, *op. cit.*, p. 19.

98. "As the economy falters, Mr. Xi will rely ever more on Chinese nationalism as a source of legitimacy and popularity." Simon Long, "China's chairman of everything," *The Economist: The World in 2017,* December, 2016, p. 21. ". . . the party-state has only one other significant source of support [besides economic growth]: nationalism." Shambaugh, *op. cit.*, p. 96. See also *Ibid.*, p. 169. "[China's political] system reposes unsteadily on a two-legged stool. Its legitimacy is sustained mostly by fast economic growth, but also by nationalism." French, *op. cit.*, p. 22. See also *Ibid.*, p. 21.

99. In addition to trying to stop the North Korean nuclear weapons program, the countries negotiating with it were playing for time, hoping that the regime would collapse before it acquired these weapons. This did not happen.

100. Like the Putin regime in Russia and the communist government in China, the North Korean leadership apparently also regarded an

aggressive foreign policy as a way of consolidating domestic support. According to B.R. Meyers, a scholar of North Korea, "It is the regime's awareness of a pending legitimacy crisis, not a fear of attack from without, which makes it behave ever more provocatively on the world stage." Quoted in Max Fisher, "Why a Solution to North Korea's Nuclear Threat Has Proved So Elusive," *The New York Times*, April 18, 2017, p. A8.

101.   While China acceded to the NPT in 1992, before then it had not always opposed nuclear proliferation. To the contrary: "China had conducted a nuclear test for Pakistan in May 1990, had secretly sold Algeria a nuclear reactor with military applications, and aided North Korea's nuclear program, too." Pomfret, *op. cit.*, p. 547.

102.   Christensen, *The China Challenge*, p. 122.

103.   Not all Chinese were convinced that closing the border would have the desired effect. According to one, "The fundamental reason for not cutting oil is they [the Chinese government] don't want to sacrifice the buffer zone, and they also know that if they cut off the oil supply, it will not force Kim Jong-un to surrender his weapons." Quoted in Jane Perlez, "China's Silence Reinforces Its North Korea Calculus," *The New York Times*, September 12, 2016, p. A6.

104.   James Kynge, "China froze exports to North Korea in run-up to Kim's meeting with Xi," *Financial Times*, March 31/April 1, 2018, p. 1.

105.   Christensen, *The China Challenge*, pp. 123–126.

106.   "As for the Korean War, to this day Chinese textbooks maintain that South Korea, backed by America, started that conflagration, when in truth it was the North Koreans supported by Joseph Stalin and Mao." Pomfret, *op. cit.*, p. 5. During the Korean War Mao used anti-American nationalism to generate support for his regime. *Ibid.*, p. 388.

107.   *Ibid.*, pp. 119, 126–127, 130–132.

108.   "Not the least dangerous aspect of North Korea has been its willingness to sell its nuclear and ballistic missile technology to other countries, including nominal friends of the United States, such as Pakistan." Cohen, *op. cit.*, p. 162.

109.   The preceding five paragraphs are adapted from Michael Mandelbaum, "Will Nuclear History Repeat Itself in Korea?" *Project Syndicate*, April 4, 2017, www.project-syndicate.org/print/north-korea-nuclear-weapons Two considerations in particular may well have reinforced NATO's deterrence of the Soviet Union despite the vulnerability of the American homeland to Soviet nuclear strikes. First, Soviet officials actively planning to launch an attack westward, if there were such, could not be certain that NATO and the United States would *not* respond militarily, even using nuclear weapons, risky though that would have been for the United States itself. Second, while the non-nuclear superiority of the Soviet Union and the other members of its alliance, the Warsaw Pact,

over the NATO armies that opposed them passed for an established
fact in the Western discourse about European defense, Soviet military
planners might not have been entirely confident of it. They would in
fact have had good reason to doubt that their forces would easily win—
or win at all—a non-nuclear war in Europe. See John Mearsheimer,
Conventional Deterrence, Ithaca, New York: Cornell University
Press, 1983.

110. Just how much damage a DPRK artillery attack on South Korea would
do is a matter of debate, with some observers giving relatively low
estimates of the likely toll in death, injuries, and property damage. Still,
successive South Korean governments were sufficiently concerned about
what the totals might be, as well as sufficiently reluctant to incur the
costs of taking responsibility for the North Koreans if the DPRK should
collapse, that they opposed attacking the North under virtually any
circumstances short of a North Korean attack.

111. The Chinese government objected, asserting that the prospective missile
defense system would counteract its own nuclear-armed missiles and
so degrade China's nuclear deterrent. Western experts judged the likely
impact on China's military capacity to be minimal.

112. Ashton Carter and William J. Perry, "If Necessary, Strike and Destroy,"
The Washington Post, June 22, 2006. Perry later expressed his reservations
about such a course.

113. Rajan Menon, "Asia's New Balance of Power, *The National Interest*,
November/December, 2016, pp. 71–73. See also Lam, *op. cit.*,
pp. 225–226.

114. Pomfret, *op. cit.*, p. 628.

115. Hayton, *op. cit.*, p. 234.

116. Smith, *op. cit.*, p. 231.

117. Helene Cooper, "Pentagon Chief Adds 'Secretary of Reassurance' to His
Portfolio," *The New York Times*, August 4, 2015, p. A10.

118. ". . . Australia, New Zealand, Japan, Korea, Taiwan, the Philippines
and Thailand have had defence treaties or agreements with the US
for decades. More recently, seven ASEAN members have agreed
to some form of partnership with Washington (the exceptions are
Myanmar, Vietnam, and land-locked Laos—and the first two are
moving cautiously toward some kind of engagement)." Hayton, *op.
cit.*, pp. 203–204. See also Miller, *op. cit.*, pp. 245–246. Two members
of the American-centered coalition wavered in their opposition to
China: South Korea and the Philippines, the first because of the extent
of its economic dealings with China and hopes that Beijing would
restrain North Korea, the second because of the erratic foreign policy of
its president, Rodrigo Duterte, who resented American criticism of his
harsh campaign against suspected Filipino drug dealers.

119. Lam, *op. cit.*, p. 210.

120.   India and Australia "agreed a 'Joint Declaration on Security
        Cooperation' in 2009 and talks in June 2013 produced agreements
        on joint naval exercises and regular consultations about regional
        security issues. India is developing other relationships too: a 'strategic
        partnership' with Vietnam, a 'Defense Policy Dialogue' with Japan,
        and a 'trilateral dialogue with Japan and South Korea. It has provided
        Vietnam with $100 million in cheap loans to buy patrol boats to protect
        Indian-operated oilfields off the Vietnamese coast and holds joint
        exercises with Malaysia, Singapore, Thailand and Japan." Hayton, *op.
        cit.*, p. 203. Other Australian initiatives are mentioned in Luttwak, *op.
        cit.*, pp. 112–118.
121.   "Japan: We May Patrol South China Sea," *The American Interest*, June 25,
        2015, www.the-american-interest.com/2015/06/25/japan-we-may-patrol-
        south-china-sea; Harsh V. Pant, "Asia's New Geopolitics Takes Shape
        Around India, Japan, and Australia," *The Diplomat*, July 28, 2015, http://
        thediplomat.com/2015/07/asias-new-geopolitics-takes-shape-around-
        india-japan-and-australia. Auslin, *op. cit.*, p. 133.
122.   Michael Mandelbaum, *The Fate of Nations: The Search for National
        Security in the Nineteenth and Twentieth Centuries*, New York:
        Cambridge University Press, 1988, pp. 49–50.
123.   "Hot water," *The Economist*, October 31, 2015, p. 42. The United States
        Navy repeated the exercise subsequently, including in May, 2017,
        drawing a rebuke from the Chinese government. Jeremy Page, "China
        Protests U.S. Naval Patrol," *The Wall Street Journal*, May 26, 2017,
        p. A10.
124.   Lam, *op. cit.,* p. 193.
125.   ". . . nationalist humiliation, particularly as it pertains to issues such as
        Japan or Taiwan independence, is the third rail of Chinese Communist
        politics." Christensen, *The China Challenge*, p. 110. See also Hayton, *op.
        cit.*, p. 178, and French, *op. cit.*, pp. 23–26. After one of the incidents
        with Japan over the Senkakus, "anti-Japanese protests were staged in
        more than a hundred Chinese cities, with Japanese stores, restaurants,
        automobiles and even factories coming under widespread attack."
        French, *op. cit.*, p. 217. "While patriotism creates a sense of unity and
        shared identity, anti-foreign sentiments have led to repeated protests
        against Japan, the U.S., and other countries. These outpourings of anger
        become a cause of concern for the Party when criticisms against the
        actions of other countries turn into criticisms of the Chinese government
        for not doing enough to defend the country's interests." Dickson, *op. cit.*,
        p. 233.
126.   On Vietnam, for example, see Hayton, *op. cit.*, pp. 153–154. On Japan see
        Smith, *op. cit.*, pp. 224–226.
127.   French, *op. cit.*, pp. 26–27.
128.   Christensen, *The China Challenge*, p. 105; Hayton, *op. cit.*, p. 218.

129.   By some accounts the traditional Chinese approach to geopolitics also supplies a layer of insulation from a shooting war, emphasizing as it does the goal of outflanking, surrounding, and reducing the adversary in the manner of the board game *wei chi*, without resorting to the overt use of force.

130.   The United States and China had many non-economic ties with each other as well. Shambaugh, *op. cit.*, pp. 150–151.

131.   Christensen, *The China Challenge*, p. 42; Gat, *The Causes of War & The Spread of Peace*, p. 220.

132.   At the outset of 2018 China held an estimated $1.18 trillion in the form of United States Treasury bills and had total foreign-exchange holdings of $3.16 trillion. It therefore had, in theory, the means to injure the United States economically by selling them in large quantities; but that would have weakened China as well, driving down the value of its holdings.

133.   "Intra-Asian trade makes up by far the largest share of exchange for all Asian countries: close to 40 percent of ASEAN's trade is with China, while trade with American firms had dropped to just 10 percent of ASEAN's total by 2011." Auslin, *op. cit.*, p. 208.

134.   Shambaugh, *op. cit.*, p. 142.

135.   Christensen, *The China Challenge*, pp. 43–44. On supply chains see Baldwin, *op. cit.*, pp. 129, 136, 176.

136.   On the potential economic and political costs of war for China, see Arthur Waldron, "Could Four Simmering Global Crises Boil Over?" *Orbis*, Spring, 2016, p. 176.

137.   " 'In East Asia, with the exception of North Korea, growth far more than any abstract political theory is the primary means by which governments legitimate their rule,' says Bilahari Kausikan, Singapore's ambassador-at-large." Tricks, *op. cit.*, p. 5.

138.   ". . . as with the old maritime tribute system, China's aim is to maximally leverage access to its immense market. In doing so, the none too subtle message it radiates to its neighbors is a familiar one that can be summed up in the following way: *In order to ensure your prosperity, hitch your wagons to us. Yes, we expect deference, but isn't that a small price to pay for stability and co-prosperity?* It is a message that in substance could have been penned by an emperor of old." French, *op. cit.*, p. 120. "South Korea ships one-quarter of its exports to China, Australia one-third. Taiwan's economy would stall without the mainland's vast markets for high-tech electronics. That makes the region highly susceptible to Chinese political pressure." Andrew Browne, "Seoul's Predicament: Protection or Prosperity," *The Wall Street Journal*, February 22, 2017, p. A18. See also Miller, *op. cit.*, p. 11, and Auslin, *op. cit.*, p. 18.

139.   Smith, *op. cit.*, p. 192.

140. Motoko Rich, "A Reliance on China Jeopardizes the South Korean Economy," *The New York Times*, March 9, 2017, p. A4. See also Kurlantzick, *op. cit.*, p. 123.

141. Shambaugh, *op. cit.*, p. 143. Ben Bland, Tom Hancock, and Bryan Harris, "Boycott diplomacy," *Financial Times*, May 4, 2017, p. 7.

142. ". . . for the Defense Department as a whole and for the U.S. Air Force and Navy more decidedly, China has unambiguously become the prospective 'Main Enemy,' at least for planning and procurement purposes." Luttwak, *op. cit.*, p. 239.

143. In Japan, few conservatives "wanted to alter Japan's economic relations, and no one wanted to abandon the formula of working toward mutually beneficial relations [with China] based on common interests." Smith, *op. cit.*, p. 254. On the Asians' ambivalence toward China see Auslin, *op. cit.*, p. 145.

144. Smith, *op. cit.*, p. 22.

145. "U.S. policymakers have relied on a two-pronged approach of hedging and engagement" to China. Minxin Pei, "How China and America See Each Other," *Foreign Affairs*, March/April 2014, p. 147.

146. China's cyberattacks fit this description. Many were directed at the United States, seemingly undertaken mainly, although not exclusively, for economic purposes—to steal the commercial secrets of American firms. In the event of a shooting war in the Asia-Pacific region, China would presumably launch such attacks on the systems of the United States and its allies. Adam Segal, *The Hacked World Order: How Nations Fight, Trade, Maneuver and Manipulate in the Digital Age*, New York: PublicAffairs, 2016, pp. 7–8, 113–114.

147. Jakub J. Grygiel and A. Wess Mitchell, *The Unquiet Frontier: Rising Rivals, Vulnerable Allies, and the Crisis of American Power*, Princeton, New Jersey: Princeton University Press, 2016, pp. 9, 48.

148. "China's moves in the region—such as efforts to gain ground via occasional provocations—have often been likened to salami slicing, meaning that when they work well, they are calibrated so finely as to never draw direct involvement from the United States or galvanize its Southeast Asian neighbors to meaningfully coalesce in self-defense." French, *op. cit.*, p. 246. This general approach has also been compared to pulling an artichoke apart leaf by leaf. Grygiel and Mitchell, *op. cit.*, p. 74.

149. As one of his first acts as president, Trump withdrew the United States from the Trans-Pacific Partnership (TPP), a trade agreement involving almost all the countries of Asia except China. The withdrawal cast doubt on his personal commitment to the longstanding American role in the region. The prime minister of Singapore called American adherence to the TPP "a 'litmus test of [American] credibility and seriousness of purpose' in Asia." Gideon Rachman, "America's Pacific pivot is sinking," *Financial Times*, September 20, 2016, p. 9.

150.   This is a theme of Michael Mandelbaum, *The Frugal Superpower: America's Global Leadership in a Cash-Strapped World*, New York: PublicAffairs, 2010.

Chapter 3

1.   Quoted in Ramy Aziz, "Iran's Old Aspirations and New Role in the Region," Fikra Forum, The Washington Institute for Near East Policy, August 21, 2015, http://fikraforum.org/?p=7501

2.   Martin Kramer, *The War on Error: Israel, Islam, and the Middle East*, New Brunswick, New Jersey: Transaction Publishers, 2016, p. 151.

3.   To refine the metaphor, China, with a population of 1.3 billion and a growing economy, and Russia, with 150 million souls and a stagnant economy, were fraternal rather than identical twins.

4.   Neither Israel nor Turkey offered an attractive political model to the Arabs, Israel because it was Jewish and Turkey because it descended from the Ottoman Empire that had governed much of the Arab world for four centuries and was thus distrusted as a former imperial overlord.

5.   "The fact is that the territorial state, especially in the sense that Max Weber described the modern state, is alien to Arab history and culture . . . Most Middle Eastern states, upon independence if not before, took on the superficial appearance of Western states—constitutions, parliaments, presidents and prime ministers, and so on—but these were in effect standard-size Savile Row suits draped on bodies of other shapes." Adam Garfinkle, "The Geopolitical Frame in the Contemporary Middle East," *Orbis*, Fall, 2015, p. 538.

6.   "Tahseen Bashir (1925-2002) put the matter pithily: 'Egypt is the only nation-state in the Arab world; the rest are just tribes with flags.'" Ofir Haivry, "The Great Arab Implosion and Its Consequences," *Mosaic*, July 5, 2016, http://mosaicmagazine.com/essay/2016/07/the-great-arab-implosion

7.   ". . . where more than one nationality inhabits a sovereign state in appreciable numbers, democracy has proven difficult to establish. In a stable democracy, people must be willing to be part of the minority. They will accept minority status if they feel confident that the majority will respect their liberties. In a multinational state, depending on the history of relations between and among the different constituent nations, such confidence is not always present." Michael Mandelbaum, *Democracy's Good Name*, New York: PublicAffairs, 2007, p. 30. "Almost all Muslim countries are really multi-ethnic or multi-tribal societies, usually composed of one large ethnic community plus several smaller ones . . . These ethnic or tribal communities are the actual basis for most political behavior in Muslim countries. Most people act to preserve or promote the interests of their own ethnic community or tribe against the interests of other ones . . ." James R. Kurth, "Ignoring History: U.S. Democratization in the Muslim World," *Orbis*, Spring, 2005, pp. 319–320.

8. The two European countries had initially established themselves in the Middle East in the nineteenth century, with France conquering Algeria in 1830 and the British assuming a dominant position in Egypt in 1882.

9. This is the subject of Michael Doran, *Ike's Gamble: America's Rise to Dominance in the Middle East*, New York: Free Press, 2016.

10. The unimportance for the Middle East as a whole of the Israeli-Palestinian conflict became clear during the Arab Spring, when regimes fell and wars erupted entirely independently of it.

11. The United States did manage to broker peace treaties between Israel and two of its other Arab neighbors—Egypt, while the Cold War was still under way in 1979, and Jordan in 1994. Each Arab country had, for reasons independent of its conflict with Israel, aligned itself closely with the United States, so the Americans were making peace within their own coalition.

12. See Michael Mandelbaum, "1967's Gift to America," *The American Interest*, June 2, 2017. https://www.the-american-interest.com/2017/06/02/1967s-gift-to-america/

13. Between 1991 and 2003 the United States considered Iraq, still governed by Saddam Hussein, to require the same approach and so pursued a policy, in the Persian Gulf region, of "dual containment."

14. During the war "[d]eath became commonplace as famine struck. Both Iranians and travelers at the time reported conditions so severe that some Iranians cannibalized the dead to feed the living. A population weakened by hunger and endemic diseases such as malaria and cholera stood little chance when the 1918 influenza pandemic struck, killing up to 20 percent of the total population." Patrick Clawson and Michael Rubin, *Eternal Iran: Continuity and Chaos*, New York: Palgrave Macmillan, 2005, p. 48.

15. *Ibid.*, p. 53.

16. In 1935 he changed the name of the country from Persia to Iran, the word for it in the Persian language, allegedly to make it seem more Aryan and thus attractive to the Nazi regime that held power in Germany.

17. "... the Iran of today is just a rump of what it once was, At its height, Iranian rulers controlled Iraq, Afghanistan, much of Central Asia, and the Caucasus." Clawson and Rubin, *op. cit.*, p. 30.

18. The first Pahlavi took as his model the post-World War I reforms in Turkey of Mustafa Kemal (Ataturk). *Ibid.*, p. 56.

19. "By 1929, religious courts held authority only over marriage and divorce. The importance of the clergy in business and daily life declined steadily over the following decade, as the shah's government purged clerics who could not pass examinations in civil code from the judiciary. Such marginalization caused dissatisfaction among clerical ranks, but they could not stand up to the shah, the army, or the bureaucracy." *Ibid.*, p. 54.

20. Michael Axworthy, *Revolutionary Iran: A History of the Islamic Republic*, New York: Oxford University Press, 2013, p. xviii.

21. Clawson and Rubin, *op. cit.*, p. 79.
22. *Ibid.*, pp. 81–82.
23. The events of 1979 in Iran also have features in common with the first and greatest of all revolutions, the one in France in 1789.
24. A crucial event in persuading the Iranian government to make peace was the accidental shooting down of an Iranian passenger airliner by American military forces. Ray Takeyh, *Guardians of the Revolution: Iran and the World in the Age of the Ayatollahs*, New York: Oxford University Press, 2009, p. 57.
25. "Khomeini declared the Iraq war to be a godsend and a blessing that had many benefits, including national cohesion." Misagh Parsa, *Democracy in Iran: Why It Failed and How It Might Succeed*, Cambridge, Massachusetts: Harvard University Press, 2016, p. 89. ". . . the [Iraqi] invasion gave the Islamist regime the necessary excuse for suppressing popular demands for political freedoms by imposing a state of emergency." Ali Alfoneh, "What the Iran-Iraq War Can Teach U.S. Officials," *Middle East Quarterly,* Spring, 2013, p. 89.
26. Clawson and Rubin, *op. cit.*, pp. 94–95.
27. Parsa, *op. cit.*, p. 7.
28. The American government was also widely, but erroneously, considered to have engineered the removal from power of the radical Iranian prime minister Mohammed Mossadeq in 1953, on behalf of the shah. The received account vastly exaggerates the American role in the events of that year, while underestimating the growing public discontent with Mossadeq and the genuine popularity of the monarch. The account also omits the fact that the Shia clerics, while hardly enthusiastic about the Pahlavi dynasty, mistrusted Mossadeq as a radical secularist with possible ties to the atheistic Soviet Union. See Ray Takeyh, "What Really Happened in Iran: The CIA, the Ouster of Mossadeq, and the Restoration of the Shah," *Foreign Affairs*, July/August, 2014, and Takeyh, "The Myths of 1953," *The Weekly Standard*, July 24, 2017.
29. Takeyh, *Guardians of the Revolution*, p. 4; Parsa, *op. cit.*, pp. 142–143.
30. "Khomeini's hostility to Israel was not a cynical strategy of appealing to the larger Arab society but an essential and enduring pillar of his ideology." Takeyh, *Guardians of the Revolution*, p. 20.
31. "The destruction of Israel is to be emblematic of Iran's transformative role: by implementing its ideological interpretation of the Shi'a faith, it is to achieve what Sunni regimes have failed to accomplish since 1948." Eran Lerman, "The Game of Camps: Ideological Fault Lines in the Wreckage of the Arab State System," Ramat Gan, Israel, The Begin-Sadat Center for Strategic Studies Mideast Security and Policy Studies No. 124, September, 2016, p. 21. https://besacenter.org/mideast-security-and-policy-studies/124-lerman-game-of-camps/
32. Clawson and Rubin, *op. cit.*, p. 7, Parsa, *op. cit.*, p. 17.

33. "While Iran's per capita GDP was slightly higher than South Korea's in 1979, by 2009 Iran's per capita GDP was less than one-third of South Korea's. Real per capita GDP (in constant 2005 dollars) was lower in 2009 than in 1978, the year before the revolution, and considerably lower than its peak in 1976 . . ." Parsa, *op. cit.*, p. 138. "Adjusted for inflation, national income fell more than 20 percent between 1977 and 1989, while population rose at a brisk clip, with the result that per capita income fell by nearly half." Clawson and Rubin, *op. cit.*, p. 103. On economic growth the shah's regime had done much better. ". . . under the shah's rule, from 1960 to 1978, Iran had a rate of growth higher than that of the Chinese miracle since 1980, and the growth was largely due to wise government policy. The factual record is in stark contrast to the image that the shah's rule was an economic failure." *Ibid.*, p. 85.

34. Parsa, *op. cit.*, p. 137, Axworthy, *op. cit.*, p. 396.

35. Parsa, *op. cit.*, pp. 100, 105, 107, 111–112, 122. "'The youth know that Porsches and Maseratis are not the fruits of start-ups,' says another government official. 'Iran's economy has become an economy for the rich kids. There is an angry army of unemployed youth who threaten Iran like a nuclear bomb.'" Najmeh Bozorgmehr, "Iran's deep divisions," *Financial Times*, May 16, 2017, p. 7.

36. Parsa, *op. cit.*, p. 131.

37. Rouhani did not try particularly hard to change them. ". . . it would be inaccurate to call Rouhani a reformist. He has always been part of a pragmatic cohort of Iranian leaders attracted to the so-called China model of offering citizens economic rewards in exchange for political passivity." Ray Takeyh, "Iran's President Isn't a Reformer. He's an Enabler," *Politico*, May 22, 2017, https://www.politico.com/magazine/story/2017/05/22/ irans-president-isnt-a-reformer-hes-an-enabler-215171

38. This paragraph is adapted from Michael Mandelbaum, "The Iran Paradox," *Project Syndicate*, July 9, 2017. https://www.project-syndicate. org/onpoint/the-iran-paradox-by-michael-mandelbaum-2017-07? barrier=accessreg

39. Axworthy, *op. cit.*, p. 415.

40. On the rise and fall of the Green Movement see Parsa, *op. cit.*, Chapters 7 and 8.

41. "The Holy Defense Museum [in Tehran] is a monument to Iranian nationalism, the Islamic revolution, and the country's historic role as the self-declared greatest power in the Middle East. Maps of the original Persian Empire show neighboring countries, such as Bahrain and Azerbaijan, as they are meant to be in the eyes of Tehran—under Iran's writ." Jay Solomon, *The Iran Wars: Spy Games, Bank Battles, and the Secret Deals that Reshaped the Middle East*, New York: Random House, 2016, p. 13.

42. Parsa, *op. cit.*, pp. 314–315. "Amid the dilution of Islamic revolutionary ideology and the global disarray of liberalism, the message one hears most insistently in Iran these days is a nationalist one." Christopher de Bellaigue, "Iran: Still Waiting for Democracy," *The New York Review of Books*, July 15, 2017, p. 27.

43. "The Islamic Republic's foreign campaigns are now part of its play for domestic legitimacy. Iranian dissidents have a harder time criticizing the regime for its 'pro-Shiite' wars when Arab Sunnis have been for so long cruel to their sect. Political dysfunction at home . . . will likely fuel more foreign aggression. Legitimacy denied at home will be found abroad." Reuel Marc Gerecht, "Perfect Partners," *The Weekly Standard*, September 18, 2017, p. 36.

44. In this way Iran had something in common with what the historian Martin Malia, referring to communist and Nazi rule, called an "ideocratic" regime, with its policy direction "governed not by pragmatic considerations of state- or nation-building, but by overriding metahistorical goals . . ." Malia, *Russia Under Western Eyes*, Cambridge, Massachusetts: The Belknap Press of Harvard University Press, 2000 paperback, p. 328.

45. Parsa, *op. cit.*, pp. 142–143.

46. Clawson and Rubin, *op. cit.*, p. 105.

47. ". . . Iran's rulers fear that if they were to allow greater freedom in Iranian society, Western influence, Western culture and the forces of globalization would gather an unstoppable momentum (such is the yearning of many ordinary Iranians for them) and would bury them." Axworthy, *op. cit.*, p. 418.

48. Solomon, *op. cit.*, pp. 30–31.

49. Ibid., p. 120.

50. *Ibid.*, pp. 114–118.

51. *Ibid.*, p. 132.

52. Anthony Cordesman, "Are North Korea and Iran Cooperating to Build Long-Range Weapons of Mass Destruction? An Assessment," *Tablet*, June 26, 2017, http://www.tabletmag.com/jewish-news-and-politics/238409/north-korea-and-iran-weapons-of-mass-destruction

53. See pp. 83–85.

54. For an argument in favor of a policy of deterring the Iranian acquisition, as distinct from the use, of nuclear weapons see Michael Mandelbaum, "How to Prevent an Iranian Bomb: The Case for Deterrence," *Foreign Affairs*, November/December 2015.

55. "Saudi officials have publicly stated their intention to produce nuclear weapons if conventional capabilities are deemed insufficient to deter a nuclear Iran. As a paper on Saudi defense put it in 2014, '. . . if Iran gets nuclear weapons . . . [we] will be forced to follow suit.'" Jakub J. Grygiel and A. Wess Mitchell, *The Unquiet Frontier: Rising Rivals, Vulnerable*

Allies, and the Crisis of American Power, Princeton, New Jersey: Princeton University Press, 2016, p. 94. "Once Iran does have nuclear weapons, or even if it is merely seen as having them, the world will have changed dramatically. Among the consequences would likely be a drive for nuclear weapons on the part of other Middle Eastern states (e.g., Saudi Arabia, Egypt, the United Arab Emirates, and Turkey) . . ." Eliot A. Cohen, *The Big Stick: The Limits of Soft Power & the Necessity of Military Force,* New York: Basic Books, 2016, p. 159.

56. Israel, America's closest Middle Eastern ally, is widely believed to have nuclear weapons but has never officially acknowledged possessing them.

57. The United States and Israel did attempt to sabotage Iran's nuclear program by introducing a computer virus into its uranium reprocessing equipment. Solomon, *op. cit.,* pp. 25, 133.

58. The sanctions authorized in 2006 proved to be the first of four rounds of them.

59. Solomon, *op. cit.,* p. 147.

60. *Ibid.,* p. 4.

61. ". . . Iran was being forced to engage in a medieval form of barter to import key commodities and everyday household goods, selling its oil, in exchange for wheat and tea from India, rice from Uruguay, and zippers and bricks from China." *Ibid.,* p. 206.

62. Matthew Kroenig, "A Nuclear Turning Point: The longstanding, bipartisan nonproliferation standard is dead," *The Weekly Standard,* April 20, 2015. The rule applied even to friendly countries. "When U.S. allies Taiwan and South Korea began reprocessing programs in the late 1970s, the United States threatened to withdraw America's security guarantee if the programs continued, and the countries relented. As one Taiwanese scientist said, 'After the Americans got through with us, we wouldn't have been able to teach physics here on Taiwan.'" Matthew Kroenig, "Why Is Obama Abandoning 70 Years of U.S. Nonproliferation Policy," *Tablet,* June 15, 2015, http://www.tabletmag.com/jewish-news-and-politics/191479/ obama-iran-nonproliferation

63. "Up until 2013, the P5+1 [the umbrella organization for negotiations with Iran] had sought to dismantle Iran's nuclear infrastructure—except perhaps for an extremely limited and mainly symbolic enrichment program of no more than 1,500 centrifuges—and to deny it the ability to develop nuclear weapons." Emily B. Landau, "Obama's Legacy, a Nuclear Iran?" *Middle East Quarterly,* Spring, 2017, http://www.meforum.org/ 6561/obama-legacy-a-nuclear-iran

64. ". . . what the deal specifies . . . is that International Atomic Energy Agency inspectors will first have to ask Iran's permission to visit a suspicious location . . . After that, Iran has the chance to propose 'alternative means' to address IAEA suspicions. All of that will take some unspecified period of time . . . this process could stretch to a lot longer than 24 days." "The

Iranian Inspections Mirage," *The Wall Street Journal*, July 22, 2015, https://www.wsj.com/articles/the-iranian-inspections-mirage-1437607825. On inspections see also William Tobey, "The Iranian Nuclear-Inspection Charade," *The Wall Street Journal*, July 16, 2015, p. A11.

65.   Some American sanctions, imposed by the Congress in response to Iranian policies other than the direct pursuit of nuclear weapons, remained in force.

66.   United Nations Security Council Resolution 2231, passed in 2015 to endorse the JCPOA, "calls upon" Iran not to develop missiles capable of delivering nuclear weapons but does not specifically forbid this.

67.   "Those who argued that a key benefit of the nuclear deal would be a moderation of Iran's behavior in the region have been sadly disappointed. Armed with substantial funds and a growing economy, Iran is challenging the United States in the region and appears as committed to maintaining the capability to pursue a nuclear weapons path as before, just a longer path." "Assessing the Iran Deal: Examining Iranian Non-Compliance with the Joint Comprehensive Plan of Action and United Nations Security Council Resolution 2231," Testimony of David Albright, president of the Institute for Science and International Security, before the House Subcommittee on National Security, Committee of Oversight and Government Reform, April 5, 2017, p. 2.

68.   Solomon, *op. cit.*, pp. 168–169.

69.   In August, 2015, Kerry "emphasized precisely the prospect of regional collaboration with Iran: 'If we can get this deal done, then we're ready to sit down and talk about the regional issues, and we may be able to work things in different places.' " Tony Badran, "America Makes a U-Turn in the Middle East," *Tablet*, February 4, 2016, http://www.tabletmag.com/jewish-news-and-politics/197368/u-turn-in-the-middle-east

70.   Solomon, *op. cit.*, pp. 181–182.

71.   "President Obama's defense of the complex and painstakingly negotiated nuclear deal that his administration reached with Iran boiled down to a simple, if controversial, contention: The only real alternative to the deal was war." Greg Jaffe, "Obama says nuclear deal staves off war," *The Washington Post*, July 16, 2015, p. A1.

72.   Solomon, *op. cit.*, pp. 198, 251.

73.   Behind the various uprisings, and indeed the stagnant, repressive politics of the Middle East over seven decades, lay "a full-fledged sociological problem in the greater Middle East, one having mainly to do with the stresses of modernization on traditional and, in many cases, still largely tribally structured societies." Adam Garfinkle, "What Orlando Doesn't Mean," *The American Interest*, June 16, 2016, https://www.the-american-interest.com/2016/06/16/what-orlando-doesnt-mean/

74.   Anti-government demonstrations also occurred in Algeria, Jordan, Oman, Sudan, Kuwait, Morocco, Lebanon, and Saudi Arabia. Steven A. Cook,

False Dawn: Protest, Democracy, and Violence in the New Middle East,
New York: Oxford University Press, 2017, p. 16.

75. Solomon, *op. cit.*, p. 213.

76. "The use of the term 'Arab Spring' to describe this collapse is both sad and ludicrous. If a natural phenomenon is to be used, it should be an earthquake, a wrenching upheaval that shattered not only regimes but long-established states." Lerman, *op. cit.*, p. 12.

77. Solomon, *op. cit.*, p. 54. Members of the administration of George W. Bush, which launched the campaign in Iraq, had hoped that a change of regime in Baghdad would weaken the clerical regime next door. In fact, the fall of Saddam strengthened the Islamic Republic. *Ibid.*, pp. 22–23, 59, 81.

78. *Ibid.*, p. 72; Clawson and Rubin, *op. cit.*, p. 150; Jonathan Spyer, "The Fall of Kirkuk: Made in Iran," *The American Interest*, October 18, 2017, https://www.the-american-interest.com/2017/10/18/fall-kirkuk-made-in-iran/

79. Solomon, *op. cit.*, p. 73. "Iran . . . provided lethal expertise in the form of roadside bombs, of which the most dangerous types—explosively formed projectiles, or EFPs—were manufactured in that country. Iran may have been indirectly responsible for five hundred American deaths in Iraq and Afghanistan, and perhaps more." Cohen, *op. cit.*, p. 52.

80. "The Alawites or Nusayris, to whom Assad's clan belongs, are not a Shi'a sect (although some give them the benefit of the doubt). In the eyes of most Muslims, they are a separate, eclectic faith that left the fold of Islam centuries ago. Iran's willingness to treat them as some sort of Shi'a Muslim faith is an important part of the relationship." Lerman, *op. cit.*, p. 23.

81. On the origins of the conflict in Syria see Fouad Ajami, *The Syrian Rebellion*, Stanford, California: Hoover Institution Press, 2012.

82. ". . . Iran never committed more than the minimum force needed to keep Syrian president Bashar al-Assad in power. It had some 700 men in Syria prior to its brief surge in late 2015—which raised force levels to about 3,000—most of whom withdrew shortly thereafter, having experienced a spike in losses. . . Iran has tried to cut its own losses in Syria by fighting to the last non-Iranian Shia proxy, even when its own forces would have been more effective." Michael Eisenstadt, "Managing Escalation Dynamics With Iran," Washington, D.C. The Washington Institute for Near East Policy, PolicyWatch 2824, July 5, 2017. http://www.washingtoninstitute.org/policy-analysis/view/managing-escalation-dynamics-with-iran-in-syria-and-beyond

83. Avi Issacharoff, "Islamic State's wane sets the stage for regional superpower Iran," *The Times of Israel*, March 19, 2017. http://www.timesofisrael.com/islamic-states-wane-sets-the-stage-for-regional-superpower-iran/

84. Solomon, *op. cit.*, pp. 224–225. "The Assad alliance with Iran has been the single most important factor in closing this gap [in manpower]. Lebanese Hizballah forces were active on the Syrian front from 2012. As the regime's predicament worsened, so Hizballah increased its

commitment. Hizballah and IRGC personnel were also vital in creating the National Defense Forces, a 90-100,000-strong mainly Alawi militia who entered the field in mid-2013. This Basij-style force was a classic Iranian proxy creation—a sectarian-based light infantry force trained by a proxy (Hizballah) under direct Iranian guidance." Jonathan Spyer, "Patterns of Subversion: Iranian Use of Proxies in the Middle East," MERIA, September 5, 2016. http://www.rubincenter.org/2016/09/patterns-of-subversion-iranian-use-of-proxies-in-the-middle-east/

85. It was also called, in the West, the Islamic State of Iraq and the Levant (ISIL) and simply the Islamic State. In the Middle East it was most commonly known as Daesh, an acronym formed from the first letters of its Arabic name.

86. ". . . many Sunnis in Iraq and Syria now feel that ISIS is the only plausible guarantor of order and security in the civil war, and their only defense against brutal retribution from the Damascus and Baghdad governments." Anonymous, "The Mystery of ISIS," *The New York Review of Books*, August 13, 2015, p. 28. Veterans of Saddam's regime actively assisted ISIS. "Captains and sergeants who once served Saddam Hussein now enlisted in [ISIS leader] Zarqawi's army, and some rose to leadership positions. Others offered safe houses, intelligence, cash, and weapons, including, investigators later concluded, the aerial munitions and artillery shells that provided the explosive force for Zarqawi's biggest car bombs." Toby Warrick, *Black Flags: The Rise of ISIS*, quoted in Kathy Gilsinan, "Is It Really Better that Saddam's Gone?" *The Atlantic*, October 26, 2015, https://www.theatlantic.com/international/archive/2015/10/saddam-tony-blair-iraq-apology/412450/

87. Solomon, *op. cit.*, pp. 229–230. Iran's nuclear negotiators told their American counterparts that American bombing of Syria would end the negotiations, leading to the surmise that Obama refrained from making good on this threat in order to protect the talks. *Ibid.*

88. " 'The way things have been going in Ukraine makes Putin look like he lost, and if his inner circle thinks that, that's dangerous for him, like for any dictator,' says Andrei Piontkovsky, a political analyst critical of the president. 'Intervening in Syria makes him look strong again in their eyes. That's what matters.' " Kathrin Hille and Courtney Weaver, "President plays to inner circle in game with high stakes," *Financial Times*, October 3/4, 2015, p. 2.

89. "The ultimate purpose of the corridors . . . is to expand Iran's reach into the Golan Heights, with the goal of tightening the noose around Israel." Ehud Yaari, "Iran's Ambitions in the Levant: Why It's Building Two Land Corridors to the Mediterranean," *Foreign Affairs*, May 1, 2017, https://www.foreignaffairs.com/articles/iran/2017-05-01/irans-ambitions-levant

" 'A corridor is more than a road,' said Brig. Gen. Michael Herzog, an Israeli national-security expert at the Washington Institute for Near

East Policy . . . 'It is shorthand for Iran's success in changing disputed territories' demography by pushing out Sunnis and replacing them with Shiite and other friendly minorities. It is Iran's effort to develop energy, economic, and military ties with the local population, particularly along heavily disputed borders, and other means of establishing a permanent presence and Shiite dominance in the region.'" Judith Miller, "Is Israel Catching Up Too Late to a Major Strategic Threat from Iran?" *Tablet*, June 27, 2017, http://www.tabletmag.com/jewish-news-and-politics/ 238846/israel-strategic-threat-from-iran

90.   Shimon Peres with Arye Naor, *The New Middle East*, New York: Henry Holt and Company, 1993.

91.   With the outbreak of the Arab Spring the Turkish foreign minister, Ahmet Davutoglu, also hailed a new era in the region, one that would, he was confident, revolve around Turkey. He adopted Peres's phrase: "A new Middle East is emerging . . . We will continue to be the master, the leader, and the servant of this new Middle East. In the new Middle East the aspirations of the people will rule; not tyranny, oppression and dictatorships . . . And a new zone of peace, stability and prosperity will emerge around Turkey." Cook, *op. cit.*, p. 237. To err as badly as Peres had about the future of the Middle East was a difficult task, but Davutoglu managed it.

92.   Grygiel and Mitchell, *op. cit.*, pp. 9, 48, 63. "Iran's strategy represents a bid for regional hegemony by 'stealth,' avoiding significant sacrifices of Iranian personnel." Spyer, *op. cit.*

93.   China protected North Korea but did not endorse its nuclear weapons program.

94.   "The policies of all contemporary Iranian leaders, regardless of where they fall on the political spectrum, have been shaped by two impulses: regime preservation and restoration—critics would say expansion—of Iran's role as a regional leader." Ali Vaez, "Trump Can't Deal With Iran If He Doesn't Understand It," *Foreign Policy*, February 23, 2017, http://foreignpolicy.com/2017/02/23/ trump-cant-deal-with-iran-if-he-doesnt-understand-it/

95.   "Carefully cultivating downtrodden Shiite populations across the Middle East, Iran has successfully replaced their former Arab allegiances with a Shiite sectarian one." Haivry, *op. cit.*

96.   In 1955 Great Britain, Iraq, Iran, Pakistan, and Turkey, with American support, founded the Middle East Treaty Organization, or Central Powers Treaty Organization, which was popularly known as the Baghdad Pact. Its purpose was to resist the spread of Soviet influence and radical Arab nationalism. It never functioned effectively.

97.   Sunni Muslim but non-Arab Turkey was a NATO member and a democracy, although, under the leadership of Recip Tayyip Erdogan an increasingly wayward one on both scores. Non-Arab and non-Muslim

Israel was a Western-style democracy that would have fitted comfortably into NATO—although unlike the European members of the Atlantic Alliance Israel had formidable armed forces.

98.   The faltering Saudi campaign against the Shia Houthis in neighboring Yemen demonstrated the Kingdom's military weakness, despite the expensive weaponry it had purchased from the United States.

99.   The Israelis did attack shipments of precision-guided missiles to Lebanon, from which they could threaten Israel's population centers.

100. Solomon, *op. cit.*, pp. 10–11.

101. Obama said in an interview that "the Saudis need to 'share' the Middle East with their Iranian foes. 'The competition between the Saudis and the Iranians—which has helped to feed proxy wars and chaos in Syria and Iraq and Yemen—requires us to say to our friends as well as to the Iranians that they need to find an effective way to share the neighborhood and institute some sort of cold peace . . .'" Jeffrey Goldberg, "The Obama Doctrine," *The Atlantic*, April, 2016, https://www.theatlantic.com/magazine/archive/2016/04/the-obama-doctrine/471525/

Obama had also said, two years previously, "It would be profoundly in the interest of citizens throughout the [Middle East] if Sunnis and Shias weren't intent on killing each other . . . if we were able to get Iran to operate in a responsible fashion—not funding terrorist organizations, not trying to stir up sectarian discontent in other countries, and not developing a nuclear weapon—you could have an equilibrium developing between Sunni, or predominantly Sunni, Gulf States and Iran." Quoted in Niall Ferguson, "The Iran Deal and the 'Problem of Conjecture,'" *The Wall Street Journal*, July 24, 2015, https://www.wsj.com/articles/the-iran-deal-and-the-problem-of-conjecture-1437780084

102. See p. 107.

103. Cook, *op. cit.*, pp. 225–226.

104. Lerman, *op. cit.*, p. 35.

105. See Thomas Erdbrink, "China's Push to Link East and West Puts Iran at 'Center of Everything,'" *The New York Times*, July 25, 2017, p. A9.

Chapter 4

1.   The nature, the spread, and the peace-inducing effects of democracy are the subjects of Michael Mandelbaum, *Democracy's Good Name: The Rise and Risks of the World's Most Popular Form of Government*, New York: PublicAffairs, 2007.

2.   NATO expansion prevented this from occurring in Europe. See pp. 9–15.

3.   For a critical discussion of this "realist" approach to the understanding of international politics see Azar Gat, *The Causes of War and the Spread of Peace*, New York and Oxford, U.K., Oxford University Press, 2017, Chapter 5.

4. This was perhaps one reason that mass murder had gone out of fashion in the twenty-first century. According to Alexander Solzhenitsyn, "The imagination and inner strength of Shakespeare's villains stopped short at ten or so cadavers. Because they had no ideology . . . It is thanks to ideology that it fell to the lot of the twentieth century to experience villainy on a scale of millions." Solzhenitsyn, *The Gulag Archipelago*, quoted in Martin Malia, *Russia Under Western Eyes: From the Bronze Horseman to the Lenin Mausoleum*, Cambridge, Massachusetts: Harvard University Press, 2000 paperback, p. 357.

5. See, for example, Brendan Simms, *Europe: The Struggle for Supremacy from 1453 to the Present*, New York: Basic Books, 2013, p. 50. For other examples of aggressive foreign policies undertaken for domestic purposes in Europe before the twentieth century see *Ibid.*, pp. 50, 119, 193, 203.

6. Demonstrations against the regime also took place in 2017. See Benjamin Nathans, "Russia: The Joyful New Activism," *The New York Review of Books*, August 17, 2017. "These were the largest demonstrations in Russia in five years. It was also the first time during Mr. Putin's 17 years in power that protests reached across the colossal country from its European enclave of Kaliningrad to the Pacific port of Vladivostok." Kathrin Hille and Max Seddon, "Young Russians test Putin," *Financial Times*, April 1-2, 2017, p. 7.

7. On the Chinese government's efforts to use digital technology to enhance its control over the Chinese population see "Creating a digital totalitarian state," *The Economist*, December 17, 2016, p. 20.

8. On Russia, for example, see Joshua Kurlantzick, *Democracy in Retreat: The Revolt of the Middle Class and the Worldwide Decline of Representative Government*, New Haven and London: Yale University Press, 2013, p. 245.

9. "The anti-Western animus of [Putin's] ideology would be difficult to overstate. . . much of it boils down to depictions of the post-modern West as Satan's project designed to subvert traditional religion and family life." John R. Schindler, "Why Vladimir Putin Hates Us," *Observer*, November 22, 2016, observer.com/2016/11/why-vladimir-putin-hates-us/

10. David Shambaugh, *China's Future*, Cambridge, U.K: Polity Press, 2016, p. 106. "China increasingly sees itself in ideological confrontation with the West. Last month, the party magazine Qiushi quoted Mr. Xi saying that some Chinese have 'unwittingly become trumpeters of Western capitalistic ideology.'" Andrew Browne, "Xi Embraces Mao's Radical Legacy," *The Wall Street Journal*, May 13, 2016, www.wsj.com/articles/in-china-xi-embraces-maos-radical-legacy-1463153126

11. Azar Gat argues that World War I began when, and in part because, economic interdependence had gone into retreat. Gat, *op. cit.*, pp. 193–194.

12. Innate aggression can take a variety of forms. The author of this book once told a colleague how remarkable he found it that the tiny state of Israel had produced so many accomplished generals. That's because of

their national circumstances, he rightly replied. If they lived in a country surrounded by peaceful neighbors they would be super-aggressive real estate salesmen.

13. The painting also shows Caucasian Americans in peaceful parley with Native Americans, which is not an entirely accurate representation of the historical relations between these two groups. The members of the first group are, however, plainly Quakers, an unusually peaceful sect.

14. It also vindicates, up to a point, Woodrow Wilson, who said in his request to Congress for a declaration of war against Germany on April 2, 1917, that "peace must be planted upon the tested foundations of liberty . . . A steadfast concert for peace can never be maintained except by a partnership of democratic nations." Quoted in Tony Smith, " 'America First's First Crackup," *Project Syndicate*, March 31, 2017, https://www.project-syndicate.org/onpoint/america-first-s-first-crack-up-by-tony-smith-2017-03?barrier=accessreg

15. Robert Zoellick, "Whither China: From Membership to Responsibility?" Remarks to the National Committee on U.S.-China Relations, New York City, September 21, 2005. https://2001-2009.state.gov/s/d/former/zoellick/rem/53682.htm

16. Nine such causes are listed in Martin Kramer, "The Myth of Linkage," https://blogs.harvard.edu/mesh/2008/06/the_myth_of_linkage/

17. Mandelbaum, *op. cit.*, p. 187.

18. Henry S. Rowen, "China's Short Road to Democracy," *The National Interest*, Fall, 1996.

19. "Several scholars have suggested that the transition to stable democracy correlates with mean incomes between $5,000 and $6,000 and becomes impregnable at the $7,000 level." *Ibid.* (The numbers are, obviously, in 1996 dollars.) On the impact of wealth on the prospects for democracy see Mandelbaum, *op. cit.*, pp. 100–103.

20. Mandelbaum, *op. cit.*, pp. 110–121.

21. That history includes three ever-larger "waves" of democracy-formation. Samuel P. Huntington, *The Third Wave: Democratization in the Late Twentieth Century*, Norman, Oklahoma: The University of Oklahoma Press, 1999.

22. China, whose economy fared comparatively well in the financial crisis and the recession, began to be seen in some quarters as offering an alternative and perhaps superior political and economic model, one of authoritarian capitalism. Bobo Lo and Lilia Shevtsova, *A 21st Century Myth— Authoritarian Modernization in Russia and China*, Moscow: Moscow Carnegie Center, 2012, p. 32; Bill Hayton, *The South China Sea: The Struggle for Power*, New Haven and London: Yale University Press, 2014, pp. 178–179; Kurlantzick, *op. cit.*, pp. 120–121, 178–179.

23. Kurlantzick, *op. cit.*, p. 10; Larry Diamond, "Facing Up to the Democratic Recession," *Journal of Democracy* 26, no. 1 (January, 2015).

24. See Michael Mandelbaum, *Mission Failure: America and the World in the Post-Cold War Era*, New York: Oxford University Press, 2016, pp. 131–132, 208–209. Germany and Japan also had the advantage, for the purpose of establishing democracy, of ethnic homogeneity, as Iraq did not.

25. Quoted in Malia, *op. cit.*, p. 57. The remark is contained in an 1802 letter to Joseph Priestly.

26. ". . . democracy may be appropriately compared to horticulture. A tree, a plant, or a flower will only take root and flourish in appropriate soil and in the proper climate. Similarly, without the appropriate mix of skills and values in a society, a democratic political system is unlikely to be successfully established . . ." Mandelbaum, *Democracy's Good Name*, p. 44.

27. Perhaps the most frequently cited listing of these preconditions is Seymour Martin Lipset, "Some Social Requisites of Democracy: Economic Development and Political Legitimacy," *American Political Science Review* 53, no. 1 (March, 1959).

28. " . . . if the existing situation continues, the predominance of private property and the market (that is, a 'normal' modern society) will in the long run produce the same effects in Russia that they have everywhere in the contemporary world: the formation of a civil society and a pluralistic culture." Malia, *op. cit.*, p. 419.

29. This is the theme of Richard Pipes, *Russia Under the Old Regime*, New York: Charles Scribner's Sons, 1974.

30. "Most Russians have come to believe that democracy was what happened in their country between 1990 and 2000, and they do not want any more of it." Walter Laqueur, *Putinism: Russia and Its Future With the West*, New York: St. Martin's Press, 2015, p. 115.

31. " 'If you look at who those people who want to emigrate are it seems that they are the most educated, the most financially secure and from Moscow where the strongest anti-Putin sentiment is.' " Lev Gudkov, head of the Levada center, a polling organization, quoted in Courtney Weaver, "Putin drives a wedge through the middle class," *Financial Times*, May 22, 2015, p. 4.

32. "There has not been a single case of . . . an authoritarian country successfully transitioning through the Middle Income Trap and not simultaneously adopting a democratic political system." Shambaugh, *op. cit.*, p. 126.

33. See Michael Mandelbaum, *The Road to Global Prosperity*, New York: Simon & Schuster, 2014, pp. 156–166. "Average factory worker wages in China have more than quadrupled over the past decade . . . Beijing's preferred solution is for companies to 'move up the value chain' and make more advanced products with stronger brands . . . But that requires financing, which is hard for many smaller private-sector manufacturers to secure when state-owned banks are pushed by the government to

maintain support for struggling state-owned industries." Ben Bland, "Adapt or die," *Financial Times*, November 4, 2015, p. 7.

34. On this point see Jie Chen, *A Middle Class Without Democracy: Economic Growth and the Prospects for Democratization in China*, New York: Oxford University Press, 2013. The pattern is not confined to China. "The fact that the middle class, long considered the linchpin to successful democratization, actually has turned against democracy in many countries is perhaps the most striking and unsettling trend in democracy's global decline . . ." Kurlantzick, *op. cit.*, p. 32.

35. "Several experts believe a neo-Maoist candidate would probably win a general election in China today, should free elections ever be allowed." Jamil Anderlini, "The return of Mao," *Financial Times*, "Life and Art," October 1–2, 2016, p. 1. Several Chinese Communist Party officials "truly believe that the political chaos or even civil war that could result from a fresh popular push for democracy would result in untold misery for hundreds of millions." Jamil Anderlini, "The logic behind China's treatment of a dissident," *Financial Times*, July 20, 2017, p. 9.

36. On emigration from China see Rosie Blau, "The New Class War," *The Economist*, July 9, 2016, pp. 14–16.

37. See Michael Auslin, *The End of the Asian Century: War, Stagnation, and the Risks to the World's Most Dynamic Region*, New Haven and London: Yale University Press, 2017, p. 89. Russia and Iran are also multi-ethnic, multi-national states. Their minorities, however, do not present as serious a threat of secession as do the non-Han Chinese. In Russia the reason is geographic: Muslim communities are surrounded by ethnic Russian populations. In Iran it is politics that makes secession unlikely: the Azeris, the largest minority, are generally well integrated into the predominantly Persian population.

38. "Young Iranians admire the US, which they see as an ideal state of freedom and prosperity, however much their rulers bombard them with anti-American slogans." Roula Khalaf, "Iran's 'Generation Normal,'" *Financial Times*, May 30/31, 2015, p. 17.

INDEX

Abe, Shinzo, 86
Abkhazia region (Georgia), 26
Afghanistan
  Al Qaeda in, 102
  democratic deficit in, 17
  Iran and, 113, 124
  Taliban regime in, 102, 113, 125
  US invasion and occupation (2001–)
    of, 40, 70, 94, 102, 113, 130
Ahmadinejad, Mahmoud, 109, 113
AKP (Turkish political party), 131
Alawite sect (Syria), 123, 126,
  129, 197n80
Aleppo (Syria), 123, 126
Al Qaeda, 102
Antiballistic Missile (ABM) Treaty,
  13, 83, 159n17
Arab-Israeli war of 1948, 100
Arab Spring (2011)
  Iran and, 126–27
  Israel-Palestine conflict and, 191n10
  misplaced optimism regarding,
    xi, 121–22
  origins of, 120

Shiism and Sunnism in, 121, 129
  Syria and, 120, 123, 126
Arak plutonium facility (Iran), 113
arms control, 7–9, 27, 118, 159n17
Asian Financial Crisis (1998), 20
Asian Infrastructure Investment Bank
  (AIIB), 64–65
Assad, Bashar
  Alawite sect and, 123, 129, 197n80
  Hezbollah and, 112
  Iranian support for, 112, 124
  Russian support for, 31–32, 126
  Syrian civil war (2011-) and, 31–32,
    124–26, 129
Assad, Hafez, 123
Athens, 51–52
Australia, 87, 152

Bahrain, 111, 120, 122–23
Balkan Wars (1990s), xii, 32
Bangladesh, 74
Beirut barracks bombing (Lebanon,
  1983), 112
Belarus, 23